TREASON

THE END TIMES IN BIBLE PROPHESY

Debra Ortiz

Epic Earth Book

For information about this title or to order other books and/or electronic media, contact the publisher: Debra Ortiz dba Epic Earth Book LLC

Epicearthbook.com contact@epicearthbook.com

ISBN: 978-0-9842510-3-2

Printed in the United States of America

Contents

i

I dedicate this book to my children, grandchildren, and every young person who wants to be prepared with biblical foreknowledge of what lies ahead.

I want to thank my husband who never stopped believing that I was writing something of eternal significance. It has taken over ten years of prayer, research, and endurance. What a long process! I honestly wondered if I would ever finish, but he never doubted it. His steadfast encouragement has been a great strength.

Through all of this, God has faithfully shepherded me. The journey has been filled with wonderment. I will never be the same.

Foreword

The two largest jigsaw puzzles on earth, entitled "Double Retrospect" and "Life's Greatest Adventure," are collectively comprised of 56,256 pieces and cover 172 square feet of surface area when assembled. Of infinitely greater scope and significance, though, is the puzzle of man's divine creation, redemption, and eternal purpose as communicated to us through the 66 books of Holy Scripture written by at least 39 authors over 1500 years of human history! This grand "divine puzzle" is comprised of some 2,500 prophecies, of which nearly 2,000 have already been intricately fulfilled! And—just as with any good puzzle—the completed work will reveal our divine "Puzzle-maker's" amazing and awe-inspiring original intention! Likewise, in *Treason: Israel and Babylon in Bible Prophesy*, author (and friend) Debra Ortiz has fastidiously researched, integrated, and presented the entire story line of our redemptive history in a clear and comprehensive work of art! I know of no other book available that weaves the depth and breadth of bible prophecy, history, and present-day events into one comprehensive story line that enables the reader to see the big picture of what God has planned for man's redemption.

In *Treason*, Debra shows how God has been connecting all the pieces of His redemptive plan from eternity past through the grand fulfillment of these exciting days in order to quash the cosmic rebellion initiated by Lucifer before man's creation and to get for Himself a glorious Bride who will reign with Him throughout eternity! *Treason* is *the book* to help serious students of human history, Bible prophecy, or apocalyptic literature, synthesize the story line of redemption out of the kaleidoscopic menagerie of Bible prophecies into an understandable worldview! *Read it soon*—before the last chapter is fulfilled in human history!

Dave Bryan, Author / Pastor / Presenter

Church of Glad Tidings and Embassy of Heaven, Yuba City, California 95992 www.ChurchofGladTidings.com

Historical Dates Used in This Book

World History and James Ussher

The Bible scholar James Ussher places the Creation of Adam at 4004 BC. Among scholars of every discipline, his work is recognized, respected, and appreciated. His historical masterpiece, The Annals of the World, was published shortly after his death in 1658, and is based on the Bible record and myriads of historical records. Few have ever produced a more researched and scholarly work.[1]

Today, world history is an amalgamation of every fragment of information collected by man through the ages. These include pictures, writings, and archaeological finds. Together, they form our historical body of knowledge.

An important source of information about the ancient world comes from writers and historians who studied in the Library of Alexandria (James Ussher referenced these sources extensively).[2]

This ancient marvel was launched around 288 BC, suffered fires, and finally vanished by AD 400. It is estimated there were as many as 700,000 scrolls in its library, and students came from many nations to study there. Today we have writings from a number of these scholars that reference scrolls that no longer exist. In fact, Callimachus the poet and scholar described the texts in the library and then organized them by subject and author, thus becoming the father of library science.

At the Library of Alexandria, seventy-two Hebrew scholars met and translated the Hebrew Old Testament into Greek—

known as the Septuagint. The apostles and early Church fathers frequently quoted from the Septuagint. Today, we no longer have the original Hebrew scrolls, but fortunately we have their translation which is a window into the more ancient texts.

The Bible is Unmatched

The Bible is a historical document of immeasurable worth. The Israelites kept a meticulous record of genealogies, national history, prophetic and poetic writings, and world events. It is a treasure trove of details and dates that allow us to reconstruct the world back to the Creation of Adam and Eve.

James Ussher was a scholar of the Bible first and foremost. In addition, he studied and utilized the ancient histories used by all historians.

In the writing of this book, I use the dates of James Ussher when referring to biblical people and events. Among scholars—biblical and secular—exact dates for some events vary by days, months, and years, but they generally stay within the same vicinity. This will always be the case, no matter how studious and careful the scholarship. In addition, there are historians who have no problem using the exact dates found in ancient fragments of archaeology, but they dismiss the exact dates found in the Bible because it is a book filled with God, miracles, prophets, prophecies, and Jesus—and they would rather die than acknowledge God.

James Ussher has given us a priceless scholarly work. It stays true to the biblical dates even though it may differ slightly from the work of other excellent Bible scholars. To me, the difference is not worth quibbling about. Therefore, for the sake of consistency when I mention dates or the ages of patriarchs, I use the Bible and James Ussher's timeline (see Timeline of Events in the Reference materials at the back of the book).

Introduction

Nearing the End of the Age

Today, we are on the brink of a new age that will commence with the physical return of Jesus Christ.

Jesus told us before His crucifixion that the Gentile nations would trample Jerusalem and the Jewish people until their times were completed. How do we know that we are close to the end of the Gentile Age? For the first time in over 2,500 years, Jerusalem is in the hands of the Israelis who have sovereign national status and an army.[3]

After the Holocaust, all nations were pricked to the heart at the despicable evils that were committed against the Jewish people. This prompted the newly formed United Nations to officially recognize them as a sovereign nation, and give them a piece of their historical homeland on May 14, 1948.[4] Then, on June 8, 1967, in response to an attack, the Israeli army converged on the Western Wailing Wall and occupied the ancient city of Jerusalem.[5] Later, in 1980, the Israeli government proclaimed Jerusalem to be a united city under Israeli authority.[6] Finally, on December 6, 2017, President Trump formally recognized Jerusalem as the capital of Israel and subsequently moved the American embassy to the city.

This turn of events is amazing because Moses warned the Jewish people before they entered the Promised Land in 1451 BC that they would be expelled from the land and taken captive by the nations if they turned away from God. Even so, Moses prophesied that they would return to their land because of God's overarching plan in the earth. Then, before Jesus departed into heaven, He informed us that Gentile nations would rule over Jerusalem until their allotted time was over. That time is now![7]

The horses of Revelation are at the gate. In our lifetime, we have witnessed the fulfillment of prophecies that date back 3,400 years to the time of Moses.

Babylon Begins the Gentile Age

In 588 BC, the Babylonian Empire burned Jerusalem to the ground and officially ushered in the Gentile Age. It has been an age of great advances alongside tragic tyranny. The Bible is very clear that this age will end under the control of a monster government that produces economic collapse and catastrophic destruction of cities, nations, and ecosystems.

At this very moment, as we race toward global tyranny, individual nations are being sifted and weighed to determine the level of cleansing calamities that are needed to bring about repentance and a course correction before we are locked into the final seven years before the return of Jesus Christ.

In 2 Peter 3:7, we are told that the judgment of the ungodly in the last days will not happen with a flood, but with fire. Then, in the book of Revelation, we are given an overwhelming picture of the destruction of the world by fire.

After a year of intense and focused study for this book, I found myself burdened by all the disturbing images in the prophetic writings. As I prayed and complained to God that I would prefer *not* to be a messenger of doom and gloom, His response was not what I expected, and it set me free to keep going. Once I had voiced my complaint, a question arose in my spirit: "Who is the apostle of love in the Bible?" "John the Beloved," I replied. "Who wrote the book of Revelation?" "John the Beloved," I replied again.

Once I realized that the apostle of love was the one that gave us the most disturbing apocalyptic book in the Bible, I was relieved. Then I thought of Daniel, the prophet who shared with us his troubling visions of mankind under Gentile rule. Daniel was a gentle and loving man who lived his entire life as a slave in Babylon. His visions came to him as he prayed for his people, the Jews, to be restored back to their homeland. In response to his prayers, he was shown the future of Israel, and the world, and it was not a pretty picture. When he learned that hundreds of years would ensue and cruel dictators would persecute and kill his people all the way to the brink of destruction before Messiah returned, he was literally ill for days.

With every breath I take, I am looking for the greatness and glory of God in these last days. I want to know what the people of God are doing and what will happen to us when the planet finds itself locked into the birth pangs of tribulation before the return of Jesus Christ. I can hear my children saying to me, "Come on, Mom, just say it. We don't care if it's perfect; we just want to know what you are hearing and seeing."

For this reason, I study and I write—for my children, grandchildren, and every person, young and old, who cares to know the truth. I want us to be prepared.

CHAPTER 1

Babylon Desecrates
the Wife of God

The demon horde sliced its way through the city of Jerusalem with the swords of the Babylonian army. Hell-stoked flames devoured homes and buildings as billows of smoke filled the sky. The sick and starving Hebrews scurried about looking for a place to hide; their screams barely a whisper above the roar of the demonized army.

Watching from a distance, Satan reveled in every blow of the sword. Today he would not be denied his prize! The wife of God—Israel the harlot—was finally in his hateful clutches, and her humiliation was just beginning.

With epic arrogance, King Nebuchadnezzar of Babylon ordered his general to plunder the temple of the Jewish God and burn it to the ground. Once done, he would place the temple artifacts in the shrine of Marduk, his patron deity. In his mind, this was the equivalent of humiliating God and forcing Him to bow to his god.

As Solomon's temple went up in smoke, a heavenly host of angels stood with their commander, Michael the Archangel, Prince over Israel, and watched the hellish frenzy unfold. Their hearts raced with anger at Satan and his horde, and yet they stood in silent agony; they were on orders from God to stand down and let the city burn.

For nineteen months, the Israelites had hidden behind their walls—dying from starvation—and clinging to a fantasy that God would deliver them from Babylon. It never happened.[8]

The year was 588 BC, and Nebuchadnezzar was blazing a trail of conquest across the earth and collecting nations and their treasures like a child collecting seashells. With the destruction of Jerusalem, it was just another day at work. But for Satan, this was a monumental victory!

Michael and the angels watched that day as mankind shifted into a new age of mega-empires headed by godless kings and powered by spiritual wickedness. It was mind-boggling how Satan had darkened the minds of humanity in just a few thousand years. It seemed everyone—except for a small remnant—believed his treasonous lies about God and bowed before idols. Was mankind hopelessly lost? The angels had to wonder . . .

King of Babylon

This new age of mega-empires became known as "The Gentile Age" with Nebuchadnezzar as its first king. He was a man filled with lust for power, who considered himself a genius chosen by the "gods" to rule. In truth, he was a mere puppet in Satan's hand. In the end he would die, and Satan's global schemes would march on.

"King of Babylon"—Satan relished the title. Nebuchadnezzar wore it like a trophy, but everyone in the spiritual world knew the true king of Babylon was Satan (Isa. 14:3-21).

Nebuchadnezzar was the human father of this new era and warfare was his method of expansion. That devotion to war is now enshrined in the family crest so that every succeeding empire has been built through conquest—including the final empire under Antichrist. Over the centuries, the names have changed: the Medes, Persians, Greeks, and Romans. Even so, this Gentile world system is one congruent entity as we shall see

Occasionally the ruler on the throne woos his subjects with acts of benevolence, and everyone gets starry eyed with hope thinking the messiah of world peace has finally arrived. This is pure theatre.

Since the Garden of Eden, Satan has been carefully crafting a narrative to lure humans into building an empire that he can control. In the end, the entire system will collapse in a fire storm of destruction (1 John 5:19 and 2 Peter 3:7).

Adam and Eve

As Satan watched Jerusalem burn on that day, his mind was filled with memories of conquest that began with Adam and Eve. At their creation, God lavished them with love and royal privileges, and this deeply angered the rebellious Satan who was overtaken with insane jealousy toward the human race.

When Adam and Eve finally met Satan, they had every reason to trust their Creator and Father and reject the lies of the arch-deceiver, but they chose not to. Satan successfully captured their affections by casting doubt on God's power and character and alleging that they were actually deity of the same caliber. By receiving Satan's lie, their hearts became a home of opposition against God. They were now carriers of unbelief—called sin. It was the highest treason against the highest power.

Before this event, they were spiritually pure and chaste, with their hearts knitted to God in love. When they yielded their hearts to Satan, they committed spiritual adultery. Immediately, Holy Spirit left them, and they realized they were naked. God is holy and pure, and He cannot and will not join Himself to an unfaithful and subversive heart.

The deception of Adam and Eve was the beginning of the spiritual affair between Satan and mankind. Satan had successfully wedged himself between Father God and His human children. As long as they believed his lies, he would control them.

And so, the debauchery began and Satan's spiritual influence continued throughout the generations. Eventually, it appeared that he might succeed in defiling every human and thereby block the birth of the dreaded "Deliverer King" who was promised to mankind in the Garden of Eden . . .

Pre-Creation God Faces the Pain of Betrayal

Long before Adam and Eve committed spiritual betrayal on the pages of time, God the Trinity had already experienced the painful event and its cascading effects all the way to the ends of eternity. In the privacy of pre-Creation, God wrapped Himself in Himself and let the impact of human betrayal thunder through His personhood.

In those moments alone with Himself, God faced the pain and violence created by man . . . yet . . . He did not turn away. By the power of His love, He maintained His peace, and gathered the sin of man and placed it on His Son—a member of the Trinity—so that mankind could be redeemed from sin and restored to a condition of spiritual purity. Throughout this entire exchange, God never acted impetuously or with reckless anger. Instead, He faced the storm, and the power of His love kept Him anchored and steadfast.

Having finished His work pre-Creation, God stepped into the pages of time at the Garden of Eden and responded to the sin of mankind by offering forgiveness and restoration of relationship for those who desired and asked for it.[9]

Humanity, through Adam and Eve, had chosen a new spiritual adviser and "god" in Satan. This was both spiritual adultery and high treason against the government of God. The result was spiritual and physical death and a future of pain and misery of astronomical proportions. Sadly, they were clueless, so it was imperative they be given time to sow into this evil delusion and reap the consequences—and also be given the opportunity to opt out through repentance.

Most importantly, God would give humanity an exhaustive education on His personhood and His holiness, as well as how to approach and respond to Him. We are created by God and He is King. Therefore, we must be educated and brought to an understanding of the high privilege of our calling before we can take our eternal position in the family.

The Promised Deliverer

On the day that Adam and Eve fell, God promised to redeem humanity by sending "The Deliverer." This is the first prophetic word given to mankind, and it foretold the coming of Jesus Christ the Messiah and His centrality to every message that comes from God (Rev. 19:10; and John 5:39).

In the Garden, God revealed that Eve would bring forth the Deliverer who would restore spiritual purity to humanity and destroy Satan and his works. This promise was given in seed form and then expounded upon and enlarged throughout the entire Bible so that today we see the big picture like no other generation.[10]

God's promise gave hope to Eve. She rejoiced in the fact that her deceiver would someday be defeated by a man-child born from woman. She now had the confidence to hate Satan and gloat over his eventual demise. For his part, Satan was enraged that a woman could hold him in derision, and this standoff began the war of hatred between them (Gen. 3:15). Going forward, women have guarded their destiny by guarding their wombs. Satan, on the other hand, has reached deep into his wicked soul in order to invent ways to defile and cheapen the motherly calling of women.

On that day in the Garden, Satan's mind reeled with fear and shock at the prospect of being defeated by a mere man. It was preposterous to think that any human could stand against his power and intellect! Satan must have reasoned that the Deliverer would have to be a new species of superhuman to come close to challenging him. Imagine his confusion when thousands of years later he laid his eyes on Jesus Christ, a man born to an average woman who had an average childhood and grew to be average in His appearance and humble in His character.

Imagine Satan's embarrassment and rage when Jesus appeared in hades—the holding place of the dead—after His resurrection, with the keys to unlock those in death and give them life! On that day, Satan was duly stripped of his power in front of the entire spiritual world! [11]

War Against the Deliverer

In the Garden, Satan realized he had no time to lose speculating about the Deliverer; it was time for action. Trembling with rage, he began to formulate his plan to block the Deliverer's birth. First and foremost, he would seek to kill every male child of the human race (as seen in the ancient occult rituals). After all, it would be much easier to damage or kill children rather than to deal with adults.

While Satan and his ilk were focused on killing babies, man was focused on gaining personal supremacy without God. In this environment, humans were easily persuaded to sacrifice their children to idols. As time went on, insecure and evil rulers like Pharaoh of Egypt and King Herod of Rome would order the death of male Hebrew babies. For those who managed to live through birth, the demonic strategy shifted to the corruption of the young mind so that he would never have the clarity to trust God.

The defilement of Adam and Eve was Satan's first victory over mankind, but it was hardly the last. The early days of the earth were some of his favorite times as he practiced and refined his ideas on the immature and gullible human race.

CHAPTER 2

Infantile Humans

The Early Days of Mankind

While Adam was still on the planet, he was a manifest reminder of the beginnings of humanity, and his life and stories were well-known. Adam was the elder human, and everyone could trace themselves back to him but no further; he was the beginning of all genealogy, and his Father was God.

Adam lived 930 years, and during this time, he watched his descendants multiply and conduct their lives without the slightest regard for God. Infected with a lust for power, wealth, and pleasure, mankind dismissed the Creator and assumed He was too impotent to govern or discipline them.

Mature Spiritual Understanding

Adam was raised by God. In Scripture, God is the Ancient of Days who rules Creation, *and* He is the Word who creates Creation and interacts with humanity in manifest form, *and* He is Holy Spirit who broods over and permeates Creation. He is the Sovereign "One." He is Father, Jesus Christ, and Holy Spirit.

Scripture indicates that Adam communed with God in His manifest form and His Spirit. In either instance, Adam would have naturally understood His "Oneness" and His supremacy as the Self-Existent One. This simple and mature truth was preserved among Adam's descendants who chose allegiance to God. We will see this in the life of Enoch, Noah, and Abraham, and from there to the nation of Israel and into the Christian Church.

Rebellion Produces Cults

Adam's descendants who rebelled against God turned their worship to wicked spirits and natural phenomenon; inventing narratives that promoted a plethora of deities to replace God. Among the ancients, this entire scheme was complicated and filled with illogical gaps. Because of that, the characters and their stories constantly changed, and new gods were added as needed. When we look back at this time, the ancient record reveals a mind-boggling array of spiritual characters that were worshipped.[12] In the Bible, God speaks through Moses and commands the Israelites:

> "They shall no more offer their sacrifices to demons, after whom they have played the harlot."—Lev. 17:7 NKJV

As man progressed, the demon-gods morphed and some are still worshipped today as national gods. Others have a lesser degree of popularity as spirit guides and alter egos. Most are secretly worshipped in sects using codes, symbols, and rituals. Today the practice of worshipping demons is called by various names such as the dark arts, the occult, Buddhism, Hinduism, Taoism, Gnosticism, New Age, the Masonic, Satanism, Kabbalah, Reiki, and the Illuminati to name a few. Collectively, these sects form the counterfeit religion of the demonic world system. One is not more important than the other in their base deception. God identifies them all as a unified lie called:

"MYSTERY, BABYLON THE GREAT, THE MOTHER OF HARLOTS AND OF THE ABOMINATIONS OF THE EARTH."—Rev. 17:5 NKJV (caps are original to the Bible)

Forgiveness in the Garden of Eden

In Eden, after their foolish act of treason, Adam and Eve watched as God pronounced judgment upon the terrified Satan who groveled helplessly before his Creator. No doubt, this powerful scene impacted them with awe and a holy fear.[13]

Before his judgment, the serpent had presented himself as God's peer when he offered Eve access into supernatural power and hidden knowledge. Now, after watching Satan's utter humiliation, both Adam and Eve renounced their misguided admiration for the arrogant deceiver and received forgiveness when God covered them with the skins of a slain animal (a prophetic act pointing to the finished work of Jesus Christ).

Unfortunately, most of Adam's descendants lacked his awe and reverence for God and his denunciation of Satan. As they began to multiply on the earth, so did their interest in "hidden knowledge" and their involvement with the demonic realm.

Man Is on a Fast Track

Fallen man abandoned his true identity as a child of God assigned to righteously rule the earth, and he disappeared into the dark world of spiritual prostitution. Even so, God experienced all of this pre-Creation and continued our education as planned.

Earth is our classroom. In order to escalate our education and limit our destructive behavior, God has placed us on a tiny planet with a short life span. In addition, our physical bodies are filled with sensual impulses that must be controlled in order to live by the code of love and inherit eternal life. Then, to accelerate our learning curve to a few thousand years, God has allowed Satan, the father of rebellion and lies, to tempt us and draw to the surface our pride so that we can quickly recognize and deal with it.

Adding to all of this, humans are bound to the law of sowing and reaping which governs every word and deed. In our personal lives and on a global level, we reap the blessings or consequences of our actions. As a feedback loop and a teacher, it holds us accountable and instills in us a healthy fear so that we avoid sowing into painful and destructive behavior. Those who are honest soon realize that life in rebellion against God is foolish, painful, and dangerous.

When we reach the end of this age, we will have a full education on two choices: choose God, worship Him, and live a privileged life for all eternity, or choose pride, reap death, and then lose your privileges in creation.[14]

The Double Danger: Deception and Carnality

Sadly, when Adam and Eve disobeyed God in the Garden, the covering of Holy Spirit departed, leaving them spiritually naked with an oversized ego and an active libido.

Without the truth and balance of Holy Spirit, mankind built his life around sensual impulses. Also, in an effort to condone his depravity and empower his treason, he sought spiritual partners from the demon realm. Everything orbited around his short-term goal of acquiring personal power to spend on personal gratification. It was a never-ending cycle of nonsense.

Our carnal nature lacks the knowledge of right and wrong. It floods us with hormonal impulses and demands to be satiated. Because of this, our first step toward maturity is to train our eternal soul to master our temporal and physical impulses. This process builds character and teaches us how to rule and reign over ever-increasing spheres of authority. If we are unable to control our appetites, we will be unfit to serve as a leader in this age and the eternal age to come.[15]

Without Holy Spirit, and under the influence of Satan's lie, mankind lost his identity. He no longer operated out of love, which is the core essence of God's heart and His goal for us.

Choose Love Not Selfishness

By design, God has given mankind rulership over the earth so that we learn firsthand the power and responsibility we are created to carry. The ultimate goal is to raise a family of thoughtful and seasoned children who have learned gratefulness and humility. By creating us as a family unit, God has surrounded us with love in order to awaken our hearts to His love and His values.[16]

In man's infancy, and fallen state, he pursued selfish pleasures. This caused him to push love aside, which eventually resulted in a hard and cold heart. Then and now, man's selfishness suits the demonic realm just fine. As men satiate themselves and perform mental gymnastics to create narratives and physical attributes for their spiritual idols, Satan is busy building his global empire.

Satan's end goal is the enslavement of humanity. Therefore, he prefers our narcissism because it allows him to dominate us.

Satan Drunk with Glee

You can imagine Satan's delight post-Creation when infantile humans discarded God from their lives, and indulged in unrestrained debauchery. From a heavenly perspective, man was hardly different from a beast in his quest to fill his stomach and pleasure himself.[17]

From Satan's perspective, it was a major victory against God. Even so, could it really be true that God would allow the weak humans to fall into his hands so easily? Did God really believe He could create humans with raging hormones and expect them to exercise godly disciplines? What was God thinking when He gave the naïve Adam and Eve dominion authority over the earth? Didn't He know the gullible humans would fall prey to temptation? What was God up to?

God Is in Control

Contrary to what man or Satan believes, God is the Creator, Owner, and Government of creation. He is sovereign and eternal without rival. Those who choose to disagree with Him and work against Him are in rebellion and high treason. There is no middle ground; you are either with God or against Him.

The juvenile party was about to end. It was now time in man's education to advance to the next stage and learn about the fear of God and His judgment of sin.

CHAPTER 3

Enoch the Prophet: Warning Before Judgment

Enoch was seven generations descended from Adam, who was over 600 years old when he was born. For most of Enoch's life, Adam was alive, and he finally died less than a hundred years before Enoch disappeared from the planet.[18]

In Enoch's day, the creation of Adam and Eve was recent history, and Adam was still on the planet as a witness that the genealogy of man began with him. In this context, men had to form an opinion on Adam's Father. Was He the Creator and King? Or, an ascended deity that happened to be farther along in the evolutionary chain as Satan postulated? The choices were that simple.

When Enoch came on the scene, mankind had largely made the decision that God was irrelevant. This resulted in selfish pursuits fueled by the demonic.

Enoch's Faith

At the age of sixty-five, Enoch had a son named Methuselah, which means "when he is gone it will come."[19] What will come? Enoch obviously had faith for a future event because he began a very loud and public campaign calling his generation to repent of their abandonment of God or face a soon-coming judgment. In fact, Enoch's life and preaching are so legendary that his story remains today as one of the most ancient pieces of sacred history. He is God's first official prophet after Adam.

Enoch the Prophet

Enoch "walked" with God in the same way that God "walked" in the Garden of Eden. This indicates that he intimately fellowshipped with the preincarnate Christ.[20]

Enoch's close relationship with God was obvious to his generation. Just by existing, he gave witness to God's active governance and brought accountability to the people. Every time they ignored or ridiculed him, they faded further into darkness and closer to destruction.

Enoch was and is a prophet. Many in his generation claimed to speak for the spiritual realm, but none of them were legitimate messengers from the throne of God. In contrast, Enoch carried the authentic Word of God, and when he released it in the earth, it was alive, eternal, and on a mission.

The true Word of God always behaves in this way. It travels the earth and penetrates hearts as it broods over events. It never disappears or loses it power. In every generation and forever, it stands as a witness to all creation that God is establishing His kingdom rule on the earth through His promised Deliverer.

All Legitimate Prophecy Declares Jesus Christ

In the Godhead, Jesus Christ is the Creator and King of all creation. He is not struggling to become the King—He is the King. On the earth, every prophetic word from heaven is about Him, as established by Father God in the Garden.[21]

Prophecy does not wish or hope that Jesus Christ will come to earth in sovereign majesty. Instead, prophecy declares it as fact so that the inhabitants of the earth can align themselves voluntarily to their King before He arrives physically to reign. To reject the rule of Jesus, is to reject the rule of God. This is high treason.[22]

The Two-Part Message of Enoch

Enoch declared a two-part message. First, he warned of a soon-coming destruction upon mankind's demonic society of treason. By naming his son Methuselah, meaning "when he is gone it will come," he gave his generation a method to calculate the fast-approaching judgment (which happened at the Flood). They were encouraged to repent and avoid destruction.

Second, Enoch prophesied a final judgment where the incarnate God (Jesus) will physically descend from heaven. With myriads of holy ones at His side, He will put an end to human and demonic rebellion and establish justice:

> "Behold, the Lord comes with ten thousands of His saints, to execute judgment on all, to convict all who are ungodly among them of all their ungodly deeds which they have committed in an ungodly way, and of all the harsh things which ungodly sinners have spoken against Him."—Jude 14–15 NKJV (the words of Enoch as quoted by Jude)

Enoch Is a Threat to Satan

Satan shuddered as he watched Enoch who was a man like Adam before the Fall. Enoch carried the glory of God and had the authority to speak as though he were speaking God's very words. Obviously, Enoch's existence was a threat to Satan who was extremely close to enslaving the whole world.

Satan wondered at Enoch's words. Could it be true that God was about to destroy all flesh in one catastrophic event?

Enoch's Disappearance Is an End-Time Message

In the year 3017 BC, Enoch had been preaching for 300 years when he suddenly disappeared into heaven. He was 365 years old, which was very young for his generation (Heb. 11:5).

Nobody wondered if Enoch was eaten by a beast or fell into a cavern. They all knew he had been taken by God. One thing is for sure, after listening to this holy man for 300 years, it was sobering to realize that he was gone without a trace. That monumental event has stayed in our sacred history for over five thousand years.

The disappearance of Enoch is an important part of his message. Today we are at the door of the last judgment that he foretold. [23] Like Enoch, I believe the saints of God will be taken to heaven before the final judgement at the end of this age (this will be covered extensively as we move on).[24]

Enoch Ignored

Enoch's disappearance was a profound event that should have convinced the people to take his message seriously and repent. However, mankind scarcely paused before pushing his warnings out of their minds and resuming their busy work of nonsense.

The Faith of Enoch is Still Alive

Right now, there are saints worldwide who walk with God like Enoch. They are humbly honored that Holy Spirit lives inside of them and gives them access to the Fathers heart. They are the authentic voice of God in the earth and the true governmental leaders anointed by heaven. Just by existing, they convey a hope of the second coming of Jesus Christ and a warning to be ready.

CHAPTER 4

Noah:
A Deliverer During
Judgement

Adam was created in the year 4004 BC, and he died in the year 3074 BC, at the age of 930. Enoch lived 57 additional years after Adam's death. When Enoch warned of the coming judgment, Adam was listening, and so was his grandson Lamech.

Lamech had the privilege of living at the same time as both Adam and Enoch. Lamech was 56 when Adam died and 113 when Enoch disappeared. Then, 69 years later, his son Noah was born.

As a farmer, Lamech struggled to produce crops from the ground that was cursed at the Fall. Apparently, he longed for the arrival of the promised Deliverer, with the hope that He would bring relief. When his son was born, he expressed his faith and named him Noah which means "rest." Was he thinking his son might be the Deliverer? Or perhaps a deliverer, as some scholars speculate?[25]

A Righteous Man

The faith of Lamech was well founded because Noah held the same reverence for God as his great-grandfather Enoch. And, he eventually delivered his family and the animals from destruction, when he built the ark. In that sense, he was a prophetic forerunner of Messiah.

At the age of 480 years, Noah began building the ark as instructed by God. It took about 120 years to complete.[26]

Meanwhile, Enoch's son Methuselah died at the age of 969, making him the oldest man to ever live (Gen. 5:27). This was a prophetic sign to his generation because his name meant "when he dies it will come," referring to the judgment that Enoch had foretold. By extending his life, God revealed His longsuffering and desire for repentance and not judgment.

The year of Methuselah's death, Noah entered the ark at 600 years old. His father Lamech had been dead for four years. Altogether, 1,655 years and ten generations had elapsed from Adam to the Flood of Noah's day. The year was 2349 BC.[27]

Adam was living proof of the Creator, and he passed the torch of faith to Enoch. The faith and preaching of Enoch left an indelible impression on his children and his great-grandson Noah.

When Noah preached of judgement, while building the ark, it was a continuation of Enoch's message. As he warned the curious onlookers of the coming destruction, they had the opportunity to repent. When they responded with ridicule and insults, they brought condemnation to themselves (Gen. 6:9–13).

In this dark period of history, Satan could boast of his control over the hearts and souls of all humanity except Noah. Even after parading sensuality and worldly vices before his eyes, Satan was unable to entice him away from God.

The Ark

When the day finally arrived for the Flood, Noah, his family, and a pair of all the animals entered the ark. At once, God closed the door of protection, and then sent sudden and violent rain. Scripture tells us that "the fountains of the great deep were broken up and burst forth, and the windows and floodgates of the heavens were opened" (Gen. 7:11). This Flood was a world changing event, that cleansed the immature human race.

The Message of the Flood

After the flood waters receded, Noah and his family stepped from the ark and onto a desolate planet. The God and Father of Adam had just destroyed all life on earth except those tucked into the ark. The Flood washed away the worthless idols and sent a message to the ancients that their entire way of life and all they had built was criminal and therefore under damnation. There was no reason to let the wickedness continue.

> As God observed how bad it was, and saw that all mankind was vicious and depraved, he said to Noah, "I have decided to destroy all mankind; for the earth is filled with crime because of man. Yes, I will destroy mankind from the earth.
> —Gen. 6:12-14 TLB

The Flood is a historical marker from God that reminds every generation that He is *the* Almighty Creator and the worship of anything else is an act of spiritual adultery which places the offender in a state of death (the definition of death is separation from God).

As Creator, God has sovereign jurisdiction over the entirety of creation. This is "His kingdom." His kingdom is the only kingdom which means all others are illegitimate. It matters not if we agree. God created and now He governs. To be opposed to Him is to become an agent of war and a participant with Satan in his campaign of treason.

Because God is love and He created us to live with Him for an eternity as family, He has an obligation to protect the peace of His kingdom by removing those who tear at the fabric of His order. To reject the rule of God is to be a law-breaker. The penalty is death. There are no optional verdicts.

We are alive and have eternal life when we accept God and abide by His immutable terms. The window of opportunity to willingly make this decision is our life-span. If we refuse the rule of God, we are assigned to the second death at the last judgment (Rev. 20:14). In this way, we will no longer be allowed to operate as an agent of war within the environs of creation.

On a global scale, the free will of civil governments is regulated by God and His overarching plans (this will become clearer as we move on). At the end of this age, the second global judgment that Enoch foretold will occur with fire. With this fire, every nation who wars against God will be destroyed. After this, the Deliverer will reign with absolute power and enforce peace.

In summary, the Flood was a wake-up call and a reminder that the striving of man is futile and ends in destruction (Ps. 33:8-11). Both personally and nationally, we have an end date. When our collective time is up, God will place His servants in the ark, so to speak, and then pour out fire on the fully mature systems of treason. After this, we will enter a new age of peace. This will be developed more as we move along.

Rebellion After the Flood

After the Flood, some of Noah's sons were still infected with Satan's lie that God is merely farther along in the evolutionary chain. Their hearts remained hard, and they yearned for their former lives. However, they feared the judgment of God and walked cautiously. Like rebellious children, they resolved to do their own thing while looking for ways to outsmart and outmaneuver God.

This childish and rebellious mind-set was the impetus for the course of events that were about to transpire. Like a dog who returns to eat his vomit, man was again revisiting the demon gods of his pre-Flood ancestors, and the results would be evil and painful.

It was now time for the next chapter in man's journey to begin: the rise of kingdoms built on greed and empowered by demons.

CHAPTER 5

Nimrod:
The Father of Antichrist

Nimrod built ancient Babylon and was actively constructing the Tower of Babel when God dispersed them around 2242 BC. The Flood was a recent event, and his great-grandfather Noah was still alive and watching.[28]

It is a fact of history that Nimrods generation understood the Flood as judgment from God because they recorded it on various stone tablets that have been discovered by archaeology.[29]

Nimrod descended from Noah's son Ham. From this line rose the Assyrians, Egyptians, Babylonians, and Canaanite people.[30] From the beginning, Ham's descendants rebelled against God and devoted themselves to demon worship in their efforts to prosper apart from God. As a people, they worshipped an array of evil deities who encouraged prostitution, human sacrifice, and other despicable practices.

Nimrod in Scripture

In Scripture, very little is said about Nimrod directly. He is introduced in the genealogies of Genesis with these details:

> "And Cush begat Nimrod: he began to be a mighty one in the earth. He was a mighty hunter before the LORD: wherefore it is said, Even as Nimrod the mighty hunter before the LORD. And the beginning of his kingdom was

Babel, and Erech, and Accad, and Calneh, in the land of Shinar. Out of that land went forth Asshur, and builded Nineveh, and the city Rehoboth, and Calah, and Resen between Nineveh and Calah: the same is a great city."— Gen. 10:8-12 KJV

That he was a mighty hunter before the Lord is repeated in 1 Chr. 1:10. Then, in Micah 5:6 Assyria is called the "land of Nimrod" (which later became synonymous with Babylon). These are the only instances of Nimrod's name in the cannon of Scripture.[31]

The respected Keil and Delitzsch Commentary on the Old Testament states:[32]

- "Nimrods name derives from maarad, "we will revolt," and this points to some violent resistance to God."
- ""a mighty hunter" relates primarily to hunting in the literal sense, [and] we must add to the literal meaning the figurative signification of a "hunter of men.""
- "Nimrod the hunter became a tyrant, a powerful hunter of men . . . in the establishment of an imperial kingdom by tyranny and power."
- ""in the face of Jehovah" can only mean in defiance of Jehovah."

The Hunter

Scripture places a negative emphasis on Nimrod's hunting ferocity. With the imagery presented, we can imagine him hunting and killing for sport with adrenaline rushing through his veins, as he stalks his prey while they attempt to escape. As an evil hunter, he is obsessed with inflicting fear and overpowering his victim, while relishing the cries of a life slipping away. In all of this, he knows that he is making himself odious before God.[33]

In many ancient cultures, a Nimrod-like person is exalted because of his hunting prowess and eventually promoted to godhood. In fact, the worship of legendary hunters has persisted to this very day with groups that participate in the hunting of human and animal as part of their occult worship.

Giant: Mortal or Hybrid?

Nimrod is called a "mighty" hunter. The word used is "gibbowr" which can be translated giant.[34]

According to legend, Nimrod was a giant birthed from sex between a demon and a human woman. In Genesis 6:4, there is a passage about giants that may indicate this occurred (but not with specific reference to Nimrod). However, scholars are sharply divided with compelling arguments for and against. Since Scripture does not elaborate or give us any clear teaching, we must be careful to avoid definitive statements of doctrine.

Having said that, my studied opinion is that Nimrod was a mere man—according to his genealogy—who fully invested himself in satanic worship as a means to achieve "godhood." Therefore, he is the biblical prototype from which all wicked rulers descend—including Antichrist.

Jesus told us that Satan has influence and spiritual control over the rebellious:

> "You are of your father the devil, and the desires of your father you want to do. He was a murderer from the beginning, and does not stand in the truth, because there is no truth in him."—John 8:44-45 NKJV

Virgin Worship and Nimrod

In the fragments of ancient Mesopotamian civilizations (Nimrods home) we can loosely trace the evolving story of a Nimrod-like character through the ages and see that he is variously depicted as either a man or a god or sometimes both. The implication is that Nimrod and his followers advocated the lie of his deity as a stratagem to gain power.

Looking at ancient iconography—pictures and drawings—we often find the mother-with-child motif as part of the narrative of the gods and their relationship with man.

Virgin worship is not Christian in origin; it is thousands of years older. None of the apostles of Jesus worshipped Mary. This was done much later when the Catholic hierarchy advanced the idea as a way to bring an ancient and widespread occult belief under the umbrella of the Catholic religion.[35]

666- Antichrist

In Scripture, Antichrist is the last king of Babylon. Nimrod founded Babylon. Therefore, Antichrist is an evil descendant of Nimrod and both are mere mortals. I take this position because the number of Antichrist is 666 according to John the Apostle in the book of Revelation:

> "Here is wisdom. Let him who has understanding calculate the number of the beast, for it is the *number of a man*: His number is 666."—Rev. 13:18 NKJV (italics mine)

The number of mankind is six because he was created on the sixth day as a human with human DNA—not a demon hybrid—and after his creation God said it was "good."

By identifying Antichrist as 666, God is telling us that he is human through and through. Not only that, he is a man without God which means he is dead. And, because he is utterly enamored with his own ideas and the systems he has built, he is the distillation and zenith of human pride.

In summary, Antichrist encapsulates and personifies every fallen human who has aligned with Satan in treason against God. At the pinnacle of his power, he is 666; a body of weakness, mortality, and foolish imaginations. This was true of the man Nimrod, and it will be true of Antichrist his final prodigy.

A Builder of Cities

Nimrod masterminded the idea of consolidated power, and Scripture credits him with building the most important ancient cities in southern Mesopotamia (modern-day Iraq and an area known as the cradle of civilization). Many archaeological discoveries from this area confirm the existence of a person who inspired city-building and rebellion against the God of the Flood.

It was natural for the people to come together and build societies where resources are consolidated. This improves the standard of living and protects against loss of life and property from wild beasts and bands of marauders. This is not bad or evil.

The problem with Nimrod's brave new society was his agenda to herd humanity into urban centers, immerse them into occultism, and then siphon off their energies to feed the system that creates sumptuous living for the few. It makes me wonder if Satan and the fallen angels are missing their home in heaven and seeking to recreate a piece of that comfort and glory by living vicariously through the lavish lifestyle of fallen humans.

The Tower of Babel

Under Nimrod's leadership, a temple was built in Babylon to honor and worship their spiritual benefactors. A key element to the design of this temple was its ascending height symbolizing stages of occult understanding that lead to the top where the "dark secrets" are divulged and supposed deity is achieved.

The clever Nimrod likely advanced the lie that God's power was limited to sending floods, and other gods were promoted who could overpower and outsmart Him. This lie gave birth to a pantheon of superhero gods with specialized powers.

It was an age of spiritual innovation. I can see the demons feverishly vying for notoriety in the new industry of superstar "idols", all the while changing the narrative and working out the kinks. It was definitely a work in progress. Like a spider building a web, they were constructing a network of lies and rearranging the players and storyline as needed.

Because the entire scheme is based on lies, narratives are fluid and filled with illogical gaps, and perverted deeds are shrouded in secrecy. Conveniently, this jumble of ancient ideas lends itself to the personalization of religious philosophies. In the modern world, the rebellious can make his god anything he wants; sort of like when a child puts together Mr Potato Head.

The Bible tells us that behind these myths and idols are demons:

> "They offered sacrifices to demons, non-gods, to gods they had not known before, to gods only recently arrived, to gods their ancestors had never feared."—Deut. 32:17, NLT

In today's pop culture, we have wildly successful books and movies that depict romances with angels, demons, vampires, and aliens. This is no different from what the ancient cults propagated in their fervor to abandon God and gain spiritual promotion. Today the masses are being conditioned to accept these ideas as harmless and fun. In reality, their widespread assimilation into culture is a harbinger of pending judgment. In the end, only those things built in relationship with God will remain.

Act of War Against God

Nimrod's Babylon was a social contract rooted in man's desire to live without God. Therefore, it was a rival kingdom and a frontal act of aggression against the sovereign government of God. It was lunacy and it was treason.

Back then, the ideas of the people were simplistic, and what they believed and built looks like child's play to us; it is hardly that. We think we have evolved, but in truth, fallen humanity has never departed from Babylon.

Today we are still building Babylon when we push God aside to pursue our ambitions. When we do this, everything we do is an "anti-act." We are actually engaging in acts of war against the government of God. From this posture, we construct intellectual narratives, controlling governments, and religious delusions to justify ourselves.

Babylon: The Idol

Because the Nimrod group looked to their city and their religious tower for power and security, the whole enterprise was an idol.

An idol is a system (government) or belief (religion) that we embrace to help us, save us, give us prosperity, or promise us eternal bliss. Only God can help, save, prosper, and give us eternal life. Therefore, an idol is an illegitimate savior and provider; it is spiritual adultery with delusions and demons.

Babylon the Harlot

In the book of Revelation, God calls Babylon a harlot because her system of government and religion is illegitimate and those who join her are fornicating with a delusion. Fallen man's love affair with magical thinking will never produce true and lasting fruit. It has only one outcome: eternal death.

There is only one God, and He is both the religion and government of creation. He is not a system of governmental or religious rules; He is I AM. He is truth and eternal life. His creation is either with Him or against Him. To be with Him is life; to be apart from Him is death.

In the book of Revelation, we are shown that every human on the planet—from Adam to the last man—either lives in a legitimate and right relationship with God or in adultery with Babylon the harlot and her demonic handlers. There are no exceptions (Rev. 17-18).

Nimrod: Hater of Humanity

At his core, Nimrod was selfish and greedy and he advanced a demonic system to control the population for his enrichment.

In contrast, God's truth is open, loving, and good. He has given us freewill because He loves us and true love would never manipulate or violate another person.

In his rejection of God, Nimrod gave himself over to demonic control resulting in a dead conscience (1 Tim. 4:1-2). Lost in the darkness of depravity, he stands out as the father of humans who hate humans—as seen in his violence as a hunter.

When we understand that Satan is the father of evil, we recognize occult practices as acts of war against the beauty and high calling of mankind.

Satan hates us because God loves us. We remind him that he is eternally dead and destined to burn in the lake of fire.

Worship

Under Nimrod, the people devoted their mental, physical, and material resources to the building of a new society. This is called worship.

Every deed of man flows from his heart and mind. Therefore, everything—absolutely everything—that man does is worship. Man's physical exertion will always flow out of what he believes. When he wholeheartedly submits to God, all his deeds, no matter how mundane, are a pleasing act of worship to God. When he dismisses God, he is actually esteeming his own ideas and abilities as superior. Therefore, he is worshipping himself.

In ancient Babylon, it appeared the people were worshipping Nimrod's new gods. In actuality, they were worshipping a system that promised personal benefits; they were worshipping themselves.

Nimrod Worships Himself

It took great arrogance and daring for Nimrod to reject the faith of his great-grandfather Noah, who was still alive and watching. By embracing a path of spiritual evil, he launched out as a free agent with the goal of defining his destiny.

In short, Nimrod worshipped himself. His occultic allegiance was a self-serving scheme to enter into the mystery world of supernatural abilities and then ascend to godhood. In this way, he had the heart of his spiritual father, Satan, the original usurper.

Just like Satan before him, Nimrod soundly rejected God the Creator. Do we really believe that he had any deep devotion for Satan or the demons? Of course not! And in the days to come, the ultimate Nimrod, called Antichrist and the "man of sin," will have the same narcissistic disorder. Paul the Apostle tells us:

> ". . . the man of sin is revealed, the son of perdition, who opposes and exalts himself above all that is called God or that is worshiped, so that he sits as God in the temple of God, showing himself that he is God."—2 Thess. 2:3–4 NKJV

Every descendant of Nimrod is a pawn in Satan's hand. Even as they solemnly grovel before Satan and the demons, their hearts burn with hatred. To this delusional faction, Satan is a forerunner who happens to be in power . . . for now.

Such is the miserable existence of Satan. He controls the masses through their rejection of God, but he never has their devotion. Man, in his preening pride is using Satan while Satan uses man. Always, there is an uneasy tension and deep-seated hatred between them.

Nimrod: A Prototype of the Antichrist

Someday soon, Antichrist will take his seat as ruler of this world system. On his way to the throne, he will lie, cheat, and kill everyone who stands in his way. Controlled by Satan, he will be ushered past every world leader who personally covets the throne.

Among the demons, Antichrist will be a laughingstock because of his extreme and vulgar groveling before Satan in an effort to prove his loyalty. In his pride, he will imagine that he can ascend higher than Satan and eventually take his throne. As a true son of Satan, Antichrist will waste his life with visons of treason, and then spend an eternity apart from God in the lake of fire.

CHAPTER 6

Babylon:
The Seed of Treason

Babylon means gate of god. It was a city, a religious tower, and a new system of civil government. Everything was an idol.

In Genesis, Nimrod built Babylon, which indicates his oversight in the construction of the Tower of Babel. Likely, he declared himself the official prophet and priest "chosen by the gods" to whom the people looked for spiritual instructions.[36]

In Scripture we see God looking down as the people worked on their utopian project like an army of ants. We can imagine them building by day and searching the skies by night looking for signs that the "starry gods" were pleased. It was a ridiculous sight to behold: masses of people baking bricks and laboring to impress a bunch of demons (Gen. 11:1-9).

This group rebelled against God like their ancestors before the Flood. However, this time they did not ignore God under the assumption that He was powerless. Instead, they zealously sought alliances with evil spirits in an effort to overpower and outsmart Him and move themselves closer to deity.

Paradise

As God and the heavenly host looked down, the people rushed about in a flurry of activity in the construction of their utopian dream.

The desire for a utopian paradise is embedded in the human heart. We are created in God's image, and God is paradise, both spiritually and physically. Spiritual paradise exists when we are joined to God in a deep bond of love, whereas physical paradise is God's tangible and eternal home. In both of these places, God sits in all-consuming power and rules with love, joy, and peace.

The first human couple lived in and experienced paradise for a season. Now man is trying to recreate it without God; an absolute impossibility. Apart from God, paradise does not exist.

God Visits Babylon

God paused all of heaven to observe this important milestone in human history.

At Babylon, mankind embraced the idea of usurping God with a rival government. From this seed, every anti-government has sprouted. In its final form, it will be a world-wide empire. In the book of Revelation, it is depicted as the mother of spiritual wickedness. She is filled with demons, decked out in worldly riches, and gorged with the blood of the saints and the martyrs of Jesus (Rev. 17:1-6).

Mystery Babylon is not a clear-cut entity that we can measure off and isolate. Instead, it is a mind-set that is rooted in man's rebellion against God. It crosses every political line and all religious creeds. It is the original sin of Adam and Eve morphing and evolving into a monster system of civil and spiritual wickedness. In the final hours of this age, it will control the minds and hearts of fallen humanity, and exercise control over the global economy.

Human Immaturity

About 107 years earlier, Noah and his family came off the ark and started over. Humanity was concentrated in one geographic area with one language and a common memory of the great Flood.

As a centralized human tribe, they were invested in the idea of a collective government ruled by a singular man who was chosen by the gods. Lovingly, God stepped in because they were historically immature.

To their young minds, God was unimpressive and morally strict. From this mistaken belief, they were building a central government under the leadership of a satanically controlled man.

God knew that such ambitions would lead to a ruthless world where tyrant kings with beastly hearts would terrorize their subjects like monsters. In fact, as we will see in the visions of the prophet Daniel, God has depicted every global government from Babylon forward as beasts—and the final incarnation as a monster (Dan. 7).

The people were in a vacuum. How could they choose to be ruled by God when they were ignorant of His personhood, power, and ways? Clearly, they needed a more comprehensive education before they were allowed to form their utopian system.

The Confusion of Language

The heavenly angels watched as the citizens of Babylon embraced a vision of life without the restraints of God. Believing they were free; they were actually in bondage to demons and Nimrod was controlled by Satan.[37]

In the midst of this busyness, God confused their language so that they spoke in a new dialect. It is easy to imagine the hysteria that ensued. As they opened their mouths to speak, their lips were unable to form the words commanded by their brains.

Terrified, the people instantly realized they were under a supernatural judgment. Mass confusion seized the crowd. Nimrod tried in vain to rally the people, but it was useless because each clan spoke a different dialect. Immediately, the work stopped as the people scattered.

With all the confusion, families began to distance themselves from one another and move geographically to establish their own communities. Nimrod continued to do what he could and even built other cities, but he never achieved his dream of global control.

God renamed the city Babel, which means "confusion"; thus, emphasizing the nonsense in their hearts and mouths.

Infected with Babylon

In His mercy, God scattered the people because they were historically immature. Even so, they were already infected with a desire for a Babylonian-style government. Therefore, as they scattered across the earth, they used the Babylonian blueprint of rebellion and demon worship to build their nations. Even so, they were regional and lacked global impact, which is precisely what God intended.

At this juncture, there were thousands of years left in the human age, and man's education was just beginning. Up ahead, God would create His own nation and use it to educate humanity on His personhood and ways. After that, He would allow the rise of world empires.

The Rise of Nations

Within the span of several hundred years after Nimrod, the Babylonian model of government was planted across the known world so that "nations and kings" replaced families and tribes.

Within each nation, the people worshipped their patron gods in temples staffed by wicked men who demanded offerings, devotion, and rituals to keep the gods happy.

Meanwhile, kings amused themselves with the belief that they were mortal gods as they amassed armies and implements of war and torture and sat upon their thrones plotting world dominion with the help of their soothsayers, astrologers, and magicians. All the while, the people bent their backs in labor to build the palaces, cities, temples, and anything else the king desired. Everyone was beholden to the system, and the labor of every hand was dedicated to keeping the Babylonian system alive.

Babylon: Then and Now

Babylon, from its earliest incarnation to the present day, is any system of government or religion that rejects God and embraces anything and everything else. It is self-worship on a *national level*.

Groups of self-appointed and self-anointed humans come together and make laws that are lifted higher than God. The collective mind agrees that God is irrelevant and has no place in public life. The individual who honors God is ridiculed and persecuted because he stands in opposition to the system.

Tyrant kings and religious councils allow all sorts of crimes against humanity, but they cannot tolerate God intruding into their evil deeds. This was true in the ancient world, and it is true today where self-worship (called humanism) is the modern and public face of the occult.

Over the years, the look of national idol worship has morphed, been groomed, and called by many names. In the final analysis, God identifies the entire rebellious system as Babylon the Harlot.

Final Babylon

In the book of Revelation, the final government of the Gentile Age is a fully mature Babylonian system. Leading up to this apex, peace and safety will be the rally cry as the people look for a leader to unify the world and usher in personal and social paradise.

Once Antichrist rises, he will be the pride of all humanity. "Finally," men will say, "we have given birth to a son that personifies our humanistic philosophies." Sadly, the people will find themselves locked in a nightmare when they realize they have created a global throne of power for one man—and this man will consider himself a god.

Antichrist will have a veneer of civility and benevolence but underneath he will be eaten up with arrogance and a hatred of the humans he pretends to love.

Like his evil predecessor, the savage Nimrod, he will hunt men and despoil their goods and life with the adrenaline of Satan running through his veins.

God's Way: Full Disclosure

As this age closes, I believe that the ugly truth about Mystery Babylon with her satanic roots and her lust for global power will be exposed. This will allow everyone the opportunity to see her true identity and thereby make an informed decision about who they will serve: God, or the Babylonian system headed by Satan.

This is God's way. He gives us prophetic revelation, space to mature, and time to repent, as He uncovers everything hidden. As a loving God, He lets us choose our final destiny armed with truth and revelation. If we still reject Him, we will be eternally separated from God.

CHAPTER 7

Abraham: The Father of the Right-Standing Ones

Noah departed from the ark, and about 107 years later Nimrod built Babylon. Noah witnessed the dispersion of the people at the Tower of Babel, and lived an additional 350 years.

Abram was born two years after Noah's death. When Abram was seventy-five years old, he was living with his wife Sarai in Ur of Chaldea, an important commercial and religious city that predominantly worshipped the moon god Sin.[38]

Ur was part of the Chaldean dynasty, and her people were called both Chaldeans and Babylonians; they were descendants of Nimrod.

By this time in human history, Babylonian-style nations were planted over the known world with each one controlled by competing demonic powers. Finally, the time arrived for God to bring forth His own nation, so He visited a man named Abram to share His plans.

After God's visit, a radical change occurred in Abram's life. With awakened eyes, he rejected the demonic culture of Ur and made a decision to follow God to the Promised Land that was bequeathed to him and his descendants as an everlasting possession. Leaving Ur, he would have crossed over the mighty Euphrates River which was a major dividing point in the ancient world and traveled to the land of Canaan. The Canaanites called him a "Hebrew"—a term derived from his forefather Eber, and the word "eeber" which means "crossing over from beyond."[39]

In Abram, God found a man who shared His heart, and He made a legally binding covenant to make his descendants a great nation and to protect and lead them. Then, over the next twenty-five years, God appeared to Abram many times to affirm His promise (Gen. 12:1–3; Josh. 24:2–3).

Abram "Helps" God

About ten years after God's first visit, Abram was still childless and his wife Sarai was barren and too old to conceive. Wondering how they would become a great nation with no children, they reasoned that Abram still had the power to give seed, so they paired him with Sarai's Egyptian maid to produce an heir. The resulting son was named Ishmael whose descendants are scattered throughout the Middle East. Abram loved Ishmael and prayed sincerely that God would fulfill His covenant through him, but God had other plans.

Then, fourteen years after the birth of Ishmael, when Abram was ninety-nine years old, God visited the couple again and changed their names to royal titles: Abraham, a father of multitudes; and Sarah, a princess. They were promised that in one year they would give birth to a son.

Abraham Believed God

It was absurd to believe that God was still on track since He had seemingly forgotten His promise or was somehow unable to fulfill it. Even so, the elderly and barren couple managed to come together in faith and Isaac was born. This son, with his miracle birth, became the legitimate heir of God's legally binding promise to make Abraham a great nation.

God could have spared everyone the drama and allowed them to produce children with no problem. Obviously, He was making the point that the nation of Israel is His idea and no man has the power to give it birth (or destroy it). Physically, it was impossible for these two to have a child, and the odds of that lone child turning into a great nation were slim to none.

The nation of Israel was created by God, and it survives because of His protection. Man is powerless to change this. Today, it has been almost 4,000 years since God promised to be the King, Father, Husband, and God of Abraham and his descendants. Over the centuries, many kings have tried in vain to annihilate the Israelites who have been scattered among the nations. Still, they survive and maintain their national identity. Clearly, they are a sign and a wonder from God.

God's Promise Changes Everything

Israel is God's personal earthly nation. Abraham and Sarah were appointed as the first royal couple. Their descendants are the legitimate heirs to the government positions and the holy priesthood (of which Jesus Christ is the ultimate king and priest).

The establishment of Israel, by way of a holy covenant that is signed, sealed, and guaranteed by the sovereign authority of God, opened a new chapter in man's history. The human population was clustered in nation groups and living under the rule of occultic kings. Against this backdrop, mankind had no grid to recognize God or understand His ways. That was about to change.

From this point forward, God would protect His nation, ensure her survival, bless her with prosperity, discipline her when she forgot her identity, and hold every person and nation accountable for every word and deed committed against her. Things were about to get serious.

For Abraham's part, the act of believing God was accounted to him as right-standing. Going forward, it was his responsibility to teach his descendants about God's covenant and their miraculous birth. Legally, they belonged to God, and there was no going back (Gen. 15:6 and 18:19).

God's Oath: A Legal Inheritance

God's promise to Abraham is a legal covenant. Abraham understood this and considered it his most valuable possession when he passed it to Isaac his son as an inheritance. After Abraham died, God appeared to Isaac and reaffirmed the covenant. Isaac then passed it to his son Jacob before he died. When Jacob was fully grown, God appeared to him, confirmed the covenant, and then changed his name to Israel.[40]

Israel died with his twelve sons at his side while living in the land of Egypt. The entire family had relocated there several years prior because of a severe famine. Before his death, Israel gathered his twelve sons and solemnly reminded them of the legal covenant that he inherited. After this, he distributed it among them and they became known as the Twelve Tribes of Israel.

The Land of Promise

God gave Abraham the land of Canaan as his inheritance. Every nation needs land and borders. Because God created the entire earth, He can partition off any land mass He desires. The legal term that God uses to designate something set apart to Him and His purposes is called "holy."

The Promised Land, has been set apart by God and therefore it is holy. Mankind is free to populate everywhere on earth except the Promised Land. When God gave Abraham this land, He did so with terms and conditions. He emphasized that the land is His and they are stewards. As such, they were warned that they would be expelled if they rebelled against God.[41] In addition, everyone who enters the holy land comes under serious accountability.

> "The land shall not be sold permanently, for the land is Mine; for you are strangers and sojourners with Me."—Lev. 25:23-24 NKJV

Being Omniscient, God set apart the Promised Land before He began Creation. He calls it the "navel of the earth," and He calls Israel the "center of the nations."[42] This language communicates the fact that God has assigned His land and His people as the highest governmental entities in the earth.

Scripture assumes this foundational truth in everything. When God speaks, He is not tendering a proposition and asking for supporters. Rather He is articulating fact. When the biblical prophets speak of the north, south, east, or west, they are pivoting from Jerusalem. When they speak of the nation of Israel as being lifted up in the last days and all nations streaming to her, they are informing us of a heavenly decree that is non-negotiable.

God Waits on Purpose

About 320 years after Nimrod and the Tower of Babel, God promised to make Abraham a nation (Exod. 12:40). After this, it took another 430 years before Israel came out of Egypt. This lapse of 430 years allowed Abraham's descendants to grow numerically while living as slaves in Egypt.

Beyond that, the Babylonian nations (which included Egypt) were given over 750 years to develop their demonic systems and grow their militaries. This gave them the opportunity to reap the bitter consequences of demonic control and perhaps choose repentance.[43]

Moses

When Jacob—who God renamed Israel—moved his family to Egypt, they were numerically small, and Pharaoh gave them the land of Goshen in which to live. Over time, they multiplied, and the Egyptian government considered them a threat because of their size and the possibility that they could join forces with an enemy in the event of a war.

Eventually, the Israelites were made slaves, and they endured horrible cruelties including the murder of their newborn sons by government appointed midwifes who killed them at birth (Exod. 1:22).

In preparation for their Exodus, God sent a baby named Moses to be their deliverer (another prophetic reminder of *the* Deliverer). At the time of his birth, midwives were actively killing babies, but some feared God and secretly let them live.

Moses was spared at his birth and hidden by his mother. When she could no longer hide him, she placed him in a waterproof basket and secretly pushed him toward Pharaoh's sister who was bathing along the Nile River. Startled, she pulled the baby from the water, and her heart opened in love. She kept the child and raised him as her own in the royal courts of Egypt.

When Moses was forty years old, he began to consider his birth and his destiny as a leader and deliverer. In an effort to help his people, he murdered a slave driver who was beating a Hebrew.

Word spread quickly, and the next day he was rebuked when he tried to break up a fight. Realizing his people despised him and that Pharaoh was seeking to kill him as a traitor, Moses ran for his life and spent the next forty years tending sheep with a Bedouin family (Exod. 2).

Finally, when the long years had eliminated his oversized ego, God visited Moses and instructed him to return to Egypt and lead His nation out and into the Promised Land (Acts 7:23–36).

The fullness of time had arrived. The Babylonian-styled nations had been given hundreds of years to mature, and the children of Abraham had grown into a population of roughly 600,000 men of fighting age.[44]

It was now time for the hidden Israelites to come forth as a nation created and governed by God. The dawn of a new era had arrived.

CHAPTER 8

The Nation of Israel
Is Born

Born of Blood

The year was 1491 BC, and the Israelites had been living in Egypt 430 years; it was now time to leave.

Before departing, they were instructed to select a blemish-free male "Passover lamb" and keep him in the house for four days. After this, they killed the lamb and applied the blood over their doorposts in preparation for a visitation from the Lord God Jehovah—the God of Adam, Enoch, Noah, and Abraham.

As each family hid in their homes behind the blood-covered doors, the angel of the Lord passed through Egypt at midnight. Every home without the blood suffered the death of the first-born males—both man and animal (Exod. 12). This date became the first month for the nation of Israel.[45]

The Passover lamb was a prophetic picture of the Deliverer that was promised in the Garden of Eden. When God sacrificed an animal to cover the transgression of Adam and Eve, it symbolically pointed to the role of Jesus as the final sacrifice.[46] This is why He is called the Lamb of God who takes away the sin of the world.

On this ominous night in Egypt, God was again pointing to the Deliverer and reminding His people that sin leads to death.

That night, when the Israelites obeyed God, He accepted the blood of the Passover lamb as payment for their sins.

Because of their act of obedience and faith, God imputed His people with right-standing or legal holiness so that His Shekinah glory (His presence) could dwell with them.

When they departed Egypt, God went before them and opened the Red Sea. His visible presence was seen as a cloud by day and fire by night. The Israelites were instantly famous and feared because God was in their midst. What was the power of Israel? What made her great and glorious? Why did the kings and demons hate and fear her? It was the Shekinah glory of God and nothing else.[47]

Blood Sacrifices

As Adam's descendants multiplied on the earth, they introduced blood rituals of animals and humans into their idol worship, and the practice is still done today. By their mockery, they turned the symbol of forgiveness into an object of stark terror.

Thankfully, the entire world was about to be educated on the true meaning of the blood sacrifice as a substitutionary payment for sin and a forerunner of the Deliverer.

However, before mankind could welcome and embrace their Deliverer, they needed a thorough education on the holy personhood of God so that they could recognize their desperate condition apart from Him. That education was just ahead . . .

The Exodus

At the Exodus, Egypt was the most powerful nation on earth, and her chariots and cities rivaled anything the ancient world had ever seen. It was Abraham's descendants who helped build and uphold the empire with their slave labor.

When Moses informed Pharaoh that God wanted His people to leave, Pharaoh scoffed at the audacity. First of all, who was this "God" that He claimed ownership over the Hebrews?

Secondly, did this "God" think He was more powerful than the gods of Egypt?

Imagine the rage and consternation of Pharaoh when a Hebrew—raised in the courts of Egyptian royalty—appeared in his palace and politely requested that he give "God" all of Egypt's slave labor! This was a first! Pharaoh responded by demanding more output with fewer provisions. Smugly, he figured this was the end of the matter.

Pharaoh resisted for a while, and God turned up the heat and sent judgments against the Egyptians while His own people were unaffected. The plagues got worse by the day, and Pharaoh's heart grew harder. After all, God was proposing that Pharaoh bankrupt his economy. This was indeed a dilemma. The entire nation believed they were superior and protected by their patron deities, and now God was pulling rank and humiliating them.

If Pharaoh capitulated to God, the gross national output would plummet, sending the nation into an economic depression and loss of national pride from which they might never recover. It was unacceptable! Clearly, they had gained their wealth and pompous lifestyle from human trafficking. Deep down, the human heart knows this is evil, but who would have guessed that God would come knocking with a polite but stern request to cease and desist or suffer the consequences?

This knocking was so unpretentious that Pharaoh dismissed it as optional. That was a big mistake. The time had arrived for a shift on the earth, and God was serious. He was ready to establish His people as a sovereign nation, and this meant that the Babylonian system would have to step aside and make room for them. The kingdom of Egypt was simply the first nation to be visited, and all the others were next.

God would have been delighted if everyone had recognized His sovereign ownership over creation and repented of trying to usurp Him. The only option offered by God was humility and repentance, which did not occur. Now we understand why

Pharaoh and every other king refused to coexist with Israel. To do so would be the same as bowing before God. They were not ready for that option. Therefore, they found themselves fighting against the Creator.

The Odds Are Against Israel

On the night that Israel departed Egypt, screams and crying filled the air as death entered every home without the covering blood of the Passover Lamb. In the palace, Pharaoh lost his first-born son—a supposed god in the royal succession. Trembling with remorse, Pharaoh ordered Moses to take his people and leave at once.

As a nation, the Israelites were an unimpressive bunch of former slaves with no battle experience. In contrast, the Canaanite nations were prosperous, well established, militarily sophisticated, and too big to fall. This was precisely God's intention so that it would be clear to every king that Israel had no ability to succeed by her own might or power.

At this time on the earth, men were warriors, and they sought the help of their gods to win military contests. Therefore, it was believed that the most powerful nations also had the most powerful gods. Against this backdrop, the God of Israel was openly humiliating Pharaoh and his gods, and before the drama was over, He would drown them in the Red Sea. This was a profound rebuke of the most powerful army on the earth at that time. The Canaanites were duly warned.

Israel left Egypt in the middle of the night along with gifts that their Egyptian neighbors gave them on their way out (Exod. 12:35-36). Each Egyptian family had suffered death, and they were desperate to appease the Hebrew God so that the calamities would stop. Evidently, they spared no expense in their offerings, because the Hebrews would later donate enormous amounts of personal gold, silver, and other treasures to build a tabernacle for God.

Once gone, Pharaoh felt like a coward for not standing up to Moses and his God. What was he thinking? He had the most sophisticated army on the earth with an arsenal of chariots that rivaled anything the world had ever known. If he allowed these people to escape, all the other nations would be lifted up in pride and scorn against Egypt, and she would lose her place of greatness on the earth. Seething with rage, Pharaoh marshaled his troops and set out in pursuit of Israel.

Born of Water

Exactly as planned by God, Israel came up against the Red Sea with no place to go and no way to defend herself. Gripped with despair, the women and children began to cry as they braced for the oncoming slaughter. Meanwhile, the men were filled with anger at Moses for putting them in this predicament. What kind of God was this that He would play games with their lives?

God knew that Egypt's power needed to be completely broken so that His people could go forward and not look back. Beyond that, Egypt was full of pride over her military might and she would always be nipping at the heels of Israel if not soundly rebuked. For these reasons, God backed His people up against the Red Sea and dared the Egyptians to come after them. Of course, they did! They had no respect for God even after all they had been through. Not a problem . . . they would before the day was over.

Pharaoh's army lunged for Israel, and God opened the Red Sea for His people to escape. As they entered the bowels of the ocean, they crossed with fear and trepidation, knowing they faced a ruthless slaughter or a possible drowning. There was no comfortable option.

While the Israelites hurried across the sea on dry ground, God held the Egyptians back with a dark cloud. Once safely across, the cloud rose and the Egyptian army charged forward, committed to their mission of madness. After fully entering the sea, God caused the wheels of their chariots to come off, creating a wave of panic among the battle-hardened soldiers who realized that God was fighting against them. In great confusion, they struggled desperately to retreat. It was too late. All of Pharaoh's impressive chariots were mired down in the mud and swallowed by the great wall of water that came crashing down.

Over on the other side, the Israelites had just come through a baptism of water. They went into the Red Sea with the filth of Egypt clinging to them, and they emerged on the other side a new nation.

The Fame of God

The children of Israel watched in awe as God fought for them. Never in the history of the world had any nation seen such a display of divine intervention. Then, to dispel any lingering unbelief, the bodies of Pharaoh's army began to wash up on the shore. The army of Pharaoh was broken that day, and Israel was lifted up in the eyes of the watching world (Exod. 14).

Suddenly God was feared and famous, and His people were despised. Buoyed by their escape, the Israelites naturally assumed they were going to march right into the Promised Land and conquer their enemies. Not so fast! They were high on adrenaline, but they lacked strength of character and a deep-seated faith in God based on long-term relationship. All of that was about to change as they faced many more life-threatening situations.

God Owns the Earth

God owns creation. Eventually, everyone will have to face this truth. It is an illogical assumption to think He is not watching or does not care.[48]

Using Israel, God has overtly laid claim to the earth. In essence, He is saying, "As Sovereign King, I have created these people and given them the land of Canaan. The earth is mine, and I do as I choose. Don't fight me on this. I have demonstrated through the plagues of Egypt and Israel's deliverance that I am serious. You can make peace with Me and live, or fight Me and die."

We might wonder why God chose Canaan; a place already occupied. After all, He is omnipresent and could have easily looked into the future and given Abraham a land without settlers. Clearly, He chose Canaan on purpose and then gave her inhabitants some 750 years to settle in, build houses, and plant vineyards before He showed up with His nation.[49]

What was God doing? He was forcing the nations to notice Him because He was about to educate them on His personhood using Israel.

Age of Accountability

The birth of the nation of Israel was also the birth of an age of accountability. The Babylonian nations had been given plenty of time to grow their ideas and live with the results. It was now time for God to encounter and challenge the evil governments and demonic religions that ruled the earth.

Beginning with Egypt, those who dared to challenge God came face-to-face with humiliation and destruction.

The age of accountability was also an age of revelation. Through Israel, God was about to reveal His personhood in an easy-to-understand format. This was not going to be esoteric or weird. It would be simple and straightforward so that a child could understand. How? God would place Israel in the center of the nations and then parent her while the neighbors watched. The lessons learned in Israel—blessings and judgment—would then be applied to all nations. I call this "judicial due diligence." Like the ancient Canaanites, the modern nations have been duly warned.

CHAPTER 9

The Education of Israel

The Wilderness Classroom

After coming through the Red Sea, God directed His people to the wilderness, their temporary home and classroom.

Before Israel could enter the Promised Land, they needed an education on the fundamental personhood of God. They had stories from the history of mankind that dated back to Adam, Enoch, Noah, and Abraham. Even so, they lacked a true understanding of His ways and how to worship Him and conduct their lives both personally and corporately.

The wilderness was their boot camp and detox center. The Israelites were infected with Babylonian culture, and some still worshipped the idols of Egypt (Ezek. 20:7-17). It would take forty years of training and a new generation before they were ready to enter the Promised Land.

When the time came for their graduation from the wilderness, they would be highly skilled at trusting God—in the crucible of crisis—even when it ran counter to human logic. This radical devotion to obedience would send shockwaves of fear through the surrounding nations.

At this juncture, the world had plenty of experience in greed and manufactured religious systems to justify evil. The rampant demon worship encouraged and condoned human sacrifice, temple prostitution, bestiality, and slavery. The Babylonian beast system gave wealth and power to the kings, priests, and high officials who lived lavishly, and it brought misery to everyone else. Nobody was safe in the beast system because their wicked rulers had no respect for human life.

Israel was called to model love in direct opposition to the beast systems that ruled the earth. But how could they model something they didn't understand? The wilderness was the classroom where they would experience God's love and faithfulness as each trial revealed their inability to save themselves.

The Testing Begins

Immediately upon arriving in the wilderness, the Israelites encountered lack of water and then food. Right away, they reacted with fear and anger toward Moses which revealed their dependence on human help. Instead of looking to God—the orchestrator of this whole drama—they looked to a man. It was an automated response that was deeply embedded in their souls after generations of slavery. That was a problem, because they no longer had an earthly king who dictated their provisions. Their only source of hope and help was God.

As they encountered frequent life and death difficulties, the people ran to Moses who ran to God. After being raised and educated as royalty, Moses had spent forty years in the desert learning humility. Before the Exodus, he overcame the fear of death when he chose to obey God and bravely face-off with Pharaoh. Once done, he was a dead man if God failed to come through. Likewise, the Israelites were forced to face their fears and depend on God for their survival. Moses knew this, and he faithfully modeled a total reliance on God.

God is entirely responsible for the creation of Israel as a people and a nation. Before Creation, He assigned their provisions all the way to the end of the age. In the wilderness, He had no intention of killing them by withholding food and water. Instead, He created extreme teaching moments that included physical and emotional anxiety in order to override their deeply embedded slave mentality. In addition, all of these life and death moments were destined to become major milestones in Israel's national history. These are the stories they remember, and so do we.

The Coronation of Israel

Like the coronation of a king, God seated Israel at the head of the nations amid the fanfare of supernatural signs and wonders. This was only fitting since she her creation comes from heaven. The miracles were royal embellishments—like a crown, a robe, and a signet ring—and they established her legitimacy and authority among the nations. With such a display of majesty, all eyes were on Israel.

Ten Commandments

In the wilderness, God gave Israel her most precious governmental document: The Ten Commandments. They became her national Constitution and the bedrock of her laws. In them, a righteous code of ethics is set forth in a brilliantly simple document. All who live by these commands enjoy God's divine protection and provision. The first commandment is to love God, and all the others revolve around loving Him and loving others. Before Israel, no nation had ever submitted itself to a rule of love. It was absolutely radical.

The Tabernacle in the Wilderness

In the wilderness, God instructed Moses to build His governmental palace, the place where He would rule the nation from His throne. It was a humble tent known as the tabernacle.[50]

God then chose men to be set aside—consecrated—to serve as mediators between Him and the people. Called "priests," they were required to offer sacrifices for their personal sins in order to remain in a state of legal holiness. After this, they were able to enter the tabernacle—God's royal chambers—without fear of death. From this position of purity, they served the people by receiving their sacrifices and taking them before God (Exod. 29:38–46).

The sacrifice of the Passover lamb in Egypt and the continual animal sacrifices offered by the priests were accepted by God as payment for the ongoing sins of the people so He could live among them in His "Shekinah glory."

Approaching God with Humility

The architectural design of the tabernacle and the layout of the furniture revealed the fearsome power of God and our inability to approach Him with our imperfections.

At the "gate of the entrance," the people brought their blood sacrifices to the "brazen altar," but they were not allowed to go any farther into the tabernacle.

Once a year, the high priest entered the deepest chamber called the "the holy of holies" where God resided in His Shekinah glory. In preparation to stand before our pure and holy God, he brought a blood sacrifice to cover his sins in order to avoid death.

This protocol communicated the sinfulness of man, the holiness of God, and the absolute necessity of approaching Him with humility and in the prescribed order. It also pointed to Jesus Christ—our heavenly High Priest—whose shed blood allowed Him to enter the holy of holies in heaven. Today He sits at the right hand of God the Father.

Jesus is our intercessor. His blood is a perpetual prayer, a perpetual covering, and a perpetual open door for us to enter into the holy presence of God without fear of death. With boldness, we can pray and ask for those things we need. When we believe on Jesus, we are clean, holy, and accepted.[51]

God's Throne

Within the holy of holies, the ark of the covenant was the most valued and sacred piece of furniture. Also called the mercy seat, it symbolized the throne of God. This is absolutely radical. No other king has ever ruled his people from a throne called mercy (Exod. 25:21–22).

Located in the deepest chamber, behind curtains and out of view, it was hidden to prevent the people and the priests from accidentally looking upon or approaching God's throne which was off limits to all except the high priest who entered annually. This caution and care inspired reverence for God who is the King of Creation. As King, He cannot be approached by an uninvited, sordid, or unclean character.

To stand in the presence of King God is a fearful thing. His holy personhood burns like a fire that destroys anyone who comes before Him covered with the filth of sin.

This typology was well understood among the ancients whose kings sat upon thrones flanked by guards. Nobody entered a king's presence uninvited, and they definitely combed their hair. To repulse a king meant certain death.

No Images

The tabernacle had no man-made images or pictures depicting God. The other nations produced idol images and brand merchandise in profusion. God is not invented, and His personhood is beyond understanding, let alone depiction. Even so, God gave us the typology of the tabernacle so that we can encounter and meditate upon elements of His personhood that we need to know in order to have fellowship. The whole point is that God wants to commune with us as He did with Adam and Eve, but our hostile posture of unbelief stands in the way. This pride must be dealt with and removed before we can enter His presence and commune.

The Tabernacle Pictures Jesus Christ

The tabernacle furniture, design, and priestly rituals are all simple and brilliant tools that help us understand God's holiness and introduce us to our need to be cleansed by blood before entering His presence and approaching His throne.

Every revelation that the tabernacle communicated is found in bodily form in Jesus Christ. The candlesticks speak of Jesus the Light of the World (John 8:12). The bread that was laid out each day speaks of Jesus the Bread of Life (John 6:35). The blood sacrifices point to Jesus the Lamb of God who takes away the sins of the world (John 1:29).

When Jesus was in Jerusalem standing outside the temple (the more modern version of the tabernacle), He loudly proclaimed to the people, "I am the way, the truth and the life. No one comes to the Father except through Me" (John 14:6). With that declaration, Jesus identified Himself as *the* Passover Lamb whose blood allows Him to enter God's presence as *the* High Priest.

On the Cross, Jesus said, "It is finished," and instantly the prophetic and preparatory work of the tabernacle / temple worship and the Israeli priesthood was fulfilled. At that very moment, the curtain that hid the throne of God was torn from top to bottom and laid bare for all to see (Matt. 27:50–51)!

> ". . . now we may walk right into the very Holy of Holies, where God is, because of the blood of Jesus. This is the fresh, new, life-giving way that Christ has opened up for us by tearing the curtain—his human body—to let us into the holy presence of God."—Heb. 10:19–20, TLB

Looking back, we understand that the tabernacle pictured and heralded Jesus Christ the Deliverer. Therefore, Jesus was in the midst of Israel from the beginning.

Holiness

When Israel emerged from Egypt, the holiness of God was a foreign idea; mankind simply had no grid to understand it. As the Creator of creation, God stands alone. He is complete and whole, and everything created comes from Him and is held together by Him. He is One God, and yet He exists in three persons: Father, Son, and Holy Spirit. Within the Triune Godhead, there is complete unity—no places of striving, no insecurities, and therefore no incongruence. He is holy.

The Triune Godhead works together in perfect unity because they submit to a system of government out of love for one another. Governmentally, Father is the head of the Trinity. Relationally, Father, Son, and Holy Spirit defer to one another out of love. On a personal level, they are each the fullness of deity, and therefore they humbly honor one another. This governmental structure helps us picture the oneness of God and His unique and uncreated status.

God's love compelled Him to create human children, and He wants us to know His heart and live with Him for all eternity. Because He is holy, the unrepentant sinner cannot approach Him. This person is out of sync with God; he is an incongruent foreigner. His thoughts and deeds are in disagreement with the will of God; therefore, he is an agent of war and treason.

The holy personhood of God burns like a fire vaporizing anti-forces and rendering the space around Him pristine, orderly, and peaceful. For this reason, humans in rebellion are being raised on planet Earth—a place removed from the manifest presence of God. This arrangement is for our safety while we are immature.

As we grow in experience and knowledge, we have the opportunity to turn away from our childish pride and honor our heavenly Father. Then, we can approach Him in His prescribed way—through Jesus Christ—and receive forgiveness, which is legal holiness. After this, we can enter His presence and not be destroyed.

Through the tabernacle and priesthood of Israel, God provided us with an education on how to live with Him.

Then, in the fullness of time, after we were sufficiently trained and prepared, God gave His only begotten Son as the "Passover Lamb" who takes away our sins.

Today, if you come to God through Jesus Christ, you are God's tabernacle, and your heart becomes His throne of mercy where He sits in His Shekinah glory (which is His Holy Spirit). This is the revelation, education, and inheritance that we have received from Israel.

CHAPTER 10

Israel: The Depository of Revelation

The Exodus was an epic event that humbled Egypt, the crown jewel of Babylonian culture. Her pompous dismissal of God brought her to her knees in front of the whole world, and 3500 years later, we producing movies as we seek to behold and understand the spectacle.

Through the Exodus, God directed worldwide attention to His power and His nation, making it clear that He would be speaking to mankind through Israel.

Going forward, Israel would experience, record, and communicate His words and deeds for the sake of all humanity. What a monumental task!

As a nation, ancient Israel is unrivaled with respect to her meticulous record keeping. Moses was her first national leader, and he was trained in the courts of Pharaoh on matters of state. Therefore, by God's design, he understood the value of documenting genealogies, policies, histories, etc.

From the start, the national scribes highly valued the Hebrew language and they recorded and replicated important national documents with attention to every point of punctuation in their quest for accuracy.

Today we have the annals of the kings, the national histories, genealogies, census records, historical dates, songs, poems, and prophetic writings. These eternal treasures are now found in the Bible.

Authentic prophecy can only come from God who is eternal and Omniscient. In the Garden of Eden, God foretold the coming of our Deliverer. Then, through Israel, He gave us prophets who continued to build upon the revelation of Messiah. Today we have a prophetic map of Jesus Christ from Genesis to Revelation. Every word is alive and active in the earth.

God's Prophetic Calendar

At the time of the Exodus, mankind had no knowledge of the prophetic calendar of God.

To correct this, God revealed the Creation process to Moses who wrote the first five books of the Bible. In Genesis, we learn that man has six days to work and the seventh day is for rest. Scripture teaches that with God a day is as a thousand years (2 Pet. 3:8). Therefore, many scholars believe that mankind has six days or 6,000 years to work, and then we enter into one-day or 1,000 years of rest.

Then, at the end of our work, our deeds and motives will be inspected and judged to determine our place in the age to come (2 Cor. 5:10).

On God's calendar, the months, seasons, and years are marked off. Within each year, there are seven annual feasts that God calls "My feasts" (Lev. 23:1–2). These are educational events that Israel has the privilege of stewarding.

These feasts point us to milestones that have been or will be fulfilled in Jesus Christ. Again, God is pointing us to our "Deliverer." As the One who created Creation, Jesus is the center from which we all orbit (John chapter 1).[52]

Sacred History is the Bedrock that Jesus Stands On

Through Israel, God has given us the Law of Moses, and the writings of the ancient prophets who were appointed to communicate His Word to the world. By establishing this standard, God has certified true prophecy which reveals Messiah's identity, His times, His work of salvation, and the main events of this earth age.

Every prophetic word that mankind has ever needed or will need is found in the Bible. God has made it very clear that there is no other foundation of truth. Jesus Christ confirmed this when He said:

> "Do not think that I have come to abolish the Law or the Prophets; I have not come to abolish them but to fulfill them. I tell you the truth, until heaven and earth disappear, not the smallest letter, not the least stroke of a pen, will by any means disappear from the Law until everything is accomplished."—Matt. 5:17-18 NIV

When Jesus came to earth, He fulfilled everything written concerning His birth, crucifixion, and resurrection. As we wait for His return, the entire prophetic record is alive and bearing witness to the unfolding events that were foretold thousands of years ago. Through Isaiah the prophet, God tells us:

> "I predicted your future long ago, announcing events before they took place, to keep you from claiming that your idols and images made them happen."—Isa. 48:5 GNT

Knowing how Satan hates us, is it any wonder that he works tirelessly to keep us from reading or studying the Old Testament which provides us with the foundation that Jesus Christ stands upon?

Israel Is for All Mankind

Jesus Christ is the summation and fulfillment of every revelation that was given to the Israeli people; and His message is for all humanity. When speaking to the Samaritan woman at the well—a person of mixed nationality—Jesus told her that she worshipped without understanding and that truth and salvation comes from the Jews. She immediately gathered a crowd of non-Jews from the town and Jesus stayed with them two days and they believed on Him to salvation (John 4:21–22).

God created all mankind to be His family and He raised up the Jews to provide education and revelation so that His prodigal children could find their way home.

On a national level, Israel has been appointed as the head of all nations. As such, she models for us the blessings and disciplines of God upon civil governments. Her experiences are meant to prepare each nation to stand before God in judgment (which has already begun).

God is not done with national Israel. He has promised to be with her forever and He has never faltered.[53] She has much more to teach us in the days to come. This will become clearer as we move on.

Israel's Lack of Virtue

Israel was not chosen because of her virtue. No person or nation is righteous without God.

> 5 It is not because of your righteousness or the uprightness of your heart that you go in to possess their land, but because of the wickedness of these nations that the LORD your God drives them out from before you, and that He may fulfill the word which the LORD swore to your fathers, to Abraham, Isaac, and Jacob. 6 Therefore understand that the LORD your God is not giving you this good land to possess because of your righteousness, for you are a stiff-necked people. —Deut. 9:5-6 NKJV

God created planet Earth as a classroom where men are free to craft governments in accordance with their beliefs. Because of this, the systems and cultures that we create become our teachers. As mankind lives in the world of his making, he comes face to face with the results. Eventually, those who choose to reject God, come to realize that their efforts and conceit are unable to save them. In the end, they are old and humbled at the prospect of stepping into death and facing the Creator.

The cycle of rebellion and then death is depressing. Instead of just learning how pathetic we are and what not to do, God wants us to know Him in our youth and walk with Him every day so that we can ask questions, enjoy the beauty of the planet, and experience love as a child, spouse, parent, and friend. These are the things that will educate us about God's personhood and fill our hearts with gratefulness and love.

But . . . before we can get there, we need to get a few things straight about God. Israel is our starting point. Through her, we learn that every person and nation is filled with sin and in need of forgiveness and redemption. Accepting this truth, and our need for the cleansing blood of Jesus Christ, is mandatory to enter into a loving relationship with God.

Israel's Failures Educate Us

For her part, Israel is expected to cleave to God, faithfully serve Him as her King, and steward the revelation she has been given. As we know, she has sometimes succeeded in this charge and oftentimes failed. This would be true no matter what people God had chosen. Even so, God is not embarrassed by her. Instead, He openly tells her story and uncovers her sins in order to illustrate His power, love, and justice which are applicable to all people and every nation.

Some argue that Israel's failures disqualify her prophetic significance or future. God disagrees. What the enemy means for evil, God uses for good when it concerns His plans and purposes in the earth (Gen. 50:20).

There is only one nation that God has established as His special possession. He is so serious about Israel that He swore on oath to be her God and King forever; something He has never done for any other people. Over the years, He has called her His wife, children, nation, army, plumb line, and the apple of His eye, among other things.

Canaan is the only land that God has set aside for Himself, and He warns every nation that He will bring judgment and disaster upon those who violate His property.

With Israel, God has created a "touch point" on the earth. She is like the Tree of the Knowledge of Good and Evil in the Garden of Eden. She sits in the middle of the nations, and the rulers are commanded to leave her fruit alone. Just by existing, she is a refining fire that exposes the dross of national hatred toward God or the gold of respect and humility.

Israel Is Controversial

Israel is controversial because King God is controversial. You either love or hate Him. There is no middle ground.

God cleansed Israel with blood, filled her with His presence, and then delivered her from Egypt, the world's most powerful beast nation. The astonishing miracles of her deliverance and Egypt's destruction, was a warning to the surrounding peoples that their demon gods were imposters. Therefore, the introduction of Israel to the world and the judgment of idolatry was one-and-the-same event.

At the completion of her wilderness training, she was commanded to destroy the demonic governments of Canaan. You can be sure that the Canaanite people were shaking in their sandals. At this point, the only intelligent response was to bow to Israel's God and forsake their worthless idols. Of course, that never happened.

As Israel lived in her land, she was protected and prospered by God. When enemies rose against her, He would rebuke and defeat them. How could she ever be conquered?

Each time that Israel destroyed a beast nation, the demons raged. People who were invested in demon worship and the lucrative idol industry hated her. There was no way to defeat her unless she compromised and turned away from God and His protection. And of course, this is what she eventually did. However, this has no power to change God's plans.

Israel's meandering path of rebellion was known by God pre-Creation. Even so, He promised to protect her survival and finally restore her as a nation in the last days. God knows that when Jesus Christ returns to His nation, the remnant will be pierced to the heart for their foolishness and they will be forgiven in His arms of love (see the story of Joseph and his brothers for a prophetic glimpse of their reunion; Gen. 45).

Israel Commits Spiritual Adultery

Scripture tells us that the Israelites have always struggled with idolatry. Right after the Exodus, three thousand were struck dead when they fashioned and then bowed down to an idol (Exod. 32). Then, about eighty years later, they sought the favor of foreign kings and their demon gods.

During all of this, God sent prophets to remind the people of their covenant with Him which was likened to a marriage vow. As Israel's husband, God pleaded with His wife to stop sleeping around, and He offered her total forgiveness and restoration if she would return home (see Hosea).

When Israel refused to repent, her rebellion became more brazen. Over time, God stepped aside and allowed her illicit lovers to abuse her through war, taxation, and slavery. Finally, He allowed the Babylonians to burn Jerusalem to the ground.

But *before* any of that ever happened, Israel was warned by Moses—while they were still in the wilderness—that continual rebellion would eventually end in slavery in other nations. Even so, God promised to someday restore them back to their land in the last days.[54] With Israel's homecoming, in our generation, we have entered into the concluding events that culminate with the return of Jesus Christ.

Watch and Learn

The squabbles, political upheavals, and outright evil within national Israel, has provided ample opportunities for God to model perfect love, fatherly discipline, and righteous judgment while the world watches.

In all of this, God is broadcasting the message of His expectations and judgments for kings and nations who will reap what they have sown; just like Israel. Nobody is exempt.

Knowing this, we should pray for national Israel who currently rejects Jesus Christ the Messiah (even so, many individual Jews are believers).

As a nation, they have been given much and they have suffered much because of their backsliding. In the end, they will be restored and honored by Jesus Christ (more in Daniel's visions). This gives hope to everyone, that our particular country can repent and be healed by God.

Ignorance Is No Excuse

This is a time to know the Scriptures. God has laid the foundations of truth in broad daylight and the ancient Israelites meticulously preserved them in the public record. God is always moving forward and our lack of historical knowledge has no power to stop the prophetic sequence of events that are unfolding.

As we enter the days ahead, God will open His Word to those who seek Him with all their hearts. He wants us to know the times so that we are not taken by surprise as the birth pangs of tribulation come upon us.

CHAPTER 11

King David:
A Man of War

Moses led the Israelites out of Egypt and lived with them in the wilderness classroom for forty years. Upon his death, his assistant Joshua led them across the Jordan River. For the next forty years, they took possession of the Land of Canaan.

After Moses and Joshua, the nation was led by judges and prophets. During this period, the people often lost sight of their miraculous history and special calling, and engaged in unholy unions with foreign kings and their demon gods. Eventually, the foreigners would attack and enslave them—just as Moses warned—and they would cry out to be rescued. In response, God would send a prophet or judge, the people would repent, and the calamities would stop. However, once the hardship was lifted, the people always backslid. It was a never-ending cycle.

Age of the Kings

About 396 years after the Exodus, in the year 1095 BC, the Israelites decided they wanted to be ruled by a human king instead of a "prophet or judge" that spoke on behalf of God. They approached Samuel—the ruling prophet at the time—with their request. Samuel took the matter to God in prayer and was directed to give them what they wanted while also warning them of the dictatorial abuses that would occur. This warning served as a reminder that earthly kings tend toward arrogance and their appetites often lead to the enslavement of their citizens. This is a lesson for every nation.

King Saul

Saul was Israel's first king. He was incredibly good looking and tall. By appearances alone, the people easily embraced him. After Samuel anointed him, he was overcome by a rush of the Spirit of God and began to praise and prophesy under divine inspiration. This event demonstrated that God was still in control of His nation and the only way for the kings to rule righteously was under the influence and guidance of Holy Spirit. Even though national Israel was shifting her attention away from God as her King, she was still under His rule. That was and is non-negotiable (1 Sam. 8:1–22).

The people marveled at the change in Saul's demeanor but it was short-lived because he was prone to compromise when pressured by the people. Eventually, Samuel was instructed to anoint his replacement from the Tribe of Judah and the family of Jesse (1 Sam. 10).

King David from the Tribe of Judah

Samuel anointed David as king; the youngest son of Jesse from the tribe of Judah (1 Sam. 16).

Judah was one of the twelve sons of Jacob (also called Israel). Right before Israel died while living in Egypt; he gathered his sons to his bedside and reminded them of God's legal covenant with their father Abraham. He then laid hands on each son and gave a blessing and a prophetic word. To Judah, he revealed that God had chosen his lineage to carry the scepter of government. After this, it was understood that Messiah—the Deliverer—would come from the Tribe of Judah.

> "The scepter or leadership shall not depart from Judah, nor the ruler's staff from between his feet, until Shiloh [the

Messiah, the Peaceful One] comes to Whom it belongs, and to Him shall be the obedience of the people."—Gen. 49:8-12, AMP

The anointing of David fulfilled the old man Israel's prophecy, and made him a prophetic forerunner of King Jesus the Messiah. To that point, David is listed in the lineage of Jesus Christ (Matt. 1:6).

David's family was shocked when Samuel chose him. He was a young shepherd, and his brothers were experienced soldiers and seemed far more qualified.

As a shepherd, David wandered the countryside with his flock looking for pastureland and guarding against wild beasts. It was a lonely and dangerous life, but for David, it was an opportunity to spend time pondering God and developing a close relationship.

Those early years imprinted David with a deep understanding of God's fatherly love and protection which was radical for his time. Back then, God was viewed as the unapproachable One behind the veil of the tabernacle—not a loving Father.

God called David a "man after His heart" because of their close Father / son relationship (1 Sam. 13:14). Centuries later, Jesus Christ spoke of God as His loving Father which infuriated the backslidden priesthood.

Jesus Christ honored David. Ponder this: Jesus Christ is the Creator who created David and He was born into the Tribe of Judah and from the lineage of King David.[55] In Revelation, He makes reference to both of these truths:

> "I am the Root [the Creator] and Offspring [born into his lineage] of David."—Rev. 22:16 NKJV [my notes in brackets]

Jerusalem: The Capital City

When David became king, national Israel had been living in Canaan for over four hundred years. Even so, there remained a city of foreigners called Jebusites, residing in the territory belonging to the Tribe of Judah.[56] Once David was established as king, he conquered the Jebusites, made their city his capital, and called it Jerusalem.

David was now seated as king over Israel with his throne in Jerusalem. After building several homes and a palace, he set his heart to build God a permanent structure in the capital city. At the time, God's throne was located in a mobile tent that was first constructed under the leadership of Moses while living in the wilderness. At the tabernacle tent's dedication, God filled the place with His Shekinah glory, and He was still there (Exod. 40:34; Num. 9:15-23 and 14:10).

David: A Man of War

God was pleased that David wanted to build Him a more permanent residence. However, David was disqualified because he was a man of war. From the day that young David killed Goliath until his death, he was engaged in military conflicts with demonized kings and nations.

> 7 And David said to Solomon: "My son, as for me, it was in my mind to build a house to the name of the LORD my God; 8 but the word of the LORD came to me, saying, 'You have shed much blood and have made great wars; you shall not build a house for My name, because you have shed much blood on the earth in My sight."—1 Chr. 22:7-8 NKJV

The Temple Is God's Home

God would not allow His temple to be built during a time of war or by a man of war. This is because it is an earthly representation of His temple in heaven where He sits in radiant majesty and absolute power (Heb. 8:5). [57] In heaven, the power of God's presence renders the atmosphere pure and peaceful. This is God's home. It is paradise.

No creature has ever approached God's throne in heaven with arrogance or treason. War is simply not possible within the environs of His all-consuming and crushing power. Forces that war against Him can only do so within preordained boundaries that are far removed from His presence (earth, for example).[58]

War Against the Creator

Rebellion exists because God has granted free will to angels and humans. The fallen angels have already been judged and sentenced to the lake of fire. With humans, we are in a time of grace. While we are alive on earth, we are free to reject and war against the Creator, for a specific period of time with the end goal of an experiential education that teaches humility.

God is not warring with us; rather, we are warring against Him in the same way a child might throw a temper tantrum. Our kicking and screaming never provokes God to respond to us in an irrational way because He is incapable of such things. Instead, He patiently and lovingly allows us to grow up and put the childish things behind us.

Maturity should lead us to a place of respect for God and a turning away from ignorant ideas. Sadly, there are some that choose to stay in rebellion, and they will be eternally separated from God and stripped of all privileges in creation, at the end of their allotted time.

God's Home Is Peace

The bottom line is that God dwells in peace and absolute power. He does not war to get peace or hold onto it. He is peace. No warmonger has ever breached His holy presence as He abides in His heavenly home. Therefore, the angel armies in heaven are not there to protect God against insurrection; they are there at His pleasure.

If God wanted to, He could immediately send all spiritual and human rebels to the lake of fire and this would eliminate any need for His holy angels to fight. However, God has decided to let His human children, and the holy angels, experience the long-term effects of righteousness and rebellion for our eternal education.

Angelic Warfare

Even though God's holy angels have nothing to fear, they are directly impacted by our warfare with one another and our involvement with demons. This is because God has commanded them to watch over and help us (Luke 4:10; Heb. 1:14; 1 Pet. 1:12; Eph. 3:10). As they do this, they are constantly involved in disputes with demons who claim legal authority over rebellious men. The demons are always pushing the envelope in their efforts to use and abuse humans. However, they are subject to any limitations imposed by God and enforced by His angels.

Because of this, the holy angels are invested in us emotionally and experientially. Together, we are learning the utter worthlessness of evil and the profound mercy and love of God.

The Abyss

When Jesus walked the earth, He encountered a man filled with demons. Upon seeing Jesus, the man fell at His feet in repentance. Simultaneously, the demons shrieked with fear while begging not to be sent to the abyss (Luke 8:26-39).

Evidently, the greatest fear of the demons was confinement in the abyss by the command of Jesus—who was filled with Holy Spirit, and protected by holy angels. They dared not challenge Him.

This illustrates that during this age, God has allowed wicked spirits to roam the earth and torment humans. Even so, God may choose to send them to the abyss at any time. Having this fear, the demons avoid overstepping their bounds.

Jesus commanded the demons to leave the man who bowed before Him. In like manner, He has instructed His disciples to cast out demons and set the captives free (to those who want freedom). This is a powerful act of love and kindness.

God Strives with Man

God does not war as we know it. Even so, He is profoundly emotional, and so are we because He created us in His image.

Because God loves us, He willingly strives with us. God's striving is not war but passion fueled by love.[59] When we scorn God, His heart is impacted with pain and a jealous desire for us to understand the power and privilege that we are trading for our momentary pleasures. As the emotions of God rise in a powerful crescendo, love remains as His intrinsic and ruling passion. Because of this, He handles us with gentleness; pulling us into His heart and His presence as much as we can endure. The center of God's heart is the paradise in which we were created to live. Nothing else will ever satisfy. God is love. Love originates with Him and is Him.

> 8 He who does not love does not know God, for God is love. —1 John 4:8 NKJV

Death

Separation from God is death. When Adam and Eve chose the lies of Satan over the truth of God, the entire human race partook of their treason. Everyone is born into this sin, and it separates us from our Creator (Rom. 5:12).

At the end of the age, every human who chooses allegiance to Satan's lie, will be relocated to the "second death," also called hell or the lake of fire.

> 14 Then Death and Hades were cast into the lake of fire. This is the second death. 15 And anyone not found written in the book of Life was cast into the lake of fire. —Rev. 20:13-15 NKJV

Where does this fire come from? It comes from God.

The Lake of Fire

God is Omniscient. Before He created, He experienced the entirety of Creation and the uttermost consequences of creating children with free will. God saw the evil in the fallen angels and the humans who would follow them. He saw and felt the horror and the pain they would inflict on Creation. In that instant, the power of His love exploded in a fire called wrath which engulfed every speck of evil for all time and restored peace in Creation.

Because God is holy—intrinsic love, absolute peace, and utter congruence—the fire of His wrath was unable to find a resting place in His personhood. Therefore, God separated it out from Himself and sent it to the farthest corner of Creation where it burns today.

The wrath of God is entirely original to Him. It is a spontaneous surge of holy love from God's heart that violently rushes upon evil, envelopes it in flames, and removes it to a graveyard called the lake of fire.

Because the wrath of God originated in His heart of love, it is eternal. This is why hell is eternal (Matt. 25:41-46; Rev. 14:10; 20:10).

By the very act of creating us with free will, God experienced wrath. Before Creation, He lived only with Himself in absolute love; evil did not exist. To gain children with the experiential ability to know Him and love Him on purpose and of their own volition, He has paid the price of experiencing evil and wrath.

The wrath of God occurred pre-Creation—before He ever started. Therefore, the judgment of evil was finished before He began. It had to be this way for God to proceed to create because His love and His holy personhood require it.

God's wrath is not war or an act of war. For God to war assumes that He has a rival who is capable of usurping Him. Since He has no equal, war as we know it is not possible for Him.

The Removal of Wrath

From Adam and Eve onward, all humans have participated in the evil of treason. Therefore, every single one of us is an object of God's wrath. When God saw evil pre-Creation, He saw us as we participated in sin (Rom. 5:8-21).

When His wrath enflamed the evil, it was us. Therefore, it could be said that our holy God judged and sentenced us to the lake of fire—the eternal location of wrath—before we ever began.

On the other hand, God would never have created us if this were the only outcome. He is love, and there is no point in creating us apart from His desire to have a family rooted in His love. So, what is the power that overcomes wrath? Love.

As God made His plans for us pre-Creation, He saw and experienced every moment and every outcome forever-all-at-once. When His wrath erupted, His saving grace was already there. Because His holiness requires the death of evil by wrath, God had already placed His only begotten Son—a member of the Godhead—on the altar and then placed every sin committed by mankind upon Him so that when His wrath went forth, it detonated upon Jesus Christ (Rev. 13:8; Rom. 5:9; 1 Peter 1:18-20; 2:24). [60]

Jesus submitted to His Father of His own volition and received every human sin upon Himself (Phil. 2:5-11). When the fiery wrath of God consumed the sin, Jesus passed through and came out unharmed and without the smell of smoke because He is pure holiness. Finally, the fire of God's wrath fled from His body and was sent to the farthest corner of Creation where it perpetually entombs evil.

Everything needed for our deliverance from sin and the punishment that God's holiness requires was done pre-Creation. In ancient Israel, they participated in the Passover sacrifice to signify their reliance upon God to cover their sins and to someday send the Deliverer, who would once-and-for-all do away with the penalty of sin which is wrath (Rom. 5:9).

God has made our salvation easy and free, which is the right thing to do. He is, after all, our Creator and we are utterly beholden to Him and at His mercy. Thankfully and gratefully, He is love and perfect holiness. He has none of our ignorant and selfish attitudes which should make us jump for joy because He can be trusted and He never changes.

Pre-Creation God removed our sins through Jesus Christ, and then brought forth an explosion of material wealth and wonder that we call Creation. He did all of this with one goal: to gain children in His image with the capacity to receive His love and respond with love. What an incredible honor that God has gone to such lengths to have an intimate relationship with us! This is the paradise we long for.

Evil Is Progressive

Mankind has been given the choice to escape wrath. Even so, there are some that refuse God's gift.

Scripture teaches that at the end of this age, Jesus will reign for a thousand years, and then Satan and the demons will be released from the abyss for a final and short opportunity to recruit humans to the side of evil (Rev. 20:7-10).

Amazingly, a vast army will follow Satan and surround Jerusalem, the capital city of Messiah. We read of this in the book of Revelation, and it seems so irrational. What are these people thinking? After living in the golden era of Messiah, why would they try to overthrow Him? What lunacy!

It seems the ages will have come full circle. Before the creation of man, Scripture teaches that Satan was created and named Lucifer. He was beautiful and intelligent and held a privileged position in heaven. Living in such close proximity to the splendor and glory of God, Lucifer was still able to fall into pride and imagine he could overthrow God. This is why he is called the father of lies, pride, and all evil (Isa. 14:12-21; Luke 10:18; 2 Peter 2:4; Rev. 12:7–9; Ezek. 28:11–19).

Knowing that Lucifer fell from the most profound and glorious place in creation, we can now imagine how a man might do the same after living under Messiah for 1000 years.

The progression of pride should wake us up! If not repented of, we eventually lose our minds to an irrational state of insanity.

Hatred of God

King David was a man of war because he was constantly provoked and attacked by demonic nations who despised Israel's audacity to claim God as her King and His dominion as absolute.

Now, over 3000 years later, Israel is perhaps the most hated nation on earth. Tellingly, her right to exist is debated daily in the governmental chambers of every nation. In fact, at this very moment, many are calling for her to shrink her borders in an effort to weaken and finally eliminate her. Is there any other nation on earth that has endured such unrelenting hatred? No.

Natural Israel teaches us that rebellious men will never agree to God's claim on any people or piece of real estate. To make this point perfectly clear, God has allowed Israel to be reduced to a remnant and her landmass to a small patch of dirt. She is physically insignificant, and, still, the nation's rage.

The same hatred is directed toward Christians. As an example (among many), some 250 years ago, a small group of Christians escaped religious persecution and tyrannical rule and came across the ocean to form a new nation that would eventually be called the United States of America. Her founding laws declared that all rights come from God, including the freedom to worship. We can historically and irrefutably track her journey as an overwhelmingly Christian people. And yet today, there are governmental forces demanding that she reject God and any claim that He is over her or has helped her. Do you know of any other nation or culture of people who are being harassed to change their history and drop their gods?

The battle against Israel and the Christian church is fueled by spiritual wickedness. The demons fear us because of our relationship with God. In addition, a Christian has the authority to ask for justice and receive it. This is scary if you are a demon.

True Christians are not trying to force anyone to follow God. We are simply living our convictions and openly sharing what we know and believe, yet we are hated and hounded by those who want to shut us up. This will never change because we are living witnesses that God is alive and actively engaged on the earth. In the natural, we are not smart enough or attractive enough to convince the world to love God and quit fighting against Him. Instead, we have been made the least of all people, and our message is the most despised. Does it appear that God is trying to impress anyone with outward appearances? No, and this is precisely the point.

Any person who comes to God must do so in brokenness and humility. If he thinks for one minute that he is accepting a popular and attractive option, he is in delusion. We must learn from Israel, and all of history, that the people of God will never be popular or accepted by the demonically inspired and man-centered society that currently rules the planet.

We War in Prayer

Like King David, the saints of God are at war with anti-forces that hate us. This will continue until the arrival of Jesus Christ to rule from Jerusalem.

However, unlike David, our warfare is waged in the spiritual realm. As we walk with God in true sonship, we have the privilege and the duty to petition Him to bring justice on the earth.

As we pray for justice and the return of Jesus Christ, we are actually praying for the destruction of evil. In our hearts, we desire peace and neighborly good will. But the harsh reality is that those who govern the economies of the world are some of the most powerful, greedy, and wicked people that have ever walked the planet. Disturbingly, many of them grovel before Satan in their quest for riches.[61]

In the book of Revelation—written almost 2000 years ago—we see a global economic collapse at the end of this age. Unfortunately, you and I have jobs, own homes, drive cars, and eat food that is dependent on this global economy. When it suffers judgment, we cannot escape the impact.

In the parable of the unjust judge, Jesus told us that upon His return, we should be found crying out, "Punish my opponent! See his crimes and bring justice!" Jesus called the bold prayers of justice "faith," and He challenged His disciples by asking them if He would find this kind of faith in action at His second coming. Will He? The answer lies with you (Luke 18:1-8).

CHAPTER 12

King Solomon and Peace

God prevented King David from building His temple in Jerusalem because David was a man of war, and the temple represents God's throne in heaven—a place of utter peace.

David's son Solomon was granted the privilege of building the temple. To that end, Solomon ruled in a time of peace, which is a prophetic picture of the reign of Jesus Christ during the millennium.

> 8 but the word of the LORD came to me [David], saying, "You have shed much blood and have made great wars; you shall not build a house for My name, because you have shed much blood on the earth in My sight. 9 Behold, a son shall be born to you, who shall be a man of rest; and I will give him rest from all his enemies all around. His name shall be Solomon, for I will give peace and quietness to Israel in his days. 10 He shall build a house for My name"— 1 Chr. 22:8-10 NKJV

The Gift of Peace

King David spent his life fighting and overcoming Israel's enemies so his son wouldn't have to.

While ruling Israel, David fought demonic nations that eagerly sought to expand their power through pillaging and warfare; and Israel was enticingly prosperous and strategically located in the middle of the trade routes and along the Mediterranean Sea.

Hatred for David ran thick and deep. One king after another marshaled troops and advanced against Israel. Each time, they would sacrifice to their gods and boast like a drunkard about their planned humiliation of God and His people. Once the audacious boasts were spoken in the presence of the world and Creation, God would give David a strategy and angelic support so that he triumphed in battle.

In the same way, God is preparing the earth for the coronation of His Son Jesus Christ. To that end, Israel is back in her land, in the center of the earth, and her presence is causing strife and ancient animosity among the nations. In addition, the Christians world-wide are located in every stratum of society and they are maturing in their devotion to Jesus, holiness, and prayer. This infuriates the fallen world system.

In this final season before the return of Jesus Christ, the rage of the nations will be met with the judgments of God in preparation for the peaceful reign of His Son.

David Transfers the Kingdom to Solomon

At the end of David's life, Israel was at peace; and he gathered the entire nation to Jerusalem to transfer the kingdom to Solomon.

With everyone present, David gave Solomon the temple blueprints that he had received by divine inspiration. In these, every piece of furniture and every utensil was listed with its size and weight. Incredibly, David had amassed the gold, silver, bronze, wood, and all the other building materials in the amounts needed for each item. Beyond that, he gave extra gold and silver from his own treasury to assure all costs were covered (1 Chr. Chapters 22, 28, 29).

This is a prophetic picture of the day when Jesus returns to sit on His throne in Jerusalem and all wealth will be at His disposal. Jesus will not plunder what's left of the nations or the people; instead, they will give freely in the day of His power (Ps. 72).

Servants

At Solomon's coronation, David called out the name of every person and family that he had personally appointed to serve at the side of his son and also in the temple. They were commanded to remain faithful to their positions and loyal to Solomon. Everyone responded with a wholehearted yes.

The preparations of David were so complete that Solomon inherited proven and seasoned servants to help him administer the affairs of the kingdom.

In the same way, Father God is watching us right now and looking for those who can be trusted to serve in the cabinet of His Son. We are each being tested and proven through the everyday affairs of life. How we respond reveals our character and our positions in the soon-coming kingdom of Jesus Christ.

Solomon, a Prophetic Type

Upon His resurrection, Jesus Christ returned to heaven and took His seat at the right hand of God the Father who said, "Sit at My right hand, till I make Your enemies Your footstool" (Ps. 110:1). It was King David who heard and recorded this for all posterity.

The Father instructed His Son to "sit" until His enemies are conquered! Jesus is not striving. He is at rest in His seat of power at the right hand of God the Father.[62]

David and Solomon are prophetic pictures of this truth. The peace that Solomon inherited was obtained for him by his father David, who was called a man of war.

The Second Appearing of Jesus

When Messiah returns, He will not engage in a military campaign to war with His enemies. Instead of warfare as we know it, Jesus Christ will simply appear in the power of His glory as King and Creator and allow His countenance to flash forth. At once, every knee will bow and every tongue will confess that

Jesus Christ is Lord. After this, Jesus will rule for a thousand years while Satan and the demons are locked away (Rev. 20:1-3).

Provocation and War

In Scripture, God is called a "man of war" (Exod. 15:3). He is the heavenly Father who conquers for His Son.

Today, we are in a season of heightened provocation and war that began with the rebirth of national Israel. This has caused the enemies of God to rear their heads and gnash their teeth. They want the earth to be a God-free zone, but national Israel and the born-again saints are in the way. If only they could shut us up!

They are trying. To the humanistic and demonic beast system, Israel and the born-again saints are loathsome, and they are churning out strategies to eliminate us. We live and breathe, and they hate. This tension is bringing evil to the surface so that the light of God can judge it.

At this very moment, the arrogant are worshipping their gods of war and bureaucracy and boasting like a bunch of drunkards about how they are going to eliminate us and rule the world. The snakes are coming out of their holes and exposing themselves in broad daylight while all of Creation watches. Evil is ripe for judgment.

This is a holy shakedown, and in the days ahead, we will witness increased violence and war as the demonically fueled world system conspires to eliminate God's people. In response to their schemes, Father God will rise as a man of war to rebuke the enemies of His Son.

After this, the Father will turn to His Son and give Him the scepter of the earth and Jesus will return to rule (Dan. 7:13-14).

CHAPTER 13

The Temple of Solomon

Three years after David's death, Solomon laid the foundation stone of the temple on the location chosen by God.

Backing up, Scripture tells us that Father God established the boundaries of everything pre-Creation (Duet. 32:8 and Acts 17:26). Therefore, He chose the earthly location of the millennial throne of His Son before He ever began.

Then, on the pages of time, He made a covenant with Abraham and gave him the chosen land. When Abraham was older, God instructed him to sacrifice his son Isaac—the promised son from whom the Deliverer would come—on a particular spot that He would show him.

God led Abraham to Mount Moriah, and the location for the altar. As Abraham placed Isaac on the altar, an angel stopped him, and God supplied the sacrifice. The willingness of Abraham to offer his son, was a prophetic act that pointed to God the Father who gave His only begotten Son as the sacrifice for all mankind before He ever created us (John 3:16 and Rev. 13:8).

Years later, this location was inhabited by the Jebusites, even though it was within the boundaries of the Promised Land. Then, in 1048 BC, King David took control over the area, named it Jerusalem, and allowed some of the Jebusites to remain.

David's Census

Thirty-one years after this, in 1017 BC, King David took a census of all the men of fighting age, which was a violation of the census-terms laid out by God through Moses. God commanded that a numbering of the people must be accompanied by an offering in order to avoid a plague. This offering served to remind the people they belonged to God and it also discouraged a capricious census done out of pride or other nationalistic designs like military conscription and taxes.

> 11 Then the Lord said to Moses, 12 "Whenever you take a census of the people of Israel, each man who is counted must pay a ransom for himself to the Lord. Then no plague will strike the people as you count them. —Ex. 30:11-12 NLT

When David ordered the census, he didn't bother to ask God, or follow His terms, which indicated a selfish motive. Angered by David's pride, God sent a destroying angel that killed 70,000 men in one day:

> 15 So the LORD sent a plague upon Israel from the morning till the appointed time. From Dan to Beersheba seventy thousand men of the people died. 16 And when the angel stretched out His hand over Jerusalem to destroy it, the LORD relented from the destruction, and said to the angel who was destroying the people, "It is enough; now restrain your hand."—2 Sam 24:10, 15-16 NKJV

The Mercy Seat on Mount Moriah

This story is retold in 1 Chronicles 21 where we learn that the destroying angel had a sword in his hand, signifying his authority to kill. In both passages, the wave of death is called a "plague." In Scripture, this could refer to war, pestilence, disease, or natural disasters. Therefore, we don't really know how these men died.

As the "plague" swept through the ranks, David and the elders clothed themselves in garments of mourning and cried out for mercy. At this, God relented (or repented in some versions) of His judgment and ordered the avenging angel to stop.

The angel then instructed Gad the prophet to tell David to build an altar to God on the spot where he had halted. David immediately purchased the land from the Jebusite owner and built an altar. Once he had prepared the sacrifice, a fire from God consumed it and the plague was stopped.

Many scholars believe that the avenging angel stopped at the location on Mount Moriah where Abraham had previously offered up Isaac and God supplied the sacrifice.

After this episode, the location became the site of Solomon's Temple where sacrifices were made for sin and mercy was given (1 Chr. 21:16-17). In fact, many scholars believe that the location of the "mercy seat"—also called the throne of God—was on this very spot.

This event illustrates that God's judgment against sin cannot go unresolved. It must go forth to bring justice. However, God has given us a place to find mercy. This is not a random location. In the Old Testament, the location was the temple of God and His throne of mercy which foreshadowed Jesus Christ, His only begotten Son. In Jesus, mercy triumphs over judgment! (James 2:13; 1 Cor. 15:26; 2 Tim. 1:10; Heb. 2:14).

The Temple Location

From that day forward, David worshipped God from this location on Mount Moriah and instructed his son Solomon to build the temple there (1 Chr. 21).

All of these historical events were orchestrated by God to supernaturally confirm the location of His throne upon the earth.

In summary:

1. On Mount Moriah, on a specific spot, God supplied the sacrifice in place of Isaac as a prophetic act directing us to His Son Jesus Christ.
2. Years later, the destroying angel was told by God to halt at this spot in response to David's prayers for mercy.
3. Later, Solomon built the Temple and likely placed the mercy seat on this spot. This was the "throne of God" as He sat in mercy over Israel.
4. In the future, I believe this spot is the location of the millennial throne of Jesus Christ who has extended grace and mercy to all who call upon His name. Currently, its precise coordinates are unclear to us, but not to God who chose it before the foundation of the world!

The Throne of Jesus Christ

The destroying angel was stopped at the location of God's mercy. King David glimpsed this truth, and the demonic realm is fully aware of the history and destiny of this spot. This is why Jerusalem and, specifically, the area of Solomon's temple is the most contested piece of real estate on the planet.

When Jesus physically rules from Jerusalem, Satan will be imprisoned. Now we understand why he hates Jerusalem. Over the generations, he has worked tirelessly to desecrate her in his effort to make the place unholy and unfit for Messiah. Beyond that, Scripture tells us that Satan intends to install Antichrist in a future temple in Jerusalem as his ultimate act of defilement (covered more in Daniels visions).

Dedication of the Temple

After eight years of construction, King Solomon gathered the nation and dedicated the temple in the year 1004 BC. It had been 3,000 years since the creation of Adam and Eve, and it was the dawn of the fourth millennium.

With great pageantry, the priests performed the required purification sacrifices for themselves and the temple so that God could dwell there. At the end of the dedication ceremony, the priests placed the ark of the covenant—also called the mercy seat and God's throne—in the most holy place and then withdrew. Immediately, the smoke of God's manifest presence filled the temple and overpowered the priests.

Dramatically, God entered the temple, and it became the place of His earthly throne.

> Now when Solomon had made an end of praying, the fire came down from heaven, and consumed the burnt offering and the sacrifices; and the glory of the LORD filled the house. And the priests could not enter into the house of the LORD, because the glory of the LORD had filled the LORD's house. And when all the children of Israel saw how the fire came down and the glory of the LORD upon the house, they bowed themselves with their faces to the ground upon the pavement, and worshipped, and praised the LORD, saying, For he is good; for his mercy endureth forever.—2 Chr. 7:1–3, KJV

At this point, God's Shekinah glory—His presence—had been in the midst of Israel from the night of the first Passover sacrifice in Egypt some 487 years earlier. Over the years, the people often forgot this important fact, but in the spiritual realm, the presence of God in the midst of Israel was crystal clear.

The Seat of Government

God kept His promise to David and gave Solomon a reign of peace. Solomon lived in lavish wealth with a throne of pure ivory overlaid with gold, and an overflowing treasury. He became the wealthiest king ever known (1 Kings 10:14–29). His wisdom was so renowned that convoys of kings brought him gifts just to enter his presence and hear him speak. In all of Israel's history, the reign of Solomon is seen as her golden age.

Eventually, Solomon compromised, married foreign wives, and built temples for their demon gods. Even so, this does not diminish the message that God has communicated to us through David and Solomon.

The rebellion of man is powerless against God's plans and the revelation that He communicates. The story of David and Solomon is a prophetic picture of the heavenly Father and His preparation of the earth for the rule of His Son.

The Return of Jesus

The coronation of Jesus Christ will eclipse the splendor of Solomon and every king. Called the "day of the Lord" in Scripture, it is a day of great pageantry—fit for *the* King (2 Pet. 3:10; Joel 2:30-32; Zeph. 1:14-16; Isa. 13:6-13).

On that day, not a single individual or nation will lift a finger in protest. In fact, it will be like the crowning of Solomon when all the nations bowed before him and pledged allegiance to his throne.

Upon His throne, King Jesus will administer mercy and true justice and enforce it with absolute power. The nations will marvel at the pure words that come from His mouth and the stunning beauty upon Him and those who serve at His side.

The majesty of Jesus will eclipse all previous kingdoms and redefine the meaning of royalty for all eternity.

CHAPTER 14

Elijah the Prophet

Israel Divided

The reigns of Saul, David, and then Solomon were the only time in Israeli history that the nation stood united under a common king. The people served David, who never worshipped idols, and his son Solomon, who started off well, but eventually built places of idol worship for his many wives and extracted heavy taxes and servitude from the people.

Once Solomon died, in the year 975 BC, his son Rehoboam took the throne and promised to be harsher than his father. Angered, ten tribes in the north broke away and formed the Northern kingdom of Israel, and two tribes based in Jerusalem stayed with Rehoboam, becoming the kingdom of Judah.

Kingdom of Judah

The Judean kingdom lasted 475 years from the selection of David in 1063 BC, until 588 BC when Nebuchadnezzar destroyed Jerusalem and burned Solomon's temple. During this era, some Judean kings served God, and many rebelled and served idols.

Northern Kingdom

Jeroboam was the first king of the Northern tribes after the death of Solomon. In an effort to keep his people from returning to Jerusalem to worship at Solomon's temple, he immediately built two locations to worship God and several others for idol worship, and he hired illegitimate prophets and priests to staff them.

All told, the Northern kingdom lasted 254 years and had twenty different kings; all of them worshipped demons.

King Ahab of the Northern Kingdom

Elijah lived during the reign of Ahab, an especially wicked king who ruled over the Northern tribes. He married Jezebel, the famous daughter of a Phoenician king and a fervent worshipper of Baal and Ashtoreth. Coming under her influence and control, King Ahab placed idols of these demons alongside the altars built for God. Then, he allowed Jezebel to slaughter hundreds of true prophets who boldly criticized the wicked government.

Because of lavish spending and royal pomp, Baal and Ashtoreth became celebrity idols, and an entire industry arose around this money-making enterprise that included brand merchandise, tourism, sexual prostitution, and child sacrifices (1 Kings 16: 29-34).

The Cup of Blood

By nationalizing idol worship, and then using its civil authority to spill the blood of the prophets, the northern kingdom moved into a new category of crimes against God. They had crossed a dangerous threshold and the wrath of God was hanging over them and destruction was locked in unless they repented.

Repentance never came and the northern tribes were finally destroyed in the year 721 BC, when the Assyrians invaded.[63]

In the book of Revelation, we see God's depiction of the final government (or any government) that persecutes and kills the saints. She is a spiritual harlot—demonic religion—dressed in royal robes and riding high on the Babylonian beast of power and military might. In her hand is a golden goblet—signifying immense wealth—filled with the blood of the saints (Rev. 17:1-5).

The Northern kingdom of Israel is an ancient example of the "bloody harlot" religion and government of the last days.

Elijah

In Scripture, Elijah came out of the wilderness and into the palace of wicked Ahab to announce a drought; and then he disappeared.

Three years and six months later, there had been no rain or dew, and the entire nation was struggling over lost crops and teetering on the edge of starvation (James 5:17-18). Meanwhile, King Ahab was desperately searching for Elijah who had gone missing since his prophetic utterance.

When Elijah finally reappeared, he directed Ahab to gather all the people with the 450 prophets of Baal and the 400 prophets of Ashtoreth to Mount Carmel for a meeting.

Anxious to end the drought, King Ahab quickly assembled everyone. Once gathered, the huge crowd stood united against Elijah, a bristly man with unruly hair and an animal-skin tunic. In the highly charged atmosphere, the people braced themselves for the rip-roaring fun of watching the humiliation of the zealous prophet who lived in the wilds (2 Kings 1:8-9).

As Elijah looked over the foolish crowd, his anger was barely contained. Mustering extreme composure, he proposed a simple test to prove the idiocy of serving Baal.

Elijah issued his challenge. The 450 prophets of Baal would offer a sacrifice and call upon him to answer with fire from heaven. After that, Elijah would offer his sacrifice to God and do the same. In the end, the one who answered with fire would be proven as the true God.

The people agreed to the terms of Elijah's challenge and then anxiously watched as Baal's prophets made their sacrifice and spent most of the day desperately yelling, dancing, and ritually cutting their flesh with knifes and lancets in an attempt to convince their blood-thirsty demon to send fire (1 Kings 18:28).

Meantime, Elijah was busy pounding the false prophets with sarcasm: "Maybe he is busy talking, or on a journey, or maybe he is asleep; yell louder and wake him up!"

After establishing Baal as a farce, Elijah took twelve stones, one for each tribe, and built an altar to God, offered a bull sacrifice, and then drenched it seven times with water. Then he prayed for God to receive his offering without begging, whining, dancing, or cutting his flesh.

God answered Elijah's prayer and sent a fireball from heaven that consumed the sacrifice, the wood, the stones, and even licked up the water; leaving the ground smoldering.

At once, the people fell on their faces in fear as they cried out "The Lord, He is God." Like a plane cruising at thirty-thousand feet that suddenly lurches into a free fall, the people were grasping for the mercy of God. Then, like a miracle, Elijah roared over the chaos and commanded the people to seize the prophets of Baal and escort them to the valley to be executed for the crimes of fraud, ritual wickedness, and treason against God (1 Kings 18:30–40).

Relieved to still be alive, the mob apprehended the terrified prophets and escorted them to their death. Just like that, the entire industry was gutted. As everyone scattered and ran home, Elijah returned to the mountain to pray for rain. As requested, God opened the heavens, and the drought was ended.

Like a giant reset button, the actions of Elijah stopped the madness and forced the people to make sweeping lifestyle changes. We would expect to see a widespread return to God—and some genuinely did—but history tells us that the masses barely paused and then continued as before. Sadly, they loved their demonic lifestyles more than truth, and this put them on a collision course with national destruction. Meanwhile, God continued to send His prophets to warn of impending doom.

Elijah Drew a Line in the Sand

Elijah drew a line in the sand by confronting civic and religious evil. Ahab accused Elijah of being "the troubler of Israel" because he called down a drought. Elijah refuted that claim by reminding Ahab that he broke the Law of Moses which placed the nation under the curse of judgment as seen in the drought.

By reminding the people of God's laws, and then building a proper altar and offering a proper sacrifice to cover their sins, Elijah forced them to face their crimes so that mercy could be given and the drought ended. This process repaired the breach of covenant that their backsliding had caused.

Those who ignored his message were duly noted and those who repented were counted among the righteous. At this point, the northern tribes had about 175 years left before being destroyed by Assyria.

Elijah Taken to Heaven

Shortly after this major event, in 896 BC, God swept Elijah from the earth in a chariot of fire. He was still alive when taken, and according to the biblical record, this makes him and Enoch the only humans to leave the earth without a physical death.

In the New Testament, we learn that at Christ's second-coming, the born-again saints who are still alive will be caught up to meet Jesus in the air and they will immediately "put off" the old body and "put on" a new one (1 Thess. 4:15–17; 1 Cor. 15:51–54).[64]

Putting this together, I believe Elijah and Enoch are prophetic forerunners of the resurrection of the born-again saints who are taken to heaven before God's final judgment falls on the ungodly (more as we continue).

Malachi Prophesies the Return of Elijah

Some 480 years after Elijah was taken to heaven, he is mentioned by Malachi the prophet (around 416 BC). By this time, the Northern kingdom was long gone, and the survivors of the Judean kingdom were back from Babylonian captivity and living in Jerusalem with a rebuilt temple. After surviving the war and captivity, the remnant no longer worshipped idols. Even so, they had settled into a lukewarm system of rote worship to keep God happy and hopefully avoid any more calamities.

Against this backdrop, Malachi emerges. In biblical history, he is considered the last official prophet to the kingdom of Judah before the birth of Jesus Christ.

Malachi's message concerned the coming of Messiah—a wildly popular subject at the time—and the need for the people to stop pretending to care about God.

To the religious elite, Malachi warned that God was listening to their conversations. In private, they had a cold heart for God, yet they talked about the coming of Messiah with excitement, fully expecting to be part of His elite crowd. Malachi shattered their grand plans and warned that Messiah would appear suddenly and expose their hypocrisy (Mal. 2 and 3).

To the people, Malachi communicated God's displeasure with their pathetic temple sacrifices of sickly animals and the unsavory portions of their crops. They had become lukewarm (Mal. 1:8; Rev. 3:16).

Finally, Malachi ended his message with the promise that Elijah would come to bring reconciliation to the fathers and the children right before the "great and dreadful day of the Lord." This unique "day" was often mentioned by the prophets as the time when Messiah comes to judge the nations.

> 5 "Behold, I will send you Elijah the prophet before the coming of the great and dreadful day of the LORD. 6 And he will turn the hearts of the fathers to the children, and the hearts of the children to their fathers, lest I come and strike the earth with a curse."—Mal. 4:5-6 NKJV

John the Baptist Has the Elijah Anointing

Some 410 years later, the angel Gabriel appeared to Zacharias—the high priest in Jerusalem—and quoted Malachi's prophecy about Elijah and his mission as a forerunner to Messiah.

Gabriel informed Zacharias that Elizabeth, his barren and aged wife, would give birth to a son who would operate in the spirit and power of Elijah. His name would be John, and he was not allowed to drink wine, which marked him as a Nazarite.[65] Instead of coming under the influence of fermented drink, he would be filled with the Holy Spirit from the womb (Luke 1:11-41).

Jesus the Son of David

Six months later, Gabriel appeared to a virgin named Mary who was engaged to a man named Joseph—both genealogical descendants of King David—and announced that she would be overshadowed by Holy Spirit and conceive and give birth to the Messiah.[66]

Gabriel instructed Mary to visit her cousin Elizabeth who was six-months pregnant. When Mary greeted Elizabeth, the baby John leaped in her womb, and both were filled with the Holy Spirit.

For Gabriel, the announcement of the birth of Messiah and John the Baptist was a profound and distinguished honor. His last recorded appearance was his visit to the prophet Daniel, when he revealed the remainder of world history (covered in detail in the chapters on Daniel).

The Pedigree of John the Baptist

John the Baptist was born into the priestly line of Aaron, the first high priest, on both his father and mother's side, and his father was the high priest at the time of his conception. This gave John the religious pedigree of a true priest, an office that historically and officially presided over the "anointing" of the kings of Israel.

As a legal official, John was sent ahead of Messiah as a herald to announce His arrival. This gave the people an opportunity to prepare their hearts before His Majesty presented Himself. In addition, John was given the honor of residing over Messiah's "anointing" ceremony that occurred when John baptized Jesus in the Jordan River and then Father God spoke confirmation from heaven, and Holy Spirit came upon Him (Matt. 3:13-17).

Jesus Identifies Himself

Immediately after baptism, Jesus went into the wilderness to fast and pray for forty days. After this, He entered the synagogue in His hometown of Nazareth and read from the ancient scroll of Isaiah, announcing that He was "anointed" by the Spirit of God (Isa. 6:1-2a; Luke 4:16-19). This shocked everyone because this passage was regarded as a prophetic reference to Messiah.

Over the next three years, the Jewish religious leaders watched as Jesus performed irrefutable miracles and taught with authority that none of them possessed. Clearly, He was from God, and they despised Him because He exposed their hypocrisy, just as Malachi had prophesied.

Jesus Speaks of Elijah

Jesus told His disciples that John the Baptist was "the Elijah" that Malachi prophesied would precede Him (as confirmed by Gabriel). In addition, Jesus referred to His second coming which is preceded by Elijah. This indicates two Elijah appearances (Matt. 11:11–14; 17:11–12; Mark 9:12-13).[67]

In fact, Gabriel told Zacharias that John would come in "the spirit and power" of Elijah, indicating he would carry his same mission and anointing (Luke 1:17). Echoing this truth, John the Baptist denied that he was the actual Elijah. Instead, when asked, he referred to himself as a voice in the wilderness crying out to prepare the way of the Lord (John 1:23).

Going back to Malachi, he prophesied that Elijah would come before "the great and terrible day of the Lord." Most scholars agree that this refers to the "bowls of wrath" in the final days of this age. Therefore, many scholars believe as I do, that the actual Elijah of history will show up in Jerusalem to herald the second coming of Jesus the Messiah right before the final bowls of wrath.

Messiah Comes Twice

Many Jewish teachers, both then and now, incorrectly assumed that Messiah would come once and put an end to godless nations and wars against Israel. However, in the Old Testament we can see two Messiah advents. We see the suffering Messiah who was rejected by Israel as foretold by Isaiah the prophet, and the soon-coming King who sits on His throne in Jerusalem to rule for a thousand years (Isa. 53). We know that Jesus Christ is both.

Jesus came the first time as the spotless Passover Lamb. During His ministry, He was thoroughly watched and questioned by the national religious leaders and no blemish was found in Him.

Then, during Passover, the Jewish religious leaders arrested Jesus and brought Him before Pontius Pilate, the Roman governor over Judea. Pilate told the gathered Jews, "I find no fault in this man," thus confirming His innocence by the mouth of two witnesses (Matt. 27:22-25).

The crowd responded, "Crucify Him! We have no king but Caesar!" In that decisive moment, national Israel rejected her Messiah and chose Roman rule. It was a seminal act, and God obliged their wishes and allowed Rome full access to His people.

Within forty years, this generation was scattered among the nations when Titus the Roman ruler—chosen by the people— burned the rebuilt temple and massacred the Jews in Jerusalem.

The Future Elijah

Today, the nation of Israel is still waiting for Elijah to proceed Messiah because they rejected their first visitation. They will not be disappointed. According to Revelation 11, in the final moments of this age, two witnesses will come to Jerusalem to announce the arrival of Messiah and I believe Elijah will be one of them along with Moses. This was prophetically foreshadowed when they both appeared with Jesus who was transfigured into His heavenly glorified state as the disciples watched:

> Now after six days Jesus took Peter, James, and John his brother, led them up on a high mountain by themselves; 2 and He was transfigured before them. His face shone like the sun, and His clothes became as white as the light. 3 And behold, Moses and Elijah appeared to them, talking with Him. —Matt. 17:1-3 NKJV

When the actual Elijah of history appears in Jerusalem, he will not mince words as he announces the second coming of Jesus Christ. We can imagine how that will go over! As we know from history, Elijah is a fiery man with nerves of steel, who only cares about obeying God. As such, he is perfectly suited to stand up to Israeli religious and national leaders, as well as the rage of Antichrist in the final hours of this age.

As a prophet, he will remind the children of Israel of their historical covenant with God and sharply condemn them for straying from the clear writings of Moses—who will be with him—and the prophets. This will bridge the gap between fathers and children. This event will bring clarity to those who are humble and repentance to many Jews who will be born again. As a result, I believe a revival will erupt in Jerusalem.

These men will be sent during the reign of Antichrist, right before the final judgment of God falls on the earth. Their ministry will be watched by the entire world and the public will rage against them. Finally, when they have finished their ministry, they will be killed by Antichrist. Then, after three days, they will be resurrected and ascend to heaven:

> 7 When they [the two witnesses] finish their testimony, the beast that ascends out of the bottomless pit will make war against them, overcome them, and kill them. 8 And their dead bodies will lie in the street of the great city which spiritually is called Sodom and Egypt, where also our Lord was crucified. 9 Then those from the peoples, tribes, tongues, and nations will see their dead bodies three-and-a-half days, and not allow their dead bodies to be put into graves.
>
> 11 Now after the three-and-a-half days the breath of life from God entered them, and they stood on their feet, and great fear fell on those who saw them. 12 And they heard a loud voice from heaven saying to them, "Come up here." And they ascended to heaven in a cloud, and their enemies saw them. 13 In the same hour there was a great earthquake, and a tenth of the city fell. In the earthquake seven thousand people were killed, and the rest were afraid and gave glory to the God of heaven. —Rev 11:4-14 NKJV

The Anointing of Elijah

In Christian circles we often hear about the power and anointing of Elijah upon the saints. Do we have that anointing?

As saints, we are filled with Holy Spirit and commanded to preach the good news that Messiah is King and returning soon (and He is living in us!). By virtue of living and preaching this message, we are connecting biblical history to this present age. In other words, we are restoring the ancient foundations and reuniting the generations; just like Elijah did. So yes, we are carriers of the message and authority of Elijah.

In our sphere of influence, we must announce the return of Jesus to judge and rule the nations and encourage kings and leaders to rule justly. By opening our mouths to speak the truth, injustice is exposed, and justice and judgment are released into the situation. In addition, our fidelity to the Bible and our commitment to rightly divide the word of truth is a powerful force that exposes deception and brings repentance.

It is a season of shaking and uncovering. Everything hidden will be brought to light. Our message will not lay dormant for some day in the future. Instead, when we speak and pray out of obedience to God, the pillars of evil are immediately weakened, and we are one step closer to the end of this age.

Prepare Now

In order to electrify the world with authentic communication from God, the saints are currently undergoing difficulties that are meant to wake us up and shake us loose from this fallen world system.

We are living in a time of opportunity and peril. Every day, we move closer to the fullness of time when both kingdoms on earth are mature and pulsating with power: the kingdom of God and His anointed saints, and the kingdom of darkness and its cabal of evil.

As both kingdoms mature, the fruit of each will be fully revealed. As saints, we will feel the weight of God's glory and the pressure of evil—both at levels never before known.

Heaven Celebrates Our Arrival

When our mission on earth is finally complete, we will be caught up into heaven like Elijah, and given new and eternal bodies. On that occasion, the heavenly citizens will gather to celebrate our homecoming. We will be an honored generation because of the gravity of lawlessness that we have lived through and because of our triumphant level of love, long-suffering, faith, and devotion to God (Rev. 1:9; 13:10; 14:12).

CHAPTER 15

Isaiah the Prophet

The Northern kingdom of Israel was taken captive by the Assyrians and ceased to exist around 721 BC.

At this time, Hezekiah was king over the southern tribe of Judah, and he avoided Assyrian capture because of God's protection. Hezekiah was a good king who followed God and heeded His prophets: Isaiah and Micah (2 Kings 18:1–8).

Around 713 BC, Hezekiah became ill, and Isaiah the prophet informed him that he would die. Grieved, Hezekiah cried out to God with deep sincerity, and Isaiah returned to announce that God had heard his prayer and added fifteen years to his life. As a sign, God caused the sun to go backward on the steps of the palace (2 Kings 20:9-11).

This sign was noticed by a northern people called the Babylonians who were avid stargazers going back to the days of Nimrod their founder. Upon hearing about Hezekiah and his miraculous cure, an envoy travelled to Jerusalem to meet him. This was also a perfect opportunity to solicit the friendship of the king who defied Assyria—a common enemy—and got away with it (2 Kings 20:12-19; 2 Chr. 32:31).

Excited by his celebrity status, Hezekiah welcomed the curious Babylonians who brought gifts to honor his miraculous healing. Softened and disarmed, Hezekiah showed his visitors the entire royal treasury of gold and silver, military armaments, and other valuables.

Once the Babylonians departed, the prophet Isaiah rebuked Hezekiah for allowing his pride to overrule his common sense. He then prophesied that at a future date, the Babylonians would return to pillage the royal treasury and carry away some of Hezekiah's direct descendants and make them eunuchs and slaves (Isa. 39:5-8).

This word came to pass in 605 BC when Babylon raided Jerusalem for the first time and took members of the royal household into captivity, including young Daniel who was castrated and made a slave.

Pivotal Prophet

Sent by God at a turning point in history, Isaiah prophetically set the stage for the end of the kingdom of Israel as a sovereign power, and the launch of the Gentile Age.

Isaiah prophesied thirty years before the northern kingdom of Israel was destroyed by the Assyrians and roughly 114 years before the southern kingdom of Judah was raided by Babylon. The entire empire was literally on the brink of disaster and God in His due diligence sent Isaiah to remind Israel of her renowned and miraculous history and connect the dots for her soon coming destruction and captivity among the nations.

Isaiah and Messiah

Jesus Christ and His disciples quoted Isaiah more than any other prophet of God. Also, Jesus read Isaiah 61 to announce His identity as Messiah and launch His public ministry, thus validating the prophetic ministry of Isaiah.

Isaiah's name, along with the name of Jesus, means "salvation of Jehovah."[68] Jewish tradition holds that he was likely from the Tribe of Judah.

Isaiah gives more Messianic prophecies than any other Old Testament prophet. Also, he gives us some of the clearest prophecies concerning His suffering for our sins. This was a puzzling concept to the Jews who were awaiting their triumphant Savior and not the bruised and broken Messiah that Isaiah spoke of.

> 4 Surely he took up our pain and bore our suffering, yet we considered him punished by God, stricken by him, and afflicted. 5 But he was pierced for our transgressions, he was crushed for our iniquities; the punishment that brought us peace was on him, and by his wounds we are healed. 6 We all, like sheep, have gone astray, each of us has turned to our own way; and the Lord has laid on him the iniquity of us all.

> 8 . . . For he was cut off from the land of the living; for the transgression of my people he was punished.

> 10 Yet it was the Lord's will to crush him and cause him to suffer, and though the Lord makes his life an offering for sin, he will see his offspring and prolong his days, and the will of the Lord will prosper in his hand.—Isa. 53:4-6, 8, 10 NIV

Prophesies Against Babylon

Isaiah lived over 100 years before Babylon captured Judah and Jerusalem. In his day, Assyria was the dominant world power—not Babylon. Even so, he prophesied extensively about Babylon, her occult practices, her cruelty, and her eventual invasion of Jerusalem (Isa. 13).

It seems likely that God first revealed Babylon as the nation who would conquer the Judean kingdom after their visit to King Hezekiah and his foolish disclosure of his wealth.

Once their identity was revealed, Isaiah looked back to the prophecies of Moses to discover the scope of the atrocities or "curses" that awaited his rebellious people (Duet. 28).

Layers of Revelation

The prophesies of Isaiah have multiple layers of application and revelation. When he foretold the destruction and captivity of Jerusalem, his words applied to the approaching Babylonian captivity, and the destruction by Titus the Roman in AD 70.

Also, when he prophesied the return of the Israeli people back to their land, his words applied to the remnant that returned after Babylonian captivity, and the recent rebirth of the nation in our generation, and also a regathering that occurs at the millennium.

Think of it: Isaiah prophesied that the Jews would return to Jerusalem over 100 years before they were dispersed by the Babylonians! In addition, he revealed that the Medes and Persians would overthrow Babylon, and he named Cyrus the Persian king as their agent of deliverance! First of all, Babylon was not seen as a threat in Isaiah's day. Secondly, the Medes and Persians were distant and seemingly insignificant, and Cyrus was not even born (Isa. 44:28—45:1–7)!

Middle East and All Nations

Isaiah's prophecies also extended to the Middle-Eastern countries around Israel. Many were called by name and given specific warnings that their treatment of Israel would be served back to them in coming days. He specifically called out Syria and Damascus and foretold their destruction which is still future (Isa. 17:1–3).

Of particular significance are his prophecies to Babylon and Lucifer. His words are clearly addressed to earthly *and* spiritual powers. He depicts them as utterly evil and announces their total destruction and imprisonment in hell (Isa. 13-14).

He also warns that only those "nations" who honor God's ownership of Israel and the earth will enter the age of peace; all others will cease to exist.

12 For the nation and kingdom which will not serve you shall perish, and those nations shall be utterly ruined. — Isa. 60:12 NKJV

As we shall see in the chapters on Daniel, many of these nation-specific prophesies are coming to pass in our days and their final fulfillment will occur in the last seven years of this age.

Final Days

Isaiah depicts the earth bathed in sorrow and bloodshed at the end of the age as the rebellious cast up their evil until finally they are devoured by their own actions and then stopped by God.

As God allows this to happen, deep and gross darkness will cover the earth and her people. The picture is grim, but Isaiah gives us hope when he reveals that the glory of God will rise upon Israel and the unsaved Gentiles will come to her light.

> Arise, shine; for thy light is come, and the glory of the Lord is risen upon thee. For, behold, the darkness shall cover the earth, and gross darkness the people: but the Lord shall arise upon thee, and his glory shall be seen upon thee. And the Gentiles shall come to thy light, and kings to the brightness of thy rising. —Isa. 60:1–3, KJV

Technically, Isaiah is speaking to national Israel who has a key role to play in the final moments of this age. Even so, it applies to the born-again saints who are filled with the light of God through the indwelling of the Holy Spirit. Right now, we are the light of the world and the glory that God has poured on us through the Holy Spirit has made us a spectacle. We are obvious, unmistakable, and not to be missed. Jesus told His disciples:

> "You are the light of the world. A town built on a hill cannot be hidden. 15 Neither do people light a lamp and put it under a bowl. Instead they put it on its stand, and it gives light to everyone in the house. 16 In the same way, let your light shine before others, that they may see your

good deeds and glorify your Father in heaven. —Matt. 5:14-16   NIV

CHAPTER 16

Jeremiah the Prophet
Josiah the King

After the reign of Hezekiah, King of Judah, his son Manasseh became king at twelve years old. Manasseh followed the path of Ahab and Jezebel when he installed idol images of Baal and Ashtoreth in the temple of Solomon and burned one of his sons on an altar to Moloch. He reigned fifty-five years, and toward the end of his life he repented for his evil ways (even demon worshippers who sacrifice their children can repent!). After him, his wicked son Amon reigned for two years until his servants murdered him and installed his eight-year-old son Josiah on the throne in 641 BC (2 Kings 21:19–24).

Josiah Inherits a Mess

Josiah came to the throne during a pivotal time in Jewish history. The citizens of Judah had participated in demonic worship for several generations while at the same time appearing to worship God. They had watched the Northern tribes fall to the Assyrian army, and they were surrounded by warfare that involved Egypt, Assyria, Babylon, and the Medes. So far, Jerusalem had been spared. They should have recognized the brewing danger and turned to God. Instead, they were smug and indifferent.

Israel's neighbors viewed her as weak and an easy target. While claiming to be protected by her moral and jealous God, she brazenly solicited protection and favors from various national idols. In the ancient mind, only a fool would betray his god and arouse his anger—exactly what Israel was doing.

Meanwhile, off in the distance, the Babylonians who had visited Josiah's great-grandfather Hezekiah, some seventy years earlier, had never forgotten the riches of Jerusalem, and they fully intended to conquer and pillage her at the first opportune moment.

Isaiah the prophet had foretold the Babylonian invasion, and his words were actively waiting to be fulfilled. The hour was late.

Josiah Gets a Wake-Up Call

When Jeremiah the Prophet came on the scene, he was around twenty years old, and King Josiah was twenty-one. They were both members of the final generation to live in Jerusalem and see the temple of Solomon before God removed His Shekinah glory and allowed the Babylonians to destroy the nation.[69]

Jeremiah's ministry began with a revelation from God—likely while reading Isaiah's prophecies—about a soon-coming invasion by Babylon that would destroy Jerusalem because of her spiritual harlotry. For the next forty-one years, he faithfully prophesied the looming destruction and called upon the king and the people to repent (Jer. 1).

For the first nineteen years of Jeremiahs ministry, Josiah was king. When Josiah was twenty-six years old, he ordered the repair of the temple of Solomon. During the renovation, the writings of Moses and the Jewish "Histories" were discovered and read to the king. As Josiah listened, he was overcome with a holy fear of God.

Israel's Covenant with God

Josiah learned that before entering the Promised Land, Moses recited a lengthy "blessings and curses" prophecy, which was a "terms and conditions" contract between God and Israel (Deut. 28). The terms clearly stated that if the people turned to idols, they would be in breach of covenant resulting in the removal of God's protection. Once this occurred, Israel would be wide open to enemy attacks.

When Moses finished reciting the conditions of the covenant, the people accepted the terms with one accord. This entire legal discourse was then recorded by Moses and made part of the national archives.

Upon hearing this, Josiah realized that his people were in breach of covenant and under judgment because of their demon worship; it was pure mercy that Jerusalem was still standing. As the fear of God seized the king's heart, he knew something had to be done before it was too late. The reading continued . . .

In the "Histories of the Kings," Josiah learned that after the death of Solomon, his son Rehoboam was placed on the throne. Under Solomon, the citizens were subjected to hard labor, and they approached the new king asking for better conditions. King Rehoboam sought the advice of his father's counselors, who encouraged leniency, and his young friends, who advised a show of force and a heavier workload.

Unfortunately, King Rehoboam heeded his young friends and spoke harshly to the people. This angered the Northern tribes who broke away from Judah and Jerusalem and appointed their own king named Jeroboam. This is the king who immediately built two places of idol worship in the northern hills to discourage his people from traveling to Solomon's temple in Jerusalem to worship (1 Kings 12:13-31).

Sometime later, Jeroboam was worshipping a golden calf at his shrine in Bethel. While performing his ritual, an unnamed prophet burst in and pronounced damnation on the king, the false priests, and the bastard altar. The prophet then foretold the birth of a Judean king named *Josiah* who would fulfill this prophecy by unearthing the bones of the false priests and then burning them on the altar before destroying it.

Amazingly, this unnamed prophet foretold the ministry of Josiah some 326 years before he was born! Stunned by the miracle of finding his name in prophecy, Josiah realized he was destined to restore the true worship of God by tearing down places of idolatry!

In fact, Josiah did tear down the altar at Bethel, and he unearthed and burned the bones of the false priests. Then, in his fury, he almost unearthed the bones of the "unnamed prophet" but stopped when he learned it was the man who foretold his birth and actions (2 Kings 23:15-18).

Josiah Repents

Learning of his destiny and the nation's history, a new clarity came to the mind and heart of Josiah. As a nation, they were guilty of every transgression, and due to receive every curse that Moses warned about.

In repentance, Josiah tore his robes and cried to God for mercy. Then, he marshaled his forces and went through the kingdom tearing down and burning places of idolatry and killing the false priests who staffed them (2 Kings 23). As the nation watched the rage of their king, they were in a state of shock and consternation over the destruction of their family members, places of worship, and economic livelihood from idol trafficking and merchandise.

When Josiah finished his purge, he summoned his citizens to Jerusalem to observe Passover (2 Kings 23:21-25). The people gathered with serious trepidation. Their king had been on a rampage, and now he was demanding a national repentance and worship service.

As everyone stood before the king and the temple of Solomon, the writings of Moses were read, and an ominous wave of fear washed over the crowd. Suddenly, the fog of deception lifted, and they realized their crimes against God, their spiritual nakedness, and their present danger. With one heart, the nation repented and then recommitted themselves to God.

Revival

King Josiah took up arms against a devious industry that trafficked in the souls of men. The false prophets and priests were underhanded, greedy, and rich. Under a cloak of spirituality, they induced the people to commit evil rituals like child sacrifice and ceremonial orgies. Once compromised, the people were easily controlled by the fear of damnation if they failed to keep their demon gods happy. They were addicted and in need of intervention. Josiah's bold and decisive action against this criminal faction set the stage for a move of God and a national revival.

The Remnant

The full reading of the writings of Moses was a decisive moment for the nation. Revisiting their founding documents and national covenants brought revelation and new accountability. Looking at it now, we realize that God was making preparations for the soon coming destruction of Jerusalem by Babylon. This Passover event was an opportunity for true repentance. Those who turned their hearts back to God were marked as His "remnant" and they would be spared from death in the coming days. The rest were given over to their stubborn rebellion, and "marked" for destruction.

It is a serious matter when Holy Spirit moves upon your heart. Never underestimate the moment. It could be your last chance to repent before God steps back and allows satanic forces to claim any rightful property that is not under the blood of Jesus.

Josiah Is Killed in Battle

Sadly, about fourteen years after the big Passover celebration, Josiah was killed in battle by the Egyptian King Pharaoh Necho. He was thirty-nine years of age and died in the valley of Megiddo, also called Armageddon in the book of Revelation (2 Kings 23:29–30; Rev. 16:16; Zech. 12:11).

The death of Josiah is recorded as one of the most heartrending events in Israel's history. The entire nation mourned for him, and Jeremiah wrote a lamentation (2 Chr. 35:20–27).

Why did God allow Josiah to die? He was such a great king, and his reforms brought a revival to the nation.

First of all, God promised Josiah that He would withhold judgment from Israel during his lifetime because he had a tender and humble heart (2 Kings 22:18–20).

Secondly, the masses were fickle and compromised in their devotion to God. Some were riding the wave of emotional and national patriotism, and life was somewhat comfortable. But what if they encountered turbulent waters? Would they turn to God or a demon for help?

God knows the real condition of our hearts—personally and nationally. If we are harboring any doubt and unbelief toward Him, it will eventually rise to the surface. Therefore, it is mercy when God allows calamities to bring us discomfort so that our compromise can be exposed and repented of.

Israel Backslides

After Josiah's death, Pharaoh Necho of Egypt took control of Jerusalem and appointed Jehoiakim, Josiah's son, as his vassal king. Jehoiakim reigned for eleven years (2 Kings 23:34-37).

Once Jehoiakim was seated, all the reforms of his father Josiah were quickly dismissed, along with the ministry of Jeremiah the prophet. From this point forward, Jeremiah urgently warned of judgment and became a serious nuisance to the king, his governmental cabinet, the wicked priesthood, and all the people.

Sounding like a crackpot to the compromised masses, Jeremiah pleaded with his people to abandon their idols because a military invasion by Babylon—an obscure and remote nation—was just around the corner. Everyone just scoffed.

Meanwhile, Israel was under Egyptian rule and paid a heavy tribute tax that depressed the economy and depleted personal and national reserves. The wealth of every citizen was affected. Even so, the people adapted to their lower standard of living and placated themselves with the fantasy that they would eventually recover their strength and overthrow Egypt. To that end, they sought the favor of idols and foreigners instead of God. Sadly, the turbulent waters exposed their compromise.

In the meantime, the demon underworld watched the harlot nation grovel at their altars and then attempt to hide behind the skirts of God (Jer. 7:9-11). From their spiritual perch, they also spied the movement of angels *away* from Israel's defense. Clearly God was removing His protection! With menacing glee, they anxiously awaited the opportune moment to pounce.

The hour was late, and the people went about their daily lives as if everything was fine. In the palace, the king was surrounded by false prophets who predicted national glory and ultimate victory. Only the pesky prophet Jeremiah was a voice of dissent. His message was depressing. Wasn't there a law somewhere that could be used to shut him up (Jer. 38:4)?

Thankfully, Jeremiah was secure in his relationship with God and void of any need to be liked by his peers. There were some who heeded his warnings and kept their hearts free of idols. They were the "remnant." As for the rest, they would soon look terror in the face because the destruction of Jerusalem was imminent.

The Prophecies of Jeremiah

For over forty years, Jeremiah prophesied destruction to Jerusalem and finally lived to see it happen.

As an eyewitness historian, Jeremiah recorded the activities and attitudes of the final generation to live in Jerusalem and worship at the temple of Solomon. Through his writings, God has preserved important details of this unique moment in history for the sake of all generations. Today, you and I have a priceless treasure of revelation in his writings.

Jeremiah stood on the shoulders of every prophet in Israeli history when he announced a shift in the times and seasons of the earth. The season of Israel as a powerful and sovereign nation was closing, and she would soon lose her national sovereignty until her rebirth on May 14, 1948.

With the arrival of Babylon, the Gentile Age would officially commence. The world was literally at a pivot point in history, and God used Jeremiah to awaken His people before turning the page to a new chapter. I call this *prophetic due diligence.* Before God does anything, He tells His prophets (Amos 3:7).

Warnings to Gentile Nations

During Jeremiah's time, the entire Middle East was ensnared by the dragnet of Babylonian power and politics. As Babylon rose in power, other nations found it politically expedient to join them and participate in the spoils of war. Against this backdrop, Jeremiah called out specific nations and warned that God was watching and keeping record of every deed done against Israel—His beloved and estranged wife. He promised destruction upon cruel nations and blessings upon those who dealt kindly with her (Jer. Chapters 46—51).

To every nation—then and now—God's judgment of Israel is a harbinger of things to come as God turns His refining fires upon the nations of the world. Whether we agree or not, God has made Israel the center of all nations, and He pivots from her to us. Her national history is our international future (Jer. 25:15–16).

Jeremiah Prepares his People

Jeremiah often calls Israel "the wife of God," and he refers to idol worship as spiritual adultery. With a heart of reconciliation, he encouraged his people to return to the loving and forgiving arms of God. Otherwise, He would give them a bill of divorce and remove His protection. Once this occurred, the demonized nations would be allowed to ravage her (Jer. 3).

When it became clear that reconciliation was not possible, Jeremiah's message shifted from an emphasis on repentance to an emphasis on preparedness for the imminent disaster and how to survive slavery in a foreign land. The people were given a prophetic map of the days ahead. They were duly informed.

Jeremiah's message was multigenerational. To the current generation, he warned that Babylon would conquer Egypt and then take control of Jerusalem. Some would be killed, others enslaved, and the city would eventually be burned. Then, after seventy years, the remnant would return to Jerusalem and national life would resume. Finally, Messiah would come and rule (Jer. 16:14–15).

The Rise of Superpowers

Jeremiah finally witnessed the full destruction of Jerusalem by Babylon—as foretold by Isaiah. However, the revelation of Babylon as the first empire in the new "Gentile Age" was given to Daniel.

As a prophet, Jeremiah helped his people transition into a new season where they would be a small remnant living among global superpowers. Israel had experienced her glory days during a time when nations were small and territorial. In this new age, the axis of power would be concentrated and global. The prophets Jeremiah, Daniel, and Ezekiel were alive when this shift occurred in the earth.[70]

131

Babylon Is Damned

Finally, Jeremiah's last message is a recital of the charges against Babylon and her damnation (Jer. 50—51).[71]

Even though we know that God is addressing the ancient nation of Jeremiah's time, we also hear a bigger message that extends to modern nations and their leaders who are controlled by Satan; and finally to the last world empire under Antichrist.

Through Jeremiah, we learn that God has marked Babylon as the spawning pool of evil in the earth. She is bigger than a date on a calendar or a spot on the planet. She is a transgenerational and bi-dimensional (natural and spiritual) house of evil. Contained within her is every act of treason against God and His creation.

Babylon, the Home of All Evil

To the demonic realm, the final Babylonian government is utopia, and it begins when global survival is controlled by Antichrist who is controlled by Satan. When this happens, humanity will realize they are locked in a prison of terror where they must serve the interests and whims of the government or be killed. It will be a moment of sheer ecstasy for the demonic realm. This is the gold ring that Satan strives for in his long despicable career of hatred toward God and His creation.

To fallen mankind, the final Babylonian government is the culmination of every aspiration to live a self-fulfilling and God-free life. It is a global community whose power and riches eclipse all other systems of government ever created. Man's early effort was thwarted at the Tower of Babel, but now, after centuries of persistence and intellectual evolution, man will finally realize his dream of a one-world government that promises peace and prosperity to all. In reality, this government will be destructive and full of internal strife because sinful man is void of harmony and incapable of manufacturing it. Even so, it will be the most complete form of unity that godless humans will ever attain even though it is gained by the murder of all opponents.

From God's perspective, the entire history of treason has been one consolidated effort to overthrow His kingdom. In the end, God will allow the spiritual descendants of Nimrod to complete their ultimate idol; a towering government built on the foundation of personal greed, self-worship, and satanic influence.

God has a name for all of man's efforts to build an anti-kingdom that is at war with His ownership of creation: Babylon.

It is a religion of self-worship and a system of self-government.

God's Focused Wrath

On the pages of Scripture, the images and emotions of God spill forth in coals of damnation upon Babylon, as He speaks through the mouth of Jeremiah and all the prophets.

Pre-Creation, God looked out across the ages and watched the birth of evil in Satan's soul and his eventual seduction of humanity in the Garden. After this, He watched man's willingness to participate with Satan in the treasonous act of building a Babylonian society. In that moment, His wrath poured out in unquenchable fire to destroy the monster of consummate evil and remove it from creation. And out of the mouth of His prophets, God roars: Babylon is fallen!

CHAPTER 17

Ezekiel the Prophet

Ezekiel's Early Years

Like Jeremiah and Daniel, Ezekiel lived at the crossroads of history; he was a member of the last generation to see Solomon's temple and live as a citizen in a sovereign Jerusalem. During his life-time, the Gentile Age was fully born.

When Ezekiel was a young man, King Josiah was killed in battle by Pharaoh Necho of Egypt who took control of Jerusalem. A few years later, the Babylonians overthrew Egypt, took control of Jerusalem, and carried young Daniel into captivity. Then in 599 BC, the Babylonians plundered the city a second time and took Ezekiel and many others to the land of Babylon; approximately 500 miles away and a four-month journey.[72]

Ezekiel Is Essential

Ezekiel came from a priestly family, and it is believed that he was around thirty years old at the time of his captivity which is the official age to enter priestly service. This distinguished him as a spiritual official among his people.[73]

While a prisoner in Babylon, God appointed him as a prophet and gave him important revelations that were close at hand and others that belong to the last days and the millennial reign of Jesus Christ.

Almost 700 years after Ezekiel, John the Apostle was caught up into heaven and given similar visions that confirm and expand what Ezekiel saw. For this reason, among many, the study of Ezekiel is essential to understand the end-times.

Anxiousness in Captivity

In Babylonian captivity, Ezekiel and his Jewish brethren were doing their best to reorder their lives, but they missed Jerusalem and wanted to go home.

During this time, it was rumored that Egypt was preparing to overthrow Babylon and reclaim Jerusalem. This was good news to the captives who preferred slavery to Egypt where they were taxed excessively, but allowed to live in their native land. Uncertainty and fear filled the minds of the captives as they clung to every bit of news and every ray of hope.

Ezekiel Commissioned as a Watchman

Against this backdrop, about four years into his captivity, God pulled Ezekiel into His fiery and powerful presence. The grandeur of God's majesty overcame Ezekiel, and every fiber of his body fell prostrate in holy fear. This immediately brought clarity and sobriety to the prophet's mind.

Awe-struck, Ezekiel saw God seated upon a sapphire throne with four living creatures below Him. The creatures, called cherubim, each had four heads with two wings and one wheel—filled with eyes—beside them. When the Spirit of God moved, the cherubim followed in perfect synchronization. The sound of their wings was like the thunder of rushing waters and Ezekiel likened it to the voice of God (Ezek. 1:4–28). In fact, Daniel describes the voice of God in the same way and Jesus Christ has the same voice in the book of Revelation.

Radiating with majesty, God commissioned Ezekiel as a prophet and warned him that his message would be unpopular and delivered to an obstinate people. Even so, he was sternly commanded to stay strong and speak as directed. Otherwise, his tongue would be heavy in his mouth. The whole exchange was very serious.

Scripture tells us that everyone is accountable for his or her words. As saints, we are held to a higher standard, and God will cause our tongues to be useless, flat, and without a true anointing, unless we speak truth as directed by Him (Pet. 4:11; Matt. 7:22-23; Matt. 12:36–37).

After this fearsome encounter with God, Ezekiel faithfully and boldly reminded his people of their sins and unwillingness to listen to the prophets.

God Departs from Israel

Five years into his captivity, in 594 BC, Ezekiel was pulled into another heavenly encounter when he was visited by a spiritual messenger with a man-like appearance who burned from the waist down and glowed like hot metal from the waist up. The fiery form of this messenger conveyed God's purity and judgement.

This "person" yanked Ezekiel into the heavens by his hair and took him to Jerusalem where he was shown the interior of Solomon's temple and the idol statues and secret rituals that the elders, priests, and women were performing.

After witnessing the depravity occurring within the temple, Ezekiel saw God in the holy of holies, upon His burning chariot throne and surrounded by the cherubim. While he watched, God and His entourage moved toward the door to leave. But first, God instructed a heavenly scribe to go through the city and mark the foreheads of those who grieved the moral collapse of the nation. Following behind, angelic executioners were commanded to kill those without the mark—man, woman, child, and the elderly (Ezek. 9:3–11).

The Mark of Allegiance

In this vision, the mark was the Hebrew letter Tau, the last in the alphabet, which is a "t". [74] Early Church fathers generally recognized this as the sign of the cross. This mark, like the blood over the doorpost of the Israelites in Egypt, was a prophetic reference to Jesus Christ. In companion passages—Rev. 7:3 and Rev. 14:1—the seal of God is stamped upon the foreheads of His servants and they are exempted from the wrath of God.

Today, the born-again followers of Jesus are filled with Holy Spirit and this is our "mark."[75] Physically, we don't walk around with a mark on our foreheads, but in the spiritual realm our identity is clear.

According to the Book of Revelation, in the final hours of this age, those who reject God and follow Antichrist, will accept a physical mark on the forehead or the hand in order to buy and sell. Those who receive this mark are given over to eternal damnation. The forehead indicates our thinking and philosophies—the seat of our soul—and the hands represent the deeds that flow from us (worship).

Because the mark of Antichrist has such serious consequences, I propose that those who take it are willfully and publicly rejecting the rule of God (John 8:44 and Rev. 13:16–18; Rev. 14:9-13). In the last chapter, we will go deeper into this subject.

In summary, every human is "marked." You are either with God or against Him. A decision to stay neutral is a decision to refrain from accepting God's ownership over your life. Your decision does nothing to change the truth. God simply gives you the freedom to accept or decline His terms.

Prelude to Judgment

Ezekiel watched as the righteous were marked for deliverance (as the remnant) and then the heavenly scribe took burning coals from beneath God's throne and threw them upon the city of Jerusalem. After this, Ezekiel was commanded to prophesy destruction to the king and all the people for breaking God's laws, living in depravity, and lacking remorse (Ezek. 11:4-13).

Finally, Ezekiel watched as God departed from the temple upon His chariot throne, accompanied by the cherubim. Together, the entire entourage went to the east side of the city, to the Mount of Olives, and stood there as the vision ended (Ezek. 11:22-23).[76]

With this experience, Ezekiel was a firsthand witness of a historic event: the departure of God from the temple of Solomon where He had resided in the holy of holies upon His throne of mercy as He ruled over Israel.

Amazingly, this reveals that God's Shekinah glory—also known as His Holy Spirit—continued to "physically" dwell in the temple of Solomon even though the people had filled it with idols and performed secret rituals in His house and under His nose (Ezek. 8).

> For after they had slain their children for their idols, on the same day they came into My sanctuary to profane it; and indeed thus they have done in the midst of My house.— Ezek. 23:39 NKJV

What Ezekiel witnessed was the unbelievable long-suffering and patience of a loving God who remained at the side of His harlot wife as long as He could before finally giving her over to her demonic lovers.

God's Patience and Orderliness

God is loving, patient, and orderly. He does nothing in haste. By the time He left the temple and Jerusalem, it had been some 900 years since He took up residence among His people on that first Passover night in Egypt. In the centuries since, they continually participated in demon worship and sought the favor of foreign kings. Incrementally, God gave them over to pestilence, drought, wars, economic hardships, and other calamities in order to awaken them. Finally, the people were so deeply embedded in their wicked lifestyle that they ignored God and His prophets. It was time to step aside and let them reap the full force of their choices.

The occasion was unprecedented and profoundly significant for Israel. God had always lived in her midst. This was the singular fact that set her apart from every other nation. Now, for the first time, she was without the "physical" presence of God and unprotected from the hatred of her enemies.

Jerusalem's destruction was locked in. Nebuchadnezzar had raided the city twice and carried off thousands of Jews, including members of the royal and priestly households. Their captivity was orchestrated by God in order to preserve a remnant and this was done *before* He abandoned the temple of Solomon. In addition, the repentant ones still living in the city, were marked to be spared in the upcoming massacre.[77]

Every arrangement was made, and Ezekiel was the chosen priest and prophet to witness the event and record it for future generations.

Israel Is Spiritually Naked

From a distance, Satan watched as an unusual amount of angelic activity occurred over Jerusalem. Suddenly, the Shekinah glory of God departed from the temple and the angels who usually kept guard over the city retreated as well! Just like that, the city and her people were left exposed and naked on the earth. It was incredible! God had finally made good on His warnings given through Moses and the prophets! As he surveyed the situation, Satan noticed some of the angels stayed behind to observe, but clearly, they were not there to protect the harlot city as in the past.

Immediately, the demon realm went into action and began stirring up mischief among the neighboring kings who obsessed over the prospect of plundering Israel; but dared not touch her because of Babylon.

Meantime, King Nebuchadnezzar heard rumors that the Jews in Jerusalem were conspiring with Egypt to overthrow his hold on the city. This was the last straw! In a rage, he ordered General Nebuzaradan to march on Jerusalem for the third and final time and utterly burn the place to the ground.

Elated, Satan and his army prepared to march with Babylon. With God gone, he would finally have full access to the royal adulteress who brazenly worshipped idols in the temple where God in His Shekinah glory had lived.

Rebuke to the Nations

From heaven, God watched as demonized kings plotted for ways to exploit Israel. Her vulnerability now stirred and exposed their deep hatred for God and His people. In this context, God directed Ezekiel to prophesy to the nations aligned against Israel—*past, present, and future*—and judicially communicate His displeasure and ultimate judgment upon those who hate her (Ezek. 25-32). These are the same warnings that Isaiah and Jeremiah gave—thus establishing them in the mouth of two or more witnesses. Today they are part of the public legal record for all nations, for all time.

As directed, Ezekiel gave damning and sometimes cryptic prophecies against Israel's neighbors including Egypt, Babylon, and Tyre. Historically, many of these prophecies have come to pass.

Even so, they clearly transcend into future generations and the spiritual realm. For instance, the king of Tyre is addressed as if he is Satan, and his city is called a *merchant* city; which is a clear connection to Babylon in the book of Revelation (Ezek. 26-28).

Through these prophecies, we realize that international hatred for Israel is demonically fueled and that it will survive and flourish all the way to the end of the age when it coalesces into a group of nations called "Babylon the great" in the book of Revelation.

God Is Judicial

God does everything with judicial righteousness. He always tells us in advance and lays out the terms *before* we go forward.

God warned the nations to be cautious and humble toward Israel *before* He departed from the temple of Solomon and allowed the Gentile Age to commence.

Likewise, in ancient Israel, Moses read the terms of God's covenant with Israel *before* she crossed over into the Promised Land.

Obviously, God knew His words would be dismissed with scorn, but it didn't matter. In His holy justice, He honors the nations with prophetic foreknowledge. To know is to be held accountable.[78]

God covered all the bases. A remnant had been forcibly removed from Jerusalem and then safely tucked away in various prisoner camps outside of Babylon. The people in Jerusalem were reminded daily by Jeremiah what was happening and why. In Babylon, the captives had the preaching of Ezekiel who witnessed the corruption in the temple of Solomon and God's departure.

Finally, Jeremiah and Ezekiel prophesied to the nations and foretold their future destruction for abusing God's people. Having laid the groundwork, it was time to give Satan and his puppet Nebuchadnezzar full access to the harlot city called Jerusalem.

Jerusalem Destroyed

On September 22, 594 BC, Ezekiel saw the vision of God's Shekinah glory leaving Jerusalem. On January 30, 590 BC—four years and four months later—the army of Babylon surrounded Jerusalem and held her under siege for the next nineteen months while the people inside slowly starved to death and resorted to cannibalism to survive.

Finally, on July 27, 588 BC, the army of Nebuchadnezzar broke down the walls of Jerusalem and ran through the streets killing, raping, and plundering. By the time they were done, the temple of Solomon and every important building and home was burned to the ground, and the walls of the city were torn down. The beautiful city had become a pile of smoldering rubble just as Moses, Isaiah, Jeremiah, Ezekiel, and all the prophets had foretold.

Six months later, on January 25, 587 BC, messengers came to the captives in Babylon and reported the news of the destruction of Jerusalem. Like a violent punch in the gut, all wishful thinking was sucked from the lungs of the prisoners, and the heavy air of reality came crashing in. It was over. Jerusalem and her magnificent temple were gone. How could they ever be restored? What about Messiah? Was He still coming?

Israel's Broken Promises

Because of Ezekiel's preaching, the remnant recognized their abandonment of God as the cause of Israel's downfall. Gone was the pride of national supremacy; they needed hope for the future.

Some 900 years earlier, the people had agreed to the legal terms laid out by God through Moses and promised to be faithful. In the intervening years, they broke their promise, worshipped demons, repented, and then started the process all over again. Clearly, they were incapable of keeping their word, and now the curse of slavery in a foreign land was upon them.

In truth, none of us are capable of living in a way that earns the blessings of God. Even so, we didn't know this about ourselves until we watched the history of Israel's never-ending failures or lived with our own. Now as we look back, we realize that no man or nation is able to serve God perfectly. This is precisely the education that God intended.

Knowing all of her weaknesses, God decided pre-Creation to make Israel His nation, Canaan her land, and Jerusalem the throne of His Son Jesus Christ. Then, on the pages of time, He appeared to Abraham and shared His predetermined plans. When Abraham believed, God placed him in a deep trance and swore on oath to make it so (Gen. 15).

Notice that Abraham was not allowed to participate, but only witness this transaction. This is because we are mere creatures and unable to guarantee something eternal. Whereas, God is the "I AM" and outside of time. Only He can make transgenerational or everlasting promises (Heb. 6:13).

When God promised to make Abraham a nation and bring Messiah through her, He swore on Himself. Therefore, His covenant is irrevocable and not subject to the fickleness of man.

Ezekiel's Vision of Dry Bones

After the fall of Jerusalem, God gave Ezekiel another vision to bring hope to the grieving captives.

In this vision, Ezekiel was transported to a vast valley of dry bones which represented the dead and scattered nation of Israel. As Ezekiel looked, God instructed him to prophesy life to the bones, and when he did, they began to rattle and come together, and their flesh returned. Finally, God instructed Ezekiel to speak to the four winds—all the corners of the earth—and call the breath of life back into the dispersed nation of Israel. When this happened, the nation came alive and stood on its feet as a large army. To have an army, you must be a sovereign nation. As captives living under foreign rule, this is not possible.

In this sweeping vision, Ezekiel saw the nation of Israel as disjointed, scattered, and long dead. The bones on the valley floor were old and bleached out. In the natural, it was impossible to put the bones back together, much less bring them back to life, and this was exactly the point.

At the time of the vision, the Jews were in captivity. Seventy years later, they returned to Jerusalem and lived under foreign rule until they were scattered again in AD 70 by Titus the

Roman. Clearly, none of this fulfilled Ezekiel's vision of Israel as a sovereign nation in her land with an army.

What Ezekiel saw was an event that would take place some 2,500 years later on May 14, 1948, when Israel officially declared her independence and reclaimed a piece of her ancient homeland.

Immediately, she mustered an army to defend her sovereign borders, and the flood gates opened as Jews from the four corners of the earth awoke and returned to the land that God gave them on oath as an everlasting possession (Joel 3:20-21; Amos 9:14-15).

The rebirth of Israel as a sovereign nation was a pivot point in history. It signaled the beginning of the end of a long era called the Gentile Age that began when Ezekiel witnessed the departure of the Shekinah glory of God from Solomon's temple.

Ezekiel the priest and prophet was alive and witnessed the commencement of the Gentile Age and then, with this vision, he witnessed the end of that age with the rebirth of national Israel! Stunning! God always tells His prophets before He does anything.

CHAPTER 18

The Battle of Gog and Magog

With the dry-bones vision, Ezekiel and his fellow captives were given new hope. God would restore Israel as a nation with an army, and then Messiah would come. What a relief!

At this point, God could have left Ezekiel with the impression that the regathered nation would automatically live in peace and security forevermore. This would have been in agreement with every prophet of Israel who warned of judgment, captivity, restoration, and finally the reign of Messiah from Jerusalem.

However, a short time after the dry-bones vision, God revealed to Ezekiel a devastating war against the restored nation of Israel by a leader named Gog from the land of Magog.

Wait a minute! Why would God allow that to happen?

Father God Prepares the Earth for His Son

Remember David and Solomon. Father God is on a mission to get the earth ready for the reign of His Son from Jerusalem. Therefore, every enemy must be brought to the surface and dealt with so that Jesus inherits a throne of peace. Today Jesus *sits* at the right hand of the Father and waits for the defeat of His enemies.

> "The Lord (God) says to my Lord (the Messiah), **Sit** at My right hand, until I make Your adversaries Your footstool."—Ps. 110:1, AMP

With the rebirth of Israel, the ancient wells of hostility have opened and Father God waits for His enemies to rise so that He can rebuke their actions in preparation for the reign of His Son.

In Scripture, God is called a "man of war" when He brings Pharaoh and his army to their knees. This same title was applied to King David because he destroyed every foe that rose against him. In this season of Israel's rebirth, God will again be called a "Man of War" (Exod. 15:3-4; Isa. 42:13; I Chr. 28:3).

Israel Without Walls

In this vision, Israel has been regathered back to her land as a distinct nation and living in *peace without walls*. This statement of peace is made several times so that we cannot dismiss it.

> After many days you [Gog] will be summoned [for service]; in the latter years you shall come into the land that is restored from [the ravages of] the sword, where people have been gathered out of many nations to the mountains of Israel, which had been a continual wasteland; but its people were brought out of the nations, *and they are living securely*, all of them. 9 You will go up [against them], you will come like a storm; you shall be like a cloud covering the land, you and all your troops, and many peoples with you."

> 10 'Thus says the Lord God, "It will come about on that day that thoughts will come into your mind, and you will devise an evil plan, 11 and you will say, 'I will go up against an open country; I will come against *those who are at rest and peaceful, who live securely, all of them living without walls and having neither bars nor gates*, 12 to take spoil and seize plunder, to turn your hand against the ruins which are now inhabited, and against the people who are gathered from the nations, who have acquired cattle and goods, who live at the center of the world [Israel].'—Ezek. 38:8-11 AMP (italics mine)

Today Israel has been regathered back to her land that was once a wasteland, but the nation is surrounded by walls and constantly vigilant against attackers. So, when will she be living without walls and in peace?

The obvious answer is during the Millennial reign of Jesus Christ. In fact, in the Book of Revelation, Satan is bound for a thousand years, and then released for a short season. Upon his release, he gathers an army called Gog and Magog to attack Israel and the throne of Messiah (Rev. 20:8). I believe this vision has application to that war, while at the same time it speaks to a war that is much closer.

So, is there another time when Israel will be at peace without walls? Many scholars propose that modern Israel will experience short term peace when she enters into a seven-year peace treaty with Antichrist (covered in detail in the visions of Daniel).

I agree, and I further propose that before Israel enters this peace treaty, she is without walls. If I am right, then something will occur before the seven-year treaty that brings her walls down. In the last two chapters of this book, we will cover an interesting war that might level the Middle East and bring down the walls that surround Jerusalem . . .

Gog and Magog

In this vision, God is speaking to Gog who is a powerful leader living in the far north. Gog has serious clout in the world because he is able to marshal many nations to attack Israel. This international confederacy is called Magog.

Many nations are called out by their ancient names. It is generally accepted that the leader Gog is from Russia and his Magog confederation reaches to the four corners of the world that Ezekiel knew about. Usually, scholars include the nations of Turkey, Syria in the north, Iran in the east, Sudan and Northern Ethiopia in the south, and Libya in the west. All of these details suggest that Gog and Magog might be Antichrist and his international allies.

The name *Gog* is a play on words which can be translated as "Gentile." Biblically speaking, a Gentile is someone of a nationality other than Israelite. Being a Gentile is neither good nor bad. In Scripture, a Gentile is a derogatory term when it is applied to self-serving and idol-worshipping people and nations. Given that distinction, many Jews—throughout history—could be called a Gentile (Rom. 2:25-29).

In this vision, Gog is a cryptic and derogatory title for a non-Jewish king who hates Israel. God calls him Gog as a designation of dishonor.

Magog, likewise, is a derogatory and cryptic name that applies to the people that Gog rules, as well as any people group that war against God and His saints.

Putting these together, Gog and Magog represent both the ancient and modern nations and people who hate God and Israel. As a unit, they are on a mission to eradicate Israel now that she has returned to her homeland.[79]

Hooks in His Jaws

Ezekiel is told this war happens in the latter days when Gog has thoughts in his mind of claiming the land, the wealth, and the people of Israel as his own. Knowing his heart, God tells him:

> "I will turn you around, put hooks into your jaws, and lead you out."—Ezek. 38:4 NKJV

We could argue that God made him do it. This is not the case. Rather, God knows our hearts and allows or disallows our evil actions based on His overarching will.

Why does Gog need hooks when his heart is already turned toward evil? Perhaps he hesitates because of Israel's peace treaty? If Gog is Antichrist, as some postulate, then he might hesitate because he would be breaking his own treaty which would put him at odds with some nations.

Merchants of the Earth

Several nations inquire about the spoils of war. This happens at the onset of the war because Gog and Magog are annihilated and never have the chance to distribute spoils.

> 13 Sheba, Dedan, the merchants of Tarshish, and all their young lions will say to you, "Have you come to take plunder? Have you gathered your army to take booty, to carry away silver and gold, to take away livestock and goods, to take great plunder?"—Ezek. 38:12-13 NKJV

The peoples identified as Sheba, Dedan, and Tarshish have long been considered by many scholars as wealthy merchants who live along the coastal trade routes of the ancient world.

Their ability to question Gog and his war, may indicate their influence in the earth and possibly their opposition. If anything, this indicates a lack of international unity. From the above passage, it is unclear if this group is wicked or benevolent.

Tarshish and Tyre

I want to add a note about Tarshish the merchant. In the Bible, Tarshish and Tyre are closely aligned and both are called merchants.[80] In a different section of Ezekiel they are both addressed together:

> 1 The word of the LORD came again to me, saying, 2 "Now, son of man, take up a lamentation for Tyre, 3 and say to Tyre, 'You who are situated at the entrance of the sea, merchant of the peoples on many coastlands.—Ezek. 27:1-3 NKJV

> 12 "Tarshish was your [Tyre] merchant because of your many luxury goods."—Ezek. 27:12 NKJV

In Ezekiel chapters 26—29, Tyre is addressed as a city, a people, a prince, and a king who is Satan. This is the famous portion of Scripture where we learn that Satan fell from heaven because of his greed for the riches of creation. Described as a very successful trader or *merchant,* Satan turned to violence in his quest for riches and glory.

> 12 "Son of man, take up a lamentation for the king of Tyre, and say to him, 'Thus says the Lord GOD:
>
> "You were the seal of perfection, Full of wisdom and perfect in beauty. 13 You were in Eden, the garden of God; every precious stone was your covering: The sardius, topaz, and diamond, Beryl, onyx, and jasper, Sapphire, turquoise, and emerald with gold. The workmanship of your timbrels and pipes was prepared for you on the day you were created. 14 "You were the anointed cherub who covers; I established you; you were on the holy mountain of God; you walked back and forth in the midst of fiery stones. 15 You were perfect in your ways from the day you were created, till iniquity was found in you. 16 *"By the abundance of your trading you became filled with violence within, and you sinned;* therefore I cast you as a profane thing out of the mountain of God; and I destroyed you, O covering cherub, From the midst of the fiery stones.—Ezek. 28:16 NKJV (emphasis mine)

Throughout the Old Testament we get glimpses of God's wrath toward those who are wicked *merchants.* Then, in the book of Revelation, God's climactic bowls of wrath destroy Babylon because she is a violent and murderous *merchant,* trafficking in people, worldly treasures, and satanic worship (Rev. 18:1–24 and Isa. 14:12–21).

Satan the Original Evil Merchant

Putting this together, we realize that Satan is the original evil merchant and his craft entered world governments through Nimrod. Throughout history, this system has persisted and will emerge as the final Babylon in the book of Revelation.

We have to wonder, why is Satan so infatuated with riches? From the above passage, he clearly lived in opulence and beauty before he defiled himself with greed and turned to violence. I theorize that after living in heaven, he is trying to recreate a piece of that paradise on earth by sponsoring evil merchants to acquire sumptuous riches so that he can live vicariously through them.

No matter his covetous greed, Satan remains fallen, eaten with strife, void of anything lovely, and destined for the lake of fire (Isa. 14:3-21). Clearly, the love of money is the root of all evil (1 Tim. 6:10).

The Battle

In Ezekiel's vision, Gog makes plans to surprise Israel with a blanket of firepower and snuff her out in one fell swoop:

> 16 You will come up against My people Israel like a cloud, to cover the land. —Ezek. 38:16 NKJV

An attack of this size requires a great deal of preparation. First, the participating nations must be aligned with Gog. Second, they must be heavily armed with weapons that are in sufficient quantity and power to achieve Israel's quick destruction and to discourage others from coming to her defense. Third, they must attack when Israel least expects it, thus limiting her retaliation.

When Gog and the Magog strike, a great earthquake levels the mountains and God pummels the invaders with fire, flooding rain, and sulfur:

> Surely in that day there shall be a great earthquake in the land of Israel . . . The mountains shall be thrown down, the steep places shall fall, and every wall shall fall to the ground. I will call for a sword against Gog throughout all My mountains says the Lord GOD. Every man's sword will be against his brother. And I will bring him to judgment with pestilence and bloodshed; I will rain down on him, on his troops, and on the many peoples who are with him,

flooding rain, great hailstones, fire, and brimstone. —Ezek. 38:19-22 NKJV

God Fights for Israel

In Ezekiel, God takes the credit for saving Israel. It is entirely possible that God fights using natural phenomenon like the earthquake, volcanos, asteroids, or anything else He wants. That is not out of the question. For example, He flooded the earth during Noah's time, and rained down fire and brimstone on Sodom and Gomorrah.

On the other hand, God has often used wicked tyrants to execute His judgments. In those instances, He steps aside and allows them the space to carry out their plans and use their armory—just as He did with Babylon.

In this vision, the "pestilence" of burning fire and brimstone could be asteroids, volcanos, or possibly modern explosives or nuclear war. If the method is modern warfare, some might argue that Israel's military weapons save her.

Supposing they do, it is God who oversees the rise and fall of nations. Therefore, it is by His permission and providence that any nation possesses military might. Even so, do not think that God condones any nation or her military apparatus. Rather, He allows a nation to mature in its ideology and obtainment of power within certain boundaries. These boundaries restrain and allow, based on God's overarching purposes and plans on the earth.

Aftermath of the Day of the Lord

This war is an international event and God calls to the predatory birds and beasts to feast upon the wicked. In addition, God tells us that this "day" is one that He has already told us about:

> 4 You will fall [dead] on the mountains of Israel, you and all your troops and the nations who are with you. *I will give you to every kind of predatory bird and animal of the field*

as food. 5 You will fall in the open field, for I have spoken," says the Lord God. 6 "I will also send fire on Magog and on those who live securely in the coastlands; and they will know [without any doubt] that I am the Lord.

7 "I will make My holy name known in the midst of My people Israel, and I will not let them profane My holy name anymore; and the nations will know that I am the Lord, the Holy One of Israel. 8 Behold, it is coming and it will be done," says the Lord God. *"That is the day of which I have spoken."*—Ezek. 39:4-9 AMP (italics mine)

This war and Israel's victory, is referred to by God as "the day of which I have spoken." This statement points us to the "Day of the Lord" (Isa. 13:6; Joel 1:15; Amos 5:18; Obad. 15; Zeph. 1:7; Acts 2:20).

When the "Day of the Lord" is mentioned in prophetic writings, God often calls for the predatory birds and animals to feast upon the slaughter of the wicked. In prophetic typology, this can refer to evil people and rulers. Therefore, the wicked of the earth are actually engaged in devouring each other.

After this war, Ezekiel tells us it will take Israel seven months to bury the bodies and cleanse the land. In addition, the weapons of the fallen army will be so numerous that it will take Israel seven years to recycle them (Ezek. 39:1–16).

Pulling this together, I believe this war might be Armageddon, which is also the climax of "The Day of the Lord" (covered more as we continue). If I am correct, the seven years of cleanup probably occurs under the earthly reign of Jesus Christ.

Israel and Messiah

Ezekiel tells us that after this war, God will pour out His Spirit on Israel. How does that happen?

Now that Jesus Christ has ascended to heaven, the Spirit of God is poured out on us when we believe on Him for salvation. Therefore, I believe that this war results in widespread repentance among the Jews in preparation for the return of Messiah.

> 29 And I will not hide My face from them anymore; for I shall have poured out My Spirit on the house of Israel,' says the Lord GOD."—Ezek. 39:29 NKJV

The Battle of Armageddon?

In summary, there are strong indications that this war happens during Israel's final days under Antichrist when she is living without walls and with a false sense of peace. Other details such as a great earthquake, and terrible hail, connect this war with "the Day of the Lord," which occurs when God pours out His bowls of wrath to end the reign of Antichrist. These details connect us to the battle of Armageddon that is mentioned in the book of Revelation:

> 14 These miracle-working demons conferred with all the rulers of the world to gather them for battle against the Lord on that great coming Judgment Day of God Almighty . . . 16 And they gathered all the armies of the world near a place called, in Hebrew, Armageddon—the Mountain of Megiddo.

> 17 Then the seventh angel poured out his flask into the air; and a mighty shout came from the throne of the temple in heaven, saying, "It is finished!" 18 Then the thunder crashed and rolled, and lightning flashed; and there was a great earthquake of a magnitude unprecedented in human history. 19 The great city of "Babylon" split into three sections, and cities around the world fell in heaps of rubble; and so all of "Babylon's" sins were remembered in God's thoughts, and she was punished to the last drop of anger in the cup of the wine of the fierceness of his wrath. 20 And islands vanished, and mountains flattened out, 21 and there was an incredible hailstorm from heaven; hailstones weighing a hundred pounds fell from the sky

onto the people below, and they cursed God because of the terrible hail. —Rev. 16:14, 16-21 TLB

CHAPTER 19

Ezekiel's Temple
Ezekiel: 40-48

God gave Ezekiel a panoramic view of Jewish history. After witnessing the departure of God from Solomon's temple, the rebirth of national Israel in the valley of dry bones, and the rage of the nations against Israel in Gog and Magog, Ezekiel receives his final vision. In this experience, he is transported to a serene and picturesque land of Israel where he witnesses the return of the glory of God to a spiritually pure temple in Jerusalem. Before we go into the future and look at this temple, we must visit the last temple the Jews worshipped in.

The Second Temple

Seventy years after Nebuchadnezzar destroyed Solomon's temple, a group of remnant Jews returned to Jerusalem to rebuild the temple on the same site where it once stood.

By this time, the Medes and Persians had conquered Babylon to become the reigning world power. King Cyrus the Mede gave permission to the Jewish captives to go home and rebuild their house of worship, and he restored many of the temple treasures that Nebuchadnezzar had taken.

When the foundation stones were placed over the ruins of Solomon's temple, the older men began to weep bitterly as they remembered its past magnificence. How could this one ever compare?

After a good start, the Jews were thwarted by their hostile neighbors, and the work stopped for fifteen years. Eventually, Haggai the prophet rose up and encouraged the people to finish the temple; promising that its glory would be greater than Solomon's (Hag. 2:9). The people responded, completed the temple, and restored the sacrifices and worship.[81]

It was an exciting and emotional time, but something very important was missing: the manifest presence / Shekinah glory of God. Where was the fulfillment of Haggai's prophecy of a greater glory? The second temple was lovely, but sadly we have no history of God returning on His chariot throne with His cherubim.

The Shekinah Glory

Some 545 years later, Herod the Great (a mixed-race Jew appointed by the Romans to govern Jerusalem) enlarged and refurbished the second temple which became known as Herod's temple. Then, a few years after the birth of Jesus, Herod died (Matt. 2:19-20).

When Jesus Christ turned thirty years old, He went to the Jordan River to be baptized by John the Baptist. Immediately, Holy Spirit came upon Him and God the Father spoke confirmation from heaven (Matt. 3:17).

This event introduced and confirmed Jesus as the long-awaited Messiah and it heralded the return of Holy Spirit to abide in a man as He once did with Adam and Eve.

Filled with Holy Spirit, Jesus went into the wilderness to fast and pray for forty days and came face to face with Satan the tempter who had already succeeded in recruiting mass-humanity into his rebellion (Matt. 4:1-11).

Satan propositioned Jesus to join him and the fallen human race in the same way that Adam was tempted to follow the rebellion of Eve. This was a legitimate temptation because Jesus came to earth as our "Bridegroom and second Adam" in order to redeem us.

Technically, Jesus could have been reunited with us by joining our rebellion (the choice Adam made). Instead, He chose to go to the Cross to and free us from the prison of death.

Jesus Brings Back the Shekinah

Sometime after being filled with Holy Spirit, Jesus entered Herod's temple (Holy Spirit is identified as the Shekinah glory in Isa. 63:11).

Finally, the promise of Haggai the prophet came to pass, and the second temple was filled with a greater glory: Jesus Christ the Messiah (Matt. 12:5–8; Eph. 2:19–22).

Israel Rejects Her True Temple: Messiah

At the time of Jesus, the religious establishment had spent centuries studying Messiah and trying to calculate the time of His arrival from the writings of the prophets and especially Daniel. They knew His time was imminent, and they were expecting Him. However, when He suddenly appeared in the temple and drove the money changers out—exercising authority over the temple without consulting them first—they were embarrassed and offended. In the confrontation that ensued, Jesus revealed His identity as the true temple:

> 19 Jesus answered and said to them, "Destroy this temple, and in three days I will raise it up." 20 Then the Jews said, "It has taken forty-six years to build this temple, and will You raise it up in three days?" 21 But He was speaking of the temple of His body."—John 2: 19-21 NKJV

When the angry religious establishment organized the death of Jesus Christ, they actually crucified the dwelling place of God's Shekinah glory.

By declaring "we have no king but Caesar," they chose allegiance to Rome. Then, forty years later in AD 70, Titus the

Roman burned Herod's temple, and not one stone was left standing upon another.

In reality, the rulers of Israel had rejected their "temple" when they rejected Jesus the Messiah, and it was only a matter of time before their meaningless building was dismantled.

Jesus Restores Us

As our second Adam, Jesus broke the curse of death on mankind and led us back into fellowship with God.

When we accept Jesus as Lord and Savior, Holy Spirit comes to live inside us. Then, like Jesus and through Jesus, we become the temple—the dwelling place—of God.

Religious and Political Israel in Delusion

After centuries of performing the demanding rituals of temple worship, which taught man's need for salvation and foreshadowed the Deliverer, the politicized Jewish priesthood came face-to-face with Jesus Christ the Messiah. This meant that their priestly role as an intermediary between God and man was now complete. Instead of rejoicing, they were outraged.

Jesus the Messiah did not curry their favor or play their political games as a means of gaining acceptance. Instead, He did the works of God the Father and left the Pharisees with no choice but to concede to His preeminence or reject Him to protect their positions.

After rejecting Jesus Christ the Messiah, and demanding His crucifixion, the Jewish religious establishment began to reinterpret the clear teachings of Moses and the prophets in order to dismiss Jesus and open the door for a different messiah who would come through their system and under their authority.[82] Over time, some of these teachings have become more disconnected from Scripture and more deeply immersed in occult mysticism. To the casual observer, the heretical strands of teaching appear to be the ancient Jewish religion, but to the biblically literate, they bear no resemblance.

162

Do We Need a Temple?

Since the destruction of "Herod's" temple, there has never been another Jewish temple in Jerusalem.

The temple served to educate us and to demonstrate that God wants to live with us. In ancient Israel, He lived in the "temple" and could only be approached after the proper blood sacrifice was made. When Jesus came along, the Shekinah glory / Holy Spirit returned to live in a man as He did in the Garden. Now, through Jesus Christ, we are filled with Holy Spirit and become the dwelling place of God. So, what is the need for a building called a temple?

Some Bible scholars believe that the perfect and pure temple described by Ezekiel in this vision is literal, and it will be built in the last days and serve as an educational center where we continue to mediate upon and learn about the things of God. In addition, because this temple will be located in Jerusalem, they believe it will serve as the headquarters for Jesus Christ during His millennial reign (Ezek. 37:26-27; Zech. 2:10-12; Zech. 8:3; Ps. 2:4-9; Luke 1:32-33).

Other scholars believe this temple is an Old Testament representation of the New Testament "temple" which is Jesus Christ and His born-again followers who come from all nationalities.

To Ezekiel's fellow captives in Babylon, this vision gave them hope that they will someday enter into the age of Messiah's perfect rule.

Ezekiel's Temple

At the time of Ezekiel's vision, it had been about thirteen years since the fall of Jerusalem and twenty-six years since Ezekiel went into captivity. The vision opens when Ezekiel is seized by the Spirit of God and transported to a high place over the land of Israel. Looking around, he notices a city on the south side of a high mountain, and he meets a heavenly being with a bronze appearance, carrying the measuring tools of a surveyor.

The bronze messenger instructs Ezekiel to pay close attention so that he can relate every detail to the Jews. Immediately, Ezekiel sees a wall completely surrounding a temple. From here, he is given a detailed tour of the new temple in a perfected land of Israel. Clearly, this temple is not the old one, and the land of Israel has changed.

Remember, Ezekiel lived in Jerusalem before his captivity, and he was familiar with Solomon's temple. In addition, God had given him a bird's eye view of the city and a tour of the inside chambers of the original temple right before He departed.

In this vision, everything is different because the temple grounds and the nation of Israel are in perfect order and spiritual purity. Biblically speaking, this perfection is only achieved under the rule of Messiah.

Animal Sacrifices

In this vision, animal sacrifices are performed in the temple which would not be applicable under Messiah who is the ultimate and final sacrifice as the Lamb of God. However, the Jewish captives did not understand this about Messiah. To them, the only path to purity was the blood sacrifice. Therefore, I believe this vision referenced the required blood sacrifice because it is directed to a Jewish audience.

Beyond that, some believe that animal sacrifices will be performed in the millennial temple of Jesus Christ as a memorial to the past. Because we don't know for sure, there is room for differing opinions.

The Shekinah Glory Returns

The bronze angel meticulously measured and described every detail as he walked Ezekiel through the inside and outside of the temple. Once on the outside, he measured the gates and walls and then took Ezekiel back to the east gate. Recognizing the glory of God from his previous vision, Ezekiel watched as it came from the east and toward the temple, filling the land with radiant light and the sound of roaring water.

At once, Ezekiel realized that God was returning to the temple in the same way and from the same direction as His departure (Ezek. 43:1).

Ezekiel fell to his face as God entered the temple through the east gate. Immediately, he found himself in the holy of holies when suddenly God spoke:

> "Son of man, this is the place of My throne and the place of the soles of My feet, where I will dwell in the midst of the children of Israel forever."—Ezek. 43:7 KJV

The Fullness of the Message to Ezekiel

In God's prophetic due diligence, He showed Ezekiel His departure and return to Israel. His departure began the Gentile Age, and His return is the absolute end of this era.

Ezekiel and Revelation Together

Many parts of Ezekiel's vision correlate with John the Apostle's vision in the book of Revelation. In Ezekiel's vision, we see the Jewish nation and her temple in perfection which is a prophetic picture of the fullness to come. In John's vision, we see a perfect New Jerusalem which is identified as the born-again Church of Jesus Christ.

In both visions, the angel who gave the tour is represented as having the tools of a surveyor (Rev. 21:15; Ezek. 40:3). Both Ezekiel and John see a river flowing from under the temple and lined with fruit trees that bring healing (Ezek. 47:1–12; Rev. 22:1–2).

The closing pages of the book of Ezekiel describe the arrangement of the land of Israel and its divisions among the twelve tribes, which signifies perfect government. Likewise, in the book of Revelation, the New Jerusalem is laid out perfectly with gates and foundations named after the twelve tribes of Israel and the twelve apostles of Jesus.

> . . ."Come, I will show you the bride, the Lamb's wife." 10 And he carried me away in the Spirit to a great and high mountain, and showed me the great city, the holy Jerusalem, descending out of heaven from God, 11 having the glory of God.
>
> 12 Also she had a great and high wall with twelve gates, and twelve angels at the gates, and names written on them, which are the names of the twelve tribes of the children of Israel . . . 14 Now the wall of the city had twelve foundations, and on them were the names of the twelve apostles of the Lamb. 15 And he who talked with me had a gold reed to measure the city, its gates, and its wall. —Rev. 21:9-12, 14-15 NKJV

Ezekiel's vision is a continuation of the message of all the prophets of Israel who foretold her perfection under Messiah. With Ezekiel, we see the return of the Shekinah glory to Jerusalem with the coming of Messiah to rule and reign. In the book of Revelation, the Shekinah glory lives in the *saints* who are the eternal temple and the "New Jerusalem" (Ezek. 43:1-7; Rev. 3:12; Rev. 21:2).

Possible Scenario's

Why would God give Ezekiel intricate architectural details of a future temple that will be filled with His Shekinah glory? I think in part, it gave the captives and every Jew the hope that Messiah will come and rule the earth from Jerusalem. To Christians, this vision reminds us that God has made promises to national Israel that He intends to keep. For both groups, it is a picture of perfection and peace that can only be achieved by Messiah.

Today, the Jews study this vision as they seek to build their third temple. Once built, they will institute the old rituals and carefully follow the mosaic law to obtain purity since they do not recognize the finished work of Jesus Christ the Lamb of God.

Eventually, this new temple will be defiled by the man of sin, when he sits in the holy of holies claiming to be God at the half-way point of the final seven years of this age (more in Daniel's visions). Finally, after all of this, Messiah will return and reign a thousand years from Jerusalem.

When Messiah comes, the rebuilt temple might already be destroyed by the wars of the Great Tribulation. Or, it might be cleansed to become His earthly headquarters. Whatever the outcome, Messiah will rule from Jerusalem.

In all of this, we must remember that the ultimate perfection and holiness portrayed in Ezekiel's temple will only be realized in the holy lives of those who accept Jesus the Messiah, and are filled with Holy Spirit. An earthly temple can never usurp this reality.

Israel in the End

This vision also conveys the honor that God has appointed to Israel. In the end, she will be known as God's personally created nation—that He loves—through whom He has educated mankind and brought forth Messiah.

God's public dealings with Israel, and His steadfast commitment to her, has led to our understanding of holiness, the judgment of sin, and the release of mercy when there is repentance. We have learned much at her expense.

19 Look, at that time I will deal with those who mistreated you. I will rescue the lame sheep and gather together the scattered sheep. I will take away their humiliation and make the whole earth admire and respect them. 20 At that time I will lead you—at the time I gather you together. Be sure of this! I will make all the nations of the earth respect and admire you when you see me restore you," says the Lord. —Zeph. 3:19-20 NET

CHAPTER 20

Daniel the Prophet

When Daniel was still a youth, King Josiah was killed in battle by Pharaoh Necho, King of Egypt, who then took control of Jerusalem and imposed a tax on the nation's output.

With Josiah dead, the succession of Judean kings was decided by foreigners and became very chaotic until finally Nebuchadnezzar appointed Zedekiah who turned out to be the last king from the line of Judah before Jerusalem was destroyed.[83]

Jeremiah's Unpopular Message

During this tumultuous time, Jeremiah the prophet preached repentance and foretold Babylon's victory over Egypt and Jerusalem, which made him a social outcast. Conveniently for the kings of Judah, Jerusalem was filled with false prophets who were happy to peddle the lies of a victorious outcome over the invaders.

Desperately wanting to believe the false prophets, every king persecuted Jeremiah in an effort to silence him.

A battle raged for the hearts and minds of the people. Would they blindly cling to their pride and insist that God was with them? Or would they recognize their national decline as a direct result of forsaking God and thus reaping the curses that Moses foretold?

Daniel Is Watching

Daniel was around eight to eleven years of age at King Josiah's death.[84] For the next four years, until he was captured by Babylon, he lived in the royal household under the wicked king Jehoiakim, and listened to the preaching of Jeremiah who warned of imminent destruction.

Daniel was young, but he paid close attention to the religious parade of "prophets and priests" who promised peace and prosperity in contrast to Jeremiah, the doom-and-gloom outcast. It didn't take much discernment to recognize that Jeremiah carried an authority that rivaled the king. He was bold, intelligent, and yet humble. When he delivered his prophecies, fear and trembling would fall on the most hardened soldier while causing extreme rage among the elite. Daniel watched Jeremiah deliver his messages with firmness and then later wander the streets crying like a baby. What kind of man was this?

Young Daniel listened as Jeremiah told his people they would be captives in Babylon for seventy years and advised them to settle into their new homes in a foreign land and to be industrious and prosper.

Wicked King Jehoiakim

During the four years of Egyptian rule—while Daniel was still in Jerusalem—Jehoiakim was the vassal king. Jewish history tells us that King Jehoiakim was a wicked ruler who had incestuous relations with his mother, step mother, and daughter in-law, and often killed men when he took their wives and property. He also tattooed his body in the tradition of the cults to separate himself from his Jewish identity. Also, to show his contempt of God, he burned the writings of Jeremiah in a fire pot while mocking him. Daniel would have been privy to the debauchery of this king.

Daniel Taken Captive

Daniel was taken captive by Babylon on their first raid of Jerusalem. Because he was a young royal from the tribe of Judah, with a promising appearance, he was chosen to receive a Chaldean education that included astronomy and sorcery so that he could join the learned men who served Nebuchadnezzar. Immediately, he was castrated and then assigned a rigorous three-year course of study. He would spend the rest of his life in service to Gentile kings.

Daniel was thrust into a violent new reality. Just barely coming into puberty, his manhood was cut from his loins. He would never know the joy of marriage or children. He was being groomed to forget his former life and bow in subservience to a king who served demons and considered himself a god. To the young Jew, it was the worst possible fate. Even so, Daniel remembered the words of Jeremiah and how he instructed the captives to pray for the welfare of their captors, settle into the land, and become productive. Daniel took these words to heart and devoted himself to remaining pure and undefiled before God while living as a slave to an evil empire.

The Flawless Character of Daniel

Though he was young, Daniel was quickly distinguished as a person of wisdom and restraint. He exhibited a flawless command over his carnal nature and formed lifelong habits of prayer and fasting as his way of staying faithful to God.

God was pleased with Daniel and gifted him with the ability to interpret dreams and solve riddles.

In Daniel's long life, he was appointed to high-ranking governmental positions under Nebuchadnezzar of Babylon, and then Cyrus and Darius of the Medes and Persians. He was well-known as a worshipper of the God of the Jews and a man who always told the truth with humility and courage. Because of the undeniable divine favor that was upon his life, he received an allotment of room and board and other material comforts from the kings he served all the days of his life.

Israel Thinks She Is Invincible

As Daniel settled into his new home in Babylon, Jeremiah was still living in Jerusalem and tirelessly warning of more Babylonian raids and a final destruction.

The fall of Jerusalem was imminent, and still the Israelites refused to believe it. Jeremiah begged them to humbly repent for living a double life of pretending to serve God while worshipping demons. The people willfully rejected Jeremiah's message and sided with their wicked rulers and false prophets. The line was drawn.

The Army of Babylon Marches to Jerusalem

About nineteen years into Daniel's captivity, Nebuzaradan, the chief military commander of Babylon, received orders to march against Jerusalem for the third and final time and utterly destroy her. By then, Daniel was around thirty-four years old, and he held a high-ranking position in King Nebuchadnezzar's administration.

Being close to the king of Babylon, Daniel would have known about this final assault on his people weeks before the army arrived at Jerusalem, some 520 miles away. Heartbroken, Daniel could only pray and seek the mercy of God for his family and his beloved homeland.

The Siege of Jerusalem

When the Babylonian army arrived at Jerusalem, the people were locked up and hiding behind its walls. For the next nineteen months, the army surrounded them and cut off all supplies of food. Meanwhile, trapped in the city, Jeremiah begged the people to surrender and avoid more bloodshed. Frightened and hungry, a small number of Jews managed to escape the city and defect to Babylon while the remainder suffered slow starvation and loss of human dignity as mothers boiled their children to survive (Lev. 26:29; Duet. 28:56; Lam. 4:10; Ezek. 5:10).

All the while, wicked Zedekiah, the last king of Judah, was huddled inside of his palace, surrounded by false prophets who continually assured him of victory even in the face of destruction. Outside his walls, the entire population was pining away from starvation and disease.

The lying prophets of Jerusalem had lulled the people into a false sense of security. They should have led the way in public repentance, but they refused. Jeremiah told the truth, and he was hated and imprisoned; the false prophets told a lie, and they were loved. Like foolish and senseless children, the people refused to come clean, and it cost them dearly.

After nineteen months of torturous starvation, the walls of Jerusalem came down, and the voracious army of Babylon ran through the streets devouring the pathetic survivors. Like demons released upon the earth, the army swooped down to plunder the remaining wealth before torching the temple of Solomon and turning the city into an inferno of destruction.

With Jerusalem and the temple of Solomon gone, it was the end of the kingdom of Judah and her dynasty of kings. There was just one problem . . . the Messiah King from the tribe of Judah had not yet taken His throne in Jerusalem. All of the prophecies from the Garden of Eden onward foretold His arrival and reign. When would this happen and how?

This is the question that Daniel would eventually ask God. In response, God gave him a revelation of world history that extends into the millennial reign of Messiah. Daniel struggled to understand his visions, and eventually he was told to safeguard them for a future generation. The future is now and we are that generation!

Daniel Watches the Humiliation of Jerusalem

Another victory for Babylon!

Like the untimely death of a loved one, Daniel grieved the news of Jerusalem's destruction. The victorious army was approaching Babylon with prisoners of war and treasure chests filled with the riches of Solomon's temple. After months of marching, their arrival was imminent, and the crowds gathered to watch the spectacle.

Daniel watched and waited anxiously in hopes that some of his family was still alive. With the loud blowing of trumpets, General Nebuzaradan entered the city waving the banner flag of Babylon as the crowds erupted with wild cheering and applause.

As the procession filed by, Daniel finally saw King Zedekiah— the last Judean king—stripped down to a loin cloth, barefoot, and bound in heavy bronze shackles. As the crowd caught sight of him, they gasped and then cheered at the sight of the torn and humiliated king whose face was disfigured and covered in dry blood from having his eyes gouged out. The last thing Zedekiah saw was the slaughter of his sons, and now he was entombed in a dark nightmare; he would stay there until his death in a Babylonian prison (Jer. 39:1-8).

Daniel's heart broke at the sight of his people. They were gaunt and sickly from the famine and disease that devoured them during the nineteen-month siege. Barely alive, they stumbled through the streets amid the jeering throng. It was a day of shame and humiliation for the once-arrogant and double-minded nation.

With his own eyes, Daniel witnessed the fulfillment of Jeremiah's prophecies: the destruction of Jerusalem and the total captivity of his people.

Israel's Destruction—A Foregone Conclusion

Daniel was grieved, and the remnant survivors were in shock; but the Babylonians were confident because they had been following the ministry of Jeremiah for forty years. They regarded him a true prophet and understood that Israel's God had forsaken her after she had forsaken Him.

The demons also followed Jeremiah's ministry, knowing that he carried the authentic Word of God. They had watched the departure of God's Shekinah glory from Solomon's temple, and they were confident of their success against Israel whose only hope was repentance. That possibility was remote because the priests and royal officials were daily groveling at idol altars and filling their minds with demonic lies.

Jeremiah Spared

When King Nebuchadnezzar gave orders to destroy Jerusalem, he instructed his commanders to find Jeremiah and treat him with kindness and honor (Jer. 39:11-14; 40:2-6).

Once located, Jeremiah was living as a prisoner under house arrest. Nebuzaradan immediately released him and recited back to him his own prophecies! Amazing! The Babylonians believed in Jeremiah even though his own people rejected him. Take note, the world is listening even when the Church is not.

Daniel: The Successor of Jeremiah

Daniel believed Jeremiah and studied his writings. This prepared him—unknowingly—to be a global prophet after the order of Isaiah and Jeremiah. In his old age, Daniel was visited by the angel Gabriel on several occasions and given the most detailed map of the rise of nations that has ever been given. When Jesus Christ came to the earth as a man, He quoted the writings of Daniel to explain the end times. And finally, when John the Beloved Apostle was given the Revelation vision, he was shown many of the same things that Daniel saw 600 years earlier. Again, God establishes His word in the mouth of two or more witnesses.

The book of Daniel contains four personal visions or dreams that concern the Age of the Gentiles, the persecution of the

Jewish people and the saints, and the reign of Messiah. In addition, Nebuchadnezzar was given two companion dreams. Together, these revelations lay out the entire history of the world from Daniel's time all the way to the end of the age of man and the coming of Messiah. In the following chapters, we will look at each of these and find ourselves in a prophetic sequence of events that are startling and sobering.

CHAPTER 21

Nebuchadnezzar's Dreams

Daniel arrived in Babylonian captivity around fifteen years of age and began his Chaldean education that lasted three years. At the end of his studies, he was questioned by Nebuchadnezzar and found to be superior over the other astrologers, sorcerers, and wise men, and then placed in the king's spiritual advisory group.

Shortly after this, in 604 BC, the king had a dream from God in which he saw a dazzling statue towering over the earth with a head of gold, breast and arms of silver, belly and thighs of bronze, legs of iron, and feet and toes of iron and clay. While watching, he saw a "Rock" strike the statue on its feet and crush it into tiny fragments that were scattered by the wind. Then, the Rock became a great mountain / kingdom established by God, and it filled the earth and remained forever.

Disturbed by his dream, the king called upon his advisors to give him both the dream and an interpretation; no one was able, except Daniel (Dan. 2).

God revealed to Daniel that the statue depicted every world empire of the Gentile Age beginning with King Nebuchadnezzar of Babylon, who was the head of gold that currently ruled. After him came successive empires that were members of the same body.

These offshoots decreased in grandeur just as the metals depicting them did; even so, they had an increase in strength. The last empire was depicted with iron legs, and feet made of iron and clay. Part strong and part weak.

Nimrod's Babylon: The First Gentile Kingdom

According to this vision, Nebuchadnezzar—a descendant of Nimrod who lived about 1,650 years earlier—was appointed by God as the head of gold and the first ruler in the Gentile Age. This was fitting since Nimrod gave birth to the idea of a centralized government fueled and ruled by occultic powers. At that time, Nimrod was not allowed to build his dream kingdom because of humanity's infancy. Even so, God held his position and pointed back to him as the seed of treason in the appointment of his descendant Nebuchadnezzar of Babylon.

The Succession of Gentile Rule

In Nebuchadnezzar's dream, the identity of the succeeding empires was not revealed; they were simply referred to as metals. That revelation was given to Daniel in later visions.

The Gentile Age began with Babylon, then the Medes and Persians, then the Greeks, and finally the Romans.

Daniel lived during the gold kingdom of Babylon and the silver kingdom of the Medes and Persians. The next kingdom of bronze was Greece, as identified by the angel Gabriel, two hundred years before they emerged as an empire.

Rome and the Kingdom of God

History reveals that Rome is the fourth kingdom with iron legs and toes of iron and clay. In Nebuchadnezzar's dream, God strikes the toes with a "Rock" that grows into a huge mountain and fills the earth (Dan 2:44-45). As we know, Jesus Christ is the Rock who came to earth during the iron rule of Imperial Rome and announced "the kingdom of God is at hand" (Mark 1:15).

Then, with His resurrection, Jesus the Rock struck Rome with the blow of death. From that time forward, the Kingdom of God on the earth (the Church) has been growing unabated. Rome on the other hand, has been under the sentence of death. From an earthly perspective, she is strong and in charge. In actual fact, she is under the sentence of God's wrath, and desperately struggling to unseat Christ and the saints.

Dream Two: Nebuchadnezzar Becomes a Beast

In Nebuchadnezzar's second dream, he was portrayed as a massive tree with far-reaching dominion when suddenly a heavenly messenger ordered the tree to be cut down and its roots preserved until the passing of seven seasons (*seven* indicating divine completion). During this season, which actually happened, Nebuchadnezzar had the mind of a beast and lived and acted like one. Finally, he came to his senses, and acknowledged and praised God, and then he was restored as the ruler over his kingdom. History indicates that he died a year later.

The fact that Nebuchadnezzar repented before his death, is a point of hope for every wicked ruler.

To God, the prideful are beasts driven by carnal impulses and demonic influence. This was true of the father of the Gentile Age—Nebuchadnezzar—and all his successors. The beast analogy will continue to be a theme in Daniel's visions and in the book of Revelation where the ultimate beast emerges.

CHAPTER 22

Daniel the Prophet
First Vision—Daniel 7

After living in captivity for about fifty-two years, Daniel had his first vision; he was around sixty-three years old. The Babylonians still ruled supreme, and it was the first year of the reign of Belshazzar, a descendant of Nebuchadnezzar. In this vision, God gave Daniel a big-picture summary of the remainder of world history. In fact, this vision was an expansion of Nebuchadnezzar's statue dream because the entire cast of characters remained the same. In successive visions, as we shall see, God continues to build upon the foundations laid in both these prophetic encounters.

The Churning Sea

As the vision begins, the four winds of heaven are blowing upon the multigenerational sea of humanity, causing a succession of four beast empires to rise from the stormy waters. Each beast takes its turn ruling the world until it gives way to the next, and finally at the end, they all give way to the kingdom of God.

In Nebuchadnezzar's dream, these nations are depicted as metals; in this vision, they are depicted as beasts. Always, God regards the striving of man to build governments opposed to His ownership of creation as an ignorant and beastly impulse.

First Beast: Babylon

Daniel watched as the first empire emerged from the sea of humanity: Babylon, the head of gold. In this vision, it is depicted as a lion with eagle wings that is unable to nest or rest upon the earth until such time as its wings are removed and it is grounded with the feet and the mind of a man.

This is exactly what happened in history. Nimrod was a lion among men, and his idea to build a system of government to usurp God made him the first of his kind; he was the "king of the beasts." However, God thwarted him at the Tower of Babel, until His initial work in Israel was complete. Meanwhile, the satanic plot of world dominion remained airborne—the wings of an eagle—nesting in the bosom of Satan, who is called the prince of the power of the air, and waiting for its opportunity to manifest on the earth (Eph. 2:1-2).

Finally, at the appointed time, God permitted the lion's descendant Nebuchadnezzar to take his stand on the earth and give expression to the generational seed of tyranny that was spawned by his forefather Nimrod in collusion with Satan.

Second Beast: Medes and Persians

The second beast empire was the chest and arms of silver: the Medes and Persians. At the time of this vision, it would be about fourteen years before they conquered Babylon.

To Daniel, this dynasty is depicted as a bear on its side with three ribs in its mouth—a few victories of war among the nations—when suddenly it is instructed to rise and eat more flesh. This indicated that at the right moment, God would allow this marginal menace to rise and conquer to become the next empire.

True to this vision, the Medes and Persians grew in power and then conquered Babylon. Once seated at the top, they dealt kindly with the Jewish captives and allowed them to return to Jerusalem and rebuild their temple. In fact, the Persian king who gave the decree is Cyrus. The prophet Isaiah foretold his birth, mission, and name—all in the public record—some 150 years earlier (Isa. 45).

Third Beast: Greece

The third beast empire was the belly and thighs of bronze: Greece. About 217 years after this vision, Greece conquered the Medo-Persians and assumed global preeminence.

To Daniel, this empire was depicted as a leopard with four heads and four wings. Historically, the first king of the Greek empire was Alexander the Great who swiftly moved across the earth—like a leopard with wings—and conquered the known world in a short span of years.

When Alexander suddenly died, his kingdom was divided among his four generals, and their regions became the four competing centers of Greek power. This is why the leopard was shown to have four wings and four heads. In prophetic writings, God often depicts a world power, nation, or leader as a head.

Fourth Beast: Rome the Monster

The fourth and final beast empire corresponds to the legs of iron and feet of iron and clay: The Roman Empire. The appearance of this beast could not be compared to an earthly animal that Daniel recognized. Instead, it was a powerful monstrosity with a bulging mouth of iron teeth, horrifying bronze claws, and ten horns on its head. It was a terrifying fusion of body parts from the preceding empires.

Daniel watched as it terrorized the whole earth by trampling, crushing, and devouring. The language used depicts a military colossus that swoops in and tramples down its opponents, while chaotically crushing neighborhoods, and sending the inhabitants into a desperate struggle for survival. Grimly, the monster is seen eating the earth as if her people and goods were delicacy's spread before him.

Imperial Rome

At the time of this vision, it would be about 409 years before the Battle of Corinth in 146 BC when the Romans conquered the Greeks and then continued to gain vast territories—crushing them with their iron legs—to become the next empire.

During the time of Jesus, Imperial Rome[85] was at the pinnacle of her power and savagery. She controlled her annexed territories (the clay parts) with a superior military (the iron parts). At this juncture, Messiah the Rock, as seen in Nebuchadnezzar's vision, struck a fatal blow to the feet of iron and clay with His crucifixion and then resurrection.

Rome, the behemoth of legislative and military might, had no idea that by crucifying Jesus the King—the highest treason—she secured her final doom. By aligning with Satan, she is dead and a kingdom of death. She is a goat nation.

Upon His resurrection, Jesus ascended to His throne at the right hand of Father God where He waits for His enemies to be made His footstool (Ps. 110.:1; Matt. 22:44; Matt. 26:64; Mark 16:19; 1 Cor. 15:25; Heb. 1:13).

Meanwhile, back on earth, the irrefutable facts of His life and resurrection caused an explosion of followers among the Jews in Jerusalem before spreading like wildfire across the Roman Empire. As a result, Imperial Rome reacted with laws against Christianity and persecuted and killed both Jews (followers of Jesus and otherwise) and Christians. Nero, for example, lit his garden parties with tarred and burning Christians. In the midst of this, the entire New Testament was written, and many of the apostles of Jesus—all Jewish—were martyred.

Then, in the year AD 70, Titus the Roman carried out a campaign to rid the empire of the pesky Jews and Christians in Jerusalem. Like ravenous wolves, his army burned down the second Jewish temple, dug up the foundation stones, and killed roughly ninety percent of the citizens of Jerusalem (Josephus puts the number at 1.1 million).

Rome Scattered

In the centuries after Jesus, Imperial Rome lost her ability to hold together the empire (iron and clay feet do not adhere) and she fragmented into independent nation-states located in the Middle East and Western Europe. The ancient lands would today include the United Kingdom, Belgium, Switzerland, Italy, France, Germany, Hungary, Spain, Lebanon, Egypt, Syria, Iraq, Saudi Arabia, Palestine, Israel, Croatia, Greece, Vatican City, Austria, Romania, Cyprus, Algeria, and many more.

In Nebuchadnezzar's dream, the final incarnation of world government has ten toes of iron and clay. In Daniel's vision, it is a freak monster with ten horns. In the book of Revelation, it is a dragon—empowered by Satan—with seven heads and ten horns. All of these are pictures of the same entity. The number ten can express literal nations and / or it can signify a fullness of human government that is hostile to God.[86]

In all these examples, the empire consists of separate and competing centers of power (as seen in the ten horns). Even so, these regions are united in their humanistic ideology and they will come together governmentally to form the final empire of Babylon in the book of Revelation. Regardless, this system will be riddled with strife because fallen mankind is incapable of manufacturing unity.

The Pause of Rome

In the statue dream, Rome is depicted as having two iron legs—a symbol of military power. Even so, her power was scattered and diluted by the clay of annexed territories which were hard to control. In this way, God frustrated her global aspirations, just as He did to early man at the Tower of Babel.

This pause of power has given the followers of Messiah a season to mature into a holy nation—spiritual and without borders—as we wait for His return. In the same way, God gave the Hebrews a season of protection in Egypt so that they could grow numerically. Then, as they approached their liberation, the Egyptians forced them into slavery and finally they used the murder of their children as a tool to break their wills and induce obedience to the empire.

I believe the saints are experiencing similar pressure and persecution as we lead up to the return of Jesus Christ. In some parts of the world, Christians are slaves and prisoners, and subject to death for their faith. In modern nations like the US, saints are pressured to obey the dictates of a humanistic government that is openly hostile to the highly dangerous act of prayer, Bible reading, and any public profession of faith.

Clearly, the Roman Empire is rising again and its acts of violence against Christians and Jews are increasing (Rev. 17).

Antichrist Emerges

In Daniel's vision, the final monster empire persecutes and pillages the saints for an indeterminate period of time (over two-thousand years so far). Then, in the final stage of its existence, three of its horns (three kings and their nations) are rooted out with the emergence of a little horn with greedy eyes and a boasting mouth.

In the New Testament, this final king is called "the man of sin and the son of perdition" (2 Thess. 2:3-4). Christians identify him as Antichrist.

Daniel watches as Antichrist makes war with the holy people (contextually Israel) and prevails against them until he is stopped by God and thrown into a fiery destruction. According to other visions, this intense persecution by Antichrist occurs near the end of the final three-and-one-half years leading up to the return of Jesus Christ (more as we move on).

> ...20 [the horn Antichrist] had human eyes and a mouth that was boasting arrogantly. 21 As I watched, this horn was waging war against the holy people and was defeating them, 22 until the Ancient One came and judged in favor of

the holy people of the Most High. Then the time arrived for the holy people to take over the kingdom.

26 "But then the court will pass judgment, and all his power will be taken away and completely destroyed. 27 Then the sovereignty, power, and greatness of all the kingdoms under heaven will be given to the holy people of the Most High. They will rule forever, and all rulers will serve and obey them."—Dan. 7:20, 26 NLT

Antichrist: Arrogant Eyes, Boasting Mouth

In Daniel's vision, we are drawn to the arrogant eyes and boasting mouth of the little horn. Perhaps he claims to be a "seer" or a prophet? No doubt, he will be possessed by Satan so that he has the eyes of a demoniac. We know that his prototype Nimrod was a narcissistic mouthpiece for the demonic realm and he instituted an occultic system to influence and dictate governmental policy.

As the final leader of the Roman monster, this little horn is the personification of selfish and arrogant humanity. He embodies all men for all time who have sought to usurp God. As the ultimate distillation of human evil, he is the descendant of Nimrod and every other wicked ruler who has wielded the scepter of Satan.

Antichrist Wars Against the Saints

As Daniel pondered the little horn with menacing eyes and a boasting mouth, an angel pointed out his obsession with changing the laws, seasons, and festivals of God. This implies an energetic effort to rewrite Jewish history and thereby obscure what God has established. This is a clever tactic because the loss of the knowledge of God is also an erasure of our created identity and prophetic future.

25 He [Antichrist] will defy the Most High and wear down the holy people of the Most High. He will try to change

their sacred festivals and laws, and they will be placed under his control for a time, times, and half a time. —Dan. 7:25 NLT

Currently there is a massive assault against the Old Testament that directly impacts both Jews and Christians. According to this vision, that assault against God and His prophetic history, will continue and reach an apex under Antichrist.

When Jesus spoke of the last days, He told us that our families and society would betray, imprison, and kill us because of our faith. This signifies a culture of ridicule and hate toward the things of God (Luke 21:12-19).

Right now, two kingdoms are growing in the earth, and as we get closer to the end, our differences will become increasingly amplified. The born-again saints will shine brightly, speak truth, and carry an undeniable anointing. As we appeal to God for justice, He will open and close doors with great power and bring judgment upon the wicked.

Like Israel of old, we will be a terror to the demonic realm and they will fight-back with fury as we expose their deeds of darkness.

Clearly, those devoted to usurping God will never peaceably co-exist with His people. They would rather destroy the planet than allow us to live. In the end, this fact will be allowed to play itself out to prove conclusively that given full license, fallen mankind will never create peace and harmony.

The Ancient of Days

After watching the little horn rage against God, attack His people, and malign His Word, Daniel found himself in a vast and seemingly endless room that was being prepared by angels for a legal proceeding. With methodical calm, thrones of judgment were set in place for the Ancient of Days and His entourage.

The atmosphere of the room was charged with power as the Ancient of Days entered and sat upon His throne. Then, a great company, too large to number, either stood or took their assigned seats. The court was in session.

Daniel marveled at the Ancient of Days—the Genesis of Creation—as He sat upon His throne surrounded by myriads of radiant angels, creatures, and saints. Wearing a blinding white robe, His hair was white, and dense power and fire streamed forth from His throne (signifying purity and judgement).

Born into royalty, and then serving kings his entire life, Daniel was well-versed in the pomp of monarchs, their show of splendor, and their meticulously dressed and well-behaved courtiers. Yet all of that paled and disappeared as feckless vanity in the face of the magnificent Ancient of Days and His regal attendants. Together in heaven, God's holy creation exuded authority and wisdom. As attendants to the Ancient of Days, they wore His graces as a testimony to His matchless beauty, love, and power.

Proceedings in Heaven

In this vision, the multiplied thousands surrounding the Ancient of Days are referred to as "attendants." In a companion vision, John the Apostle sees the same event (Rev. 4). Whereas Daniel is shown a summary glimpse, John is given layers of specific details. When John sees the thousands upon thousands in attendance, he also sees twenty-four elders seated on thrones, four living creatures filled with eyes, the seven spirits of God burning like a fire, and Jesus as the Lamb of God standing before the throne. From John's vison, the twenty-four elders are redeemed humans because they sing a new song—the song of salvation—and they worship the Lamb of God who redeemed them from sin (Rev. 7:9-17).

It is my belief that the true saints from all of human history are numbered among the "attendants" at the sentencing of Antichrist and his beast system because we are central to his judgment. God has always had a righteous remnant throughout the ages who have continually endured persecution. This has resulted in our grief over the wickedness in the world, our cries of intercession, and our pleas for justice. All of this will be remembered and answered in the courtroom of the Ancient of Days.[87]

Books of Judgment

As the little horn raged, the Ancient of Days opened the books of judgment to reveal the crimes committed by Antichrist and his accomplices who embody all treason going back to Nimrod (Dan. 7:10). Then, in the dense power of the courtroom, the Ancient of Days renders His judgment and Antichrist is thrown into the lake of fire and his army is destroyed by fire (Rev. 19:20).

Surely, this is the epic moment when the occultic empire of Babylon falls to her eternal destruction (Isa. 21:9; Jer. 51; Rev. 14:8; Rev. 18:2).

In this vision, we have no details of what that looks like on the earth. However, in John the Apostle's vision, he watches the final empire burn so fiercely that the smoke towers into the atmosphere while the merchants, nations, and peoples tremble with shock at the sudden and final destruction of such great power and wealth.

> 8 Therefore her plagues will come in one day—death and mourning and famine. And she will be utterly burned with fire, for strong is the Lord God who judges her. "The kings of the earth who committed fornication and lived luxuriously with her will weep and lament for her, when they see the smoke of her burning, 10 standing at a distance for fear of her torment, saying,' Alas, alas, that great city Babylon, that mighty city! For in one hour your judgment has come' . . .
>
> 21 Then a mighty angel took up a stone like a great millstone and threw it into the sea, saying, "Thus with

violence the great city Babylon shall be thrown down, and shall not be found anymore . . . 23 . . . For your merchants were the great men of the earth, for by your sorcery all the nations were deceived. 24 And in her was found the blood of prophets and saints, and of all who were slain on the earth."—Rev. 18:8-10, 21, 23, 24 NKJV

Some Nations Survive

After this, Daniel is told that some of the other beast nations survive for a brief time. However, they are stripped of their power.

> 11 . . . "I watched till the beast was slain, and its body destroyed and given to the burning flame. 12 As for the rest of the beasts, they had their dominion taken away, yet their lives were prolonged for a season and a time."—Dan 7:11-12 NKJV

The survival of some nations is an indication that Antichrist and his system of control are not universally embraced. This helps explain why the earth is filled with war, economic terror, ecological disasters, and near extinction (Rev. 6).

I believe some nations will recognize the prophetic times and make a stand with God and against Antichrist. It is my prayer that the United States emerges as a sheep nation. I believe this is her calling. As a nation, the US has been the greatest exporter of Christian missionaries. We have flooded the earth with Bibles and Christian media. Believers in other nations, are now praying for us to wake up and recognize the demonic attack against our assignment, and rise with humility and power in our prayers.

In fact, this is actually happening. Bold Christian leaders like Dutch Sheets have been exhorting the Church to pray for decades and the momentum is building. I believe his actions are like king Josiah who went through Israel tearing down places of idolatry and calling his nation to repentance. That season of confrontation gave the people an opportunity to repent and align with God to avoid personal destruction in the coming days.

I have been praying for America for over thirty years. In those early days, God impressed me with a vision of our nation being carried away in a flood of satanic vomit. As I prayed for mercy, I could see a generation rising out of this filth and striking fear in the demonic realm. I have held onto this promise to this very day. In fact, when I write, I hear the cries of the younger generation and their desire to know the truth and be set free from the rampant confusion of this age. I write for them.

Right now, judgement hangs over us because of the killing of our babies, our corrupt politics, and our gluttony for media fed occultism. Even so, I have not surrendered! There are wolves stalking the corridors of power, but there is a remnant that cries for mercy and justice! This remnant has been given authority to bind and loose and they have an open door into the presence of God. We each have family, friends, children, and grandchildren who need our prayers. We have heroes of the faith cheering us on. We have brothers and sisters at our side who walk in holiness and humility. We are bold like lions. We are the head and not the tail. We are not victims—we are warriors!

I believe turbulent times are ahead for America as God intervenes to cleanse us. I am praying for mercy and that we would fall into the hands of God instead of other nations. Either way, I believe the praying Church will stand at the head of the streets as Jeremiah, giving direction and hope to our nation. Now let God arise and His enemies be scattered!

Jesus Christ Receives His Kingdom

After the judgment of the little horn, Daniel watches as all of heaven turns its attention toward a glorious and heavenly "Son of Man" as He is ushered before the Ancient of Days and given glory, dominion, and an everlasting kingdom.

> 13 "I was watching in the night visions, and behold, One like the Son of Man, coming with the clouds of heaven! He came to the Ancient of Days, and they brought Him near before Him. 14 Then to Him was given dominion and glory

and a kingdom that all peoples, nations, and languages should serve Him. His dominion is an everlasting dominion, which shall not pass away, and His kingdom the one which shall not be destroyed. —Dan 7:13-14 NKJV

The splendor of this person, who is clearly Messiah, captivates Daniel. At this juncture, he is assured by an angel that the everlasting kingdom of Messiah *belongs to the saints*. At once, jubilation and praise fill heaven.

27 Then the kingdom and dominion, and the greatness of the kingdoms under the whole heaven, shall be given to the people, the saints of the Most High . . . —Dan 7:27 NKJV

Daniel has just witnessed the coronation of Jesus the Messiah by God the Father. A future event that he will be attending along with all the born-again saints from history!

I believe that after this glorious occasion, Jesus will return with His saints. This is an event that Enoch foretold *before the flood*:

14 Now Enoch, the seventh from Adam, prophesied . . . "Behold, the Lord comes with ten thousands of His saints." —Jude 14 NKJV

The Bible is full of passages that declare the coming of Messiah with His saints (Rev. 19:11-14; 1 Thess. 3:13; Col. 3:1-4; Zech. 14:5; Duet. 33:2).

Jesus Quotes Daniel

Now fast forward to Jesus Christ as He stands before the entire religious assembly of Jerusalem; He is on trial and on His way to the Cross. On this occasion, the High Priest demands that Jesus identify Himself: "are you Christ, the Son of God?" Jesus answers yes by hearkening back to this vision and calling Himself the "Son of Man sitting at the right hand of Power." Enraged, the High Priest accused Jesus of blasphemy because the Jews universally regarded this "person" in Daniels vision as Messiah.

> 63 . . . the high priest answered and said to Him, "I put You under oath by the living God: Tell us if You are the Christ, the Son of God!" 64 Jesus said to him, "It is as you said. Nevertheless, I say to you, hereafter you will see the Son of Man sitting at the right hand of the Power, and coming on the clouds of heaven."
>
> 65 Then the high priest tore his clothes, saying, "He has spoken blasphemy! What further need do we have of witnesses? Look, now you have heard His blasphemy! 66 What do you think?" They answered and said, "He is deserving of death."—Matt. 26:63-66 NKJV

Our God has never departed from His original command. He created the earth as a home for His children, and He allocated its dominion to Adam and Eve who were commanded to rule righteously. With the coronation of King Jesus—the second Adam—the earth will be restored to the righteous. Wow.

Prophetic Restart

Rome is the fourth beast empire and Antichrist is her final leader. This is clear and confirmed in all of Scripture. There is no other empire that springs up after her.

In the centuries after Jesus, Rome fell apart into nation-states and it appears her opportunity to be the end time global monster has passed. This reminds me of Nimrod who was thwarted at the Tower of Babel but his aspirations were restarted with Nebuchadnezzar.

Likewise, I believe that God placed Rome on hold after the birth of the Church. Initially, she cruelly persecuted the infant Church but then lost her place of power after a few hundred years. Meanwhile, the Church has flourished much like Israel did while living in Egypt.

It is my studied belief that with the rebirth of national Israel, the prophetic clock restarted for Rome and she is in an accelerated growth spurt. Today many of the wealthiest western and eastern European families claim they are descendants of Roman royalty. In fact, this is a very big deal in those circles. These families of immense wealth are busy funding and building technologies to control the world. We are rapidly coming under a web of control that the Roman beast was unable to construct until now. This tells me that the return of King Jesus is very close.

I am reminded of Judas Iscariot. Jesus called him the son of perdition i.e. the son of destruction and hell (John 17:12). This is also a title given to Antichrist.[88] Jesus knew of Judas' evil plan of betrayal but Judas was not released to carry it out until the time came for Jesus to finish His work at the Cross. When Jesus was ready, He turned to Judas and excused him from the table and released him to carry out his diabolical scheme.

Likewise, evil men have been scheming to rule the world and kill the undesirables since Nimrod. However, they have been thwarted from their efforts until such time as Jesus is ready. Biblically speaking, Jesus will be ready and allow Rome to take her final stand when His bride has made herself ready (Rev. 19:7).

Meanwhile, Monster Rome is busy making its plans—just like Judas Iscariot—and building its political coalition, its iron military, and its system of control through artificial intelligence. Presently, all of this is causing oppression and persecution among Christians and all people. In the midst of this increasing persecution, the born-again saints are coming into full maturity. Once we are mature, and we have finished our assignment on earth, it is my belief that we will be removed from the planet and be found in the courtroom of the Ancient of Days where we will watch the final antics of Antichrist before he is thrown into the lake of fire and his kingdom is destroyed.

Daniel was told that the little horn will "prevail" upon the saints. Primarily, this is a reference to the Jewish people and the last seven years of this age when they are united with Antichrist in a treaty (covered in detail in subsequent chapters).

Even so, we must remember that Rome has been around for a long time and her mode of operation is to persecute and kill Christians and Jews. She will be doing this all the way to the end. As she regains her supremacy in the earth (even now), she will cycle through several leaders and plenty of war, bloodshed, and religious persecution, before Antichrist finally takes the reins of power.

An Angel Gives Daniel a Summary

At the end of the vision, Daniel asked an angel to explain the meaning of the fourth monster beast and the little horn. The angel described them as the final government that persecutes the saints for a period called "time, times, and half a time" (three-and-a-half years) (Dan. 7:25). In Daniel's third vision, this calculation is explained as Israel's last three-and-one-half years under Antichrist.

The Impact of the Vision on Daniel

When the vision ended, Daniel was exhausted after watching a long succession of savage beast's rule the world until their blood thirst was ended by the Ancient of Days.

Daniel had been looking for the imminent liberation of his people from captivity and the coming of Messiah to rule and reign forever. This vision profoundly altered his understanding of the future. He wrote everything down as instructed and kept the matter to himself (Dan. 7:28).

CHAPTER 23

Daniel the Prophet
Second Vision—Daniel 8

In 553 BC, Daniel had his second vision—three years after the first—when he was about sixty-six years old. It was the third year of the reign of Belshazzar, a descendant of Nebuchadnezzar, and thirty-five years since the burning of Jerusalem.

Susa

In this vision, Daniel is visited by the angel Gabriel and transported to a palace in Susa which today is located in Iran. Historians believe Cyrus may have built a royal residence in Susa, and this is probably where Daniel was standing. Within a year of this vision, the army of Cyrus the Great, the king of the Medo-Persians, would enter the palace of King Belshazzar of Babylon, murder him, and thus establish the next world empire.[89]

In fact, Jeremiah foretold the eventual fall of Babylon *before* they conquered Jerusalem. As we have seen, the Babylonians were well-versed in Jeremiah's prophecies. Therefore, they should have been living humbly; knowing their reign at the top had an expiration date.

The situation for the Jews was about to shift. This vision was a prophetic briefing of the impending changes, and it added more details concerning the future of the Gentile Age and its impact on Israel. In fact, when God foretells the future of *nations*, He always pivots from Israel.

Once again, God was faithfully providing prophetic due diligence to all parties far in advance of world events and had them recorded in the prophetic and public record.

Medo-Persian Kings: Ram with Two Horns

While Daniel stood on the palace grounds of the next world ruler, he looked up to see a ram with two long horns standing by the water. As he watched, one horn grew longer than the other, and the ram came charging from Eastern Europe toward the west, north, and south, representing the reaches of his power. He was so fierce that no beast (nation) could stand against him. He conquered as he pleased and became great.

The angel Gabriel explained that the ram with two horns represented the kings of the Medo-Persian Empire. As we know from history, they were Cyrus the Great and then Darius, who achieved the greatest eminence, making him the longer horn.

In Daniel's previous vision, the Medo-Persian Empire was depicted as a bear with three ribs in its mouth. In this vision, the focus is on the rulers who are depicted as a ram with two horns.

The Shaggy He-Goat: Greece

After this, Daniel saw the next world empire as a shaggy he-goat with a prominent horn between his eyes coming from Western Europe and crossing the earth without touching the ground. The goat charged at the ram—the Medo-Persian Empire—with such fury that he shattered his two horns, knocked him to the ground, and then trampled him. After this, the goat became powerful on the earth until his large horn was broken and replaced by four prominent horns that grew toward the four winds of heaven.

Gabriel identified Greece, the Mediterranean people to the west, as the shaggy he-goat—and the large horn as its first king. As we know from history, this was Alexander the Great who was tutored by Aristotle until he was sixteen years old and then became king at the age of twenty. During his short twelve-year reign, Greece became the next world empire after the Medo-Persian. At the age of thirty-two, Alexander died in Babylon after a two-week illness.

In Daniel's previous vision, the Greek Empire was depicted as a leopard with four heads. In this vision, the focus is on the king who is depicted as a shaggy he-goat with a large horn that is broken and replaced by four prominent horns or kings.

Gabriel explained that upon the death of the Greek conqueror, his empire would be divided into four kingdoms as represented by the four prominent horns. History corroborates that Alexander's kingdom was divided among his four generals at his death (Dan. 8:19-22).

A Strange King

After this, Daniel was shown a "little horn" (ruler) emerging out of the four horns of the Greek Empire. This king started small, but his powers grew southward and eastward and eventually overtook Israel (Dan 8:9).

In this vision, the king is allowed to trample the Jewish temple and take away the daily sacrifices because of compromise and sin in the nation.

Keep in mind that when Daniel had this vision, his people were still in captivity and it would be several decades before they fully rebuilt their temple under Cyrus and Darius. Therefore, this vision confirmed the rebuilding of the temple, the eventual compromise of the priesthood, and a trampling of its courts by a Greek king.

Historically, this happened 388 years after Daniel's vision in the year 167 BC, when the Greek king Antiochus Epiphanes entered the holy of holies and poured pigs' blood on the altar before erecting an idol to Zeus, his patron god. This event is often referred to as the "rebellion that causes desolation" or the "abomination of desolation."

In other words, the nation and her leaders compromised their faith and position—the rebellion that causes desolation—and then God removed His protection so that a heathen king was able to perform demonic rituals in the temple—the abomination of desolation."

> "Because of rebellion, the LORD's people and the daily sacrifice were given over to it [the little horn Antiochus]."—Dan. 8:12, NIV

Antiochus Epiphanes: A Type of Antichrist

It is universally accepted among scholars that Antiochus Epiphanies is a prophetic prototype of Antichrist. As such, they are both referred to in Daniels visions as a little horn, and they share the same evil delusion that they are anointed as a god. But most importantly, Antiochus famously invaded Israel and desecrated her temple; an act that will be repeated by Antichrist.[90]

Because these men are related prophetically, it is important to understand Antiochus and the political setting that allowed him to gain the upper hand over Jerusalem and her temple.

When speaking of Antiochus, the angel Gabriel tells us he has "fierce features and understands sinister schemes" (Dan. 8:23). Historically, he seized his throne in a moment of opportunity and was so menacing that no one dared oppose him. As a masterful liar, he held his throne with cunning political rhetoric. Those in his inner circle were rewarded with wealth and favors.

Antiochus's father was a military general and a king. Coming from such privilege, Antiochus spent his formative years in Rome. He was worldly-wise with Roman, Greek, and Persian influences. He was wealthy, arrogant, and prone to public drunkenness with riffraff, which was considered scandalous for a prince.

Antiochus was groomed to be high-minded and selfish. No doubt he watched the rule of his father and then his brother and decided he could do much better. He felt enlightened and entitled. Eventually, Antiochus ruled his empire like a beast over his harem. Everything and everyone existed for his pleasure.

Antiochus: "god" Manifest

The arrogant Antiochus eventually added "Epiphanes" to his name which means "god manifest." By doing this, he claimed to be the earthly embodiment of Olympian Zeus, the leading Greek deity. By laying claim to Zeus, he invoked the idea that his ascension to the throne was secured by Zeus, and that his actions were directed by Zeus and therefore above reproach (like Nimrod before him). The pride of Antiochus was so legendary that he had coins minted with his picture and the title "Epiphanes."

Antiochus Epiphanes and the Seleucus Family

When Alexander the Great died, his conquests were divided among his four generals. The general named Seleucus I Nicator assumed the old Babylonian and Medo-Persian territories. His domain became known as the Seleucus kingdom. Today, several countries fall within these old borders, including Syria, Iraq, Iran, Turkey, Armenia, Pakistan, and Afghanistan.

Antiochus Epiphanes was a direct descendant of Seleucus but not the first in the line of royal succession because he had an older brother. This may be the reason he is depicted as a small horn that grows from the side of one of the four horns.

Antiochus's older brother became ruler when their father died, but he was soon killed. After this, the scepter should have passed to his oldest son, but he was a hostage in Rome and unable to serve. Therefore, the scepter passed to his youngest son who was a small boy. At this juncture, Antiochus seized the moment and declared himself the custodian of the young boy, who was his nephew, and became the acting king in his stead. Eventually, Antiochus killed the little boy and ruled the Seleucus dynasty until his death.

The Ptolemy Family

When Alexander died, the section of his empire that included Egypt, Palestine, and Israel came under the rule of his general, Ptolemy I Soter. This territory became known in history as the Ptolemy Empire with the capital city located in Alexandria of Egypt, which was founded by Alexander the Great.

The Ptolemy family ruled Egypt for about three hundred years. Ptolemy I Soter became the first pharaoh of Egypt in 323 BC,[91] and all his male successors kept the name Ptolemy as part of their full names. In addition, the queens of the Ptolemy family took one of three names: Berenice (the first queen), Arsinoe (the name of Ptolemy's mother) or Cleopatra.

The first Cleopatra was a princess born to the Seleucus family, and her father gave her in marriage to a prince in the Ptolemy family. The boy was sixteen, and Cleopatra was around ten years old when they married.

Prior to the marriage, the Seleucid king was attempting to conquer Egyptian territory but was held back by Rome who protected her. In an effort to avoid war with Rome, the Seleucid king gave his daughter in marriage to the Ptolemy family to soothe the tensions and gain a family tie. History confirms that this attempt to merge the two families was unsuccessful and they continued to have conflicts until Rome finally conquered them both.

Another interesting feature of the Egyptian Ptolemy's was their intentional inbreeding. They kept their kingdom holdings within the family by forcing marriages between brothers and sisters who co-ruled. Over time, this weakened the dynasty as some were born with physical or mental impairments.

The last ruler of the Ptolemy dynasty was Cleopatra VII who committed suicide in 30 BC after her Roman lover Marc Antony was defeated by Octavian. At this point, Octavian—the heir of Julius Caesar—made Egypt a territory of Rome.

Jerusalem Under Ptolemy Rule

While ruled by the Ptolemy family, the Jews enjoyed a peaceful existence. At this time in history, they were merely a small nation that consisted of Jerusalem and a few settlements around the city. They were not considered a major prize or threat.

The more important area was the land west of Jerusalem that lay between the Jordan River and the Mediterranean Sea. This area was called Palestine, and it was the major route into Egypt both by land and sea. Egypt needed this land to protect its borders, and to maintain its highly profitable trade industry. This made Palestine very important to the Egyptian economy.

Rome and Egypt

Also, during this time, Alexandria and Rome were the largest and most important cities in Western Europe, and they both maintained ports on the Mediterranean Sea. Rome depended on Alexandria for commerce and trade, and they highly valued her impressive navy that controlled the Mediterranean. For all of these reasons, Rome maintained close diplomatic ties with Alexandria and came to her aid when and if an outside power threatened her.

Antiochus Covets Egypt and Palestine

When Antiochus Epiphanes became the Seleucid king—some ninety-five years after the first Cleopatra—he embarked on a campaign to conquer Egypt and gain her territories and riches. Unfortunately for the Jews, this included Jerusalem.

The real prize for Antiochus was Alexandria Egypt, so he set about to conquer Palestine and Jerusalem in order to gain important trading routes and seaports along the Mediterranean Sea.

This strategy was designed to weaken the Ptolemy Empire while Antiochus waited for the opportunity to conquer

Alexandria. Unfortunately, this placed Jerusalem in the crosshairs of Antiochus who conquered and ruled her for approximately eleven years from 175 BC to 164 BC.[92]

The Situation Among the Jews

When Daniel had this second vision, it was about 553 BC. Then, about eighteen years later, in 535 BC, the Jews were allowed to return to Jerusalem under the rule of Cyrus the Persian and rebuild the city walls and the second temple. Finally, the temple was finished and dedicated in 515 BC during the reign of Darius the Persian. By the time of Antiochus, the Jews would be back in Jerusalem with a temple for over 350 years.

Remember, in the final days of Solomon's temple, Israel's wicked kings and priests vandalized the temple and erected idols. Therefore, with their own hands, they defiled the holy of holies. This abomination resulted in the departure of God on His chariot throne as Ezekiel watched. With God's departure, the temple was spiritually "desolate" and finally it was burned to the ground by Babylon. This sequence of events can be summed up as the "abomination that caused desolation."

In this current vision, Daniel saw the new temple which would soon be built by the Jews who had returned from Babylon after seventy years of captivity. History tells us that they were careful to keep the new temple pure and free from idols after all they had been through.

When Antiochus came along some 350 years later, the office of high priest was held by a descendant of Aaron (the first high priest), and he served as the national head of government. Having immense power, the priesthood had become politicized and corrupt with infighting and murders.[93]

Politics in Jerusalem

When Antiochus raided Jerusalem for the first time, her citizens were divided into two factions: those who wanted to follow the Law of Moses and retain purity in the temple worship, and those who wanted to become a center of Greek culture.

By this time, the Greeks had done a remarkable job of spreading their culture over conquered peoples. They did this by building city centers with gymnasiums and Greek temples and then diversifying the local population with Greek citizens who were cosmopolitan and educated. In this way, the Greeks were able to conquer far-flung territories and then put down deep roots. This strategy worked brilliantly, and it helped them retain control over areas that once belonged to the Babylonian and Persian Empires, and included what is today Pakistan, Afghanistan, Iran, Armenia, Iraq, Syria, and Turkey.

Civil Unrest in Jerusalem

When Antiochus took control of Jerusalem, the high priest was Onias III, a traditionalist descended from Aaron. However, he had a brother named Jason who wanted to do away with the old order and turn Jerusalem into a Greek metropolis.

Seeing an opportunity to supplant his brother, Jason approached Antiochus with bribe money and a plan for modernizing Jerusalem, which included the construction of an Olympian gymnasium and an altar to Zeus. Jason promised to rejuvenate the economy and increase the tribute taxes to Antiochus. The bribe money was simply a show of good faith and a promise of more to come.

Antiochus accepted Jason's proposal and made him the new high priest instead of Onias III. In the mind of Antiochus, the office of "high priest" was a political appointment. You could call this person a governor, regent, magistrate, priest, or whatever you fancied; they were all the same.

Jason ruled as Antiochus's appointee for three years until a political rival named Menelaus approached Antiochus with more money and a better proposal. Intrigued and greedy, the tyrant happily ousted Jason and installed Menelaus as the new "high priest."

Meanwhile, the followers of the Law of Moses were unhappy with the political maneuvering within the office of the high priest. Under the rule of Jason, a Grecian gymnasium was built that attracted a following among the wealthy and the young. Suddenly, in the streets of Jerusalem, the youth were sporting Greek wardrobes and paying homage to Greek gods.

The traditionalists hated the changes brought by Jason, but they tolerated them because the temple worship was unaffected. However, that changed with the appointment of Menelaus. First of all, Menelaus was not descended from Aaron. Therefore, it was illegal for him to enter the temple to perform priestly duties. In the eyes of God, anything this man presumed to do was an abomination that rendered the temple unclean.

Then, to add to the outrage, Menelaus had the old priest Onias III murdered while he was living in exile in Antioch.[94] Finally, after enduring brutal new policies and high taxes, it was discovered that Menelaus was stealing from the temple treasury in order to pay the tribute tax that he promised Antiochus. Without a doubt, he was a scoundrel, and the general population hated him.

The Line In the Sand

Against this backdrop, something unfortunate happened. Antiochus was engaged in a military campaign to overtake Cyprus and Alexandria, Egypt, and he was on the brink of succeeding when he was intercepted by a Roman commander with orders from the Senate to immediately stand down or face war with Rome.

Antiochus was so close to victory he could taste it. He had spent considerable time and money in his quest to conquer Alexandria, and he had already envisioned himself striding into Pharaoh's palace, sitting on his throne, and then pleasuring himself with his wives and concubines. With the arrival of the Romans, his heart was stabbed with alarm as the delegation surrounded him and his officers and demanded their compliance.

Antiochus mustered up a brave face and told the Roman commander, Gaius Popillius, that he would take the matter under advisement. Irritated by his arrogant response, Gaius took a stick and drew a line in the sand around Antiochus and ordered him to give an answer to Rome before stepping out of the circle.

While the troops watched, Antiochus was careful not to provoke Rome. As he stood in the circle with all eyes upon him, he was furious and embarrassed but also determined to get out alive. Finally, after what must have seemed an eternity, he capitulated to Gaius and agreed to withdraw and in the process, he humiliated himself in front of his troops and the whole world!

Looking back, it is obvious that both armies told this story thousands of times, while laughing hysterically, because we still use this phrase today: "a line drawn in the sand." It's an amusing story for us; however, it would prove to be devastating for Israel.

The Rumor that Antiochus Was Dead

During all of this, word got back to Jason—the former high priest—that Antiochus had died in battle. Upon hearing the rumor, Jason marshaled a force and entered Jerusalem to take back the position of high priest. When Menelaus heard that Jason was on his way, he ran to hide. Once Jason entered Jerusalem, he brutally murdered everyone he considered his enemy. The whole town was in an uproar as mayhem ran through the streets.

Meanwhile, Antiochus was somewhere outside of Alexandria, trying to recover from his extreme humiliation and also wondering how to pay his troops. They had just spent months trying to penetrate Alexandria and were literally on the verge of a rape and pillage payday when they were repelled by Rome.

In those days, military men were hired hands. They were land pirates who joined themselves to the army most likely to succeed so that they could live off the spoils of war.

Antiochus now faced a dilemma. In order to keep his men from mutiny or desertion, he would have to find pay dirt somewhere, and fast.

While trying to figure out what to do next, Antiochus received word that civil war had broken out in Jerusalem over news of his death! Jason had taken control of the city, ousted Menelaus, and killed the king's supporters! Antiochus was livid.

Suddenly, the perfect solution occurred to Antiochus. Surely the gods were with him! The troops were assembled, and the march to Jerusalem was on. The year was 167 BC when the army of Antiochus entered the city—under a peaceful pretense—and unleashed a hellish nightmare. For three days, his troops pillaged every home, raped the women, killed the children, and took possession of whatever they desired.

In the writings of the Maccabees, we learn that 40,000 Jews were killed and another 40,000 were sold as slaves.[95][96]

Antiochus Prospers Because of Rebellion

In Daniel's vision, the small horn—Antiochus—was allowed to trample the people of God and desecrate the temple worship because of Jewish transgressions:

> 12 And the host [the chosen people] was given [to the wicked horn] together with the continual burnt offering because of the transgression [of God's people—their abounding irreverence, ungodliness, and lack of piety]. And righteousness and truth were cast down to the ground, and it [the wicked horn] accomplished this [by divine permission] and prospered. —Dan. 8:12 AMP

Daniel had no way of knowing what kind of rebellion would allow this wicked king to prosper because he had this vision about 386 years before the actual events. For us, it is clear.

It was the backslidden religious leaders of Israel who conspired to overturn the Aaronic priesthood. They are the ones who hatched the plot to remove the high priest Onias III by using Antiochus to do their dirty work. They tapped into his greed, paid him money, and then promised to keep the cash flowing. What more could the tyrant want? He had a powerful group of insider elites who were willing to turn Jerusalem into a Greek city and do the dirty work of extracting taxes. Sweet.

What did God do? He patiently stepped aside and watched as they made a deal with a crazed demoniac. In time, the fruit of this unsavory political alliance would make itself known. Beyond that, it would serve as a prophetic dress rehearsal for things to come under Antichrist.

Antiochus's Attitude Toward Israel

Remember, Jerusalem was nothing special to Antiochus. He had claimed her land for himself, much like a dog marks his territory. She was small and off the beaten path of Palestine. Initially, he allowed her to conduct her life and business without much interference as long as she submitted to the appointed leader and paid her taxes.

In the mind of Antiochus, she was just another city that was willing to become Greek based on the commitment of her leaders. He never imagined that a large portion of the Jews would so stubbornly cling to their God and their religious traditions. In his experience, most cultures easily embraced the Greek gods and combined them with their favorite deities. Not so with the Jews.

The Abomination of Desolation

When Antiochus entered the city of Jerusalem, he went straight for the temple while his army of barbarians ripped the city apart. Inside the temple, he ransacked the inner chambers and took the precious metals and anything else of value.

It must have been strange for Antiochus when he entered the temple to find it free from idol statues. However, he did find an altar, and he wasted no time in claiming it for Zeus, the god he embodied according to his demented mind. In this way, he actually identified himself as the god of the temple. History tells us that Menelaus was there guiding Antiochus through the temple, helping him locate the wealth, and advising him to desecrate the Jewish God by sacrificing a pig—an unclean animal—upon His altar.

Menelaus knew this would be an abomination to God. With a profaned altar, it would be illegal for the priests to make any future sacrifices until such time as they could purify it. Thus, he rendered the altar physically desolate after it had been spiritually defiled by the corrupt priesthood.

After dedicating the temple to Zeus, Antiochus immediately instituted new religious laws that forced the worship of Zeus and forbade the people from engaging in Jewish practices. These included male circumcision, the reading or possession of Jewish writings, abstaining from unclean foods, and keeping the Sabbath. Anyone found engaging in any of these acts was tortured and killed.

The soldiers of Antiochus took about three days to satiate their evil appetites and when they were done, 40,000 were dead, and the city was a smoldering pile of chaos. For Antiochus, the massacre of Jerusalem was his opportunity to recover his pride and assert his prowess as the alpha dog—just in case anyone was in doubt.

At the end of the three-day blood orgy, Antiochus combed his hair, fastened his loin cloth, and then set about to lock down the city before he went on his way. As the shivering survivors looked on, he appointed a special garrison of soldiers to stay behind, patrol the city, and enforce the new religious reforms. His officers had orders to kill, without hesitation, anyone who dared to worship the Jewish God. The party was over!

The remaining troops set up living quarters in Jerusalem and ruled with an iron fist for three years.

After three years, Antiochus Epiphanes suddenly died, and his reign of terror was over. History tells us that on his death bed, he believed that his sudden sickness was due to his treatment of the Jews and his foolish disrespect of their God.

Fullness of Time and Wrath

In this vision, the little-horn Antiochus is depicted as ruling at the *latter time of wrath when wickedness has reached its fullness* (Dan. 8:17, 19, 23).

This verbiage informs us that every wickedness is given a specific time frame before wrath overtakes and destroys it.

In the time of Antiochus, the people had grown cold toward God and abused the temple, causing His wrath to hang over them. Even so, wrath was delayed, allowing time for sowing, reaping, and repentance. Finally, when wickedness was hardened and mature, God destroyed it with His wrath—through the instrument of Antiochus. This process destroyed the sin so that the people could move forward.

Today we can deal with our sins by repenting and accepting Jesus Christ as our Savior. In contrast, the unrepentant are under the sentence of wrath. Bottom line, sin must be dealt with because it wars against God's kingdom of love, peace, and order. This is why the bowls of God's wrath are poured out—as a means to destroy sin—before the second coming of Jesus Christ.

Pertaining to Israel, this order of sin and wrath is a pattern that gets played out over and over again in her history. And, as we shall see, the final episode happens under Antichrist.

To every modern nation, this pattern provides us with a template of God's governance. This is especially relevant in this current season of nation reckoning that we have entered with the rebirth of national Israel.

Judgment Shortened

Daniel's vision upset him to the point of illness. Most disturbing was the persecution of his people by the little horn. While contemplating all of this, he heard a conversation between two holy ones or angelic beings. As he listened, they discussed the stern-faced king and how long he would be allowed to prosper against Israel and pollute the temple. The answer given was 2,300 evenings and mornings, and then the temple would be restored and consecrated.

2,300 evenings and mornings computes to six years and a few months and days. It is not a full seven years. Scripture is full of examples of judgments against Israel that lasted in units of seven, yet this particular time of trouble is cut short, and it happens to be during the time of Antiochus who is a prophetic template for Antichrist.[97]

Technically, Antiochus ruled the land of Palestine and Israel for longer than seven years. Even so, his interference with temple worship officially began with the appointment of the illegitimate Menelaus as the high priest. Most scholars date the time from Menelaus to the death of Antiochus as just short of seven years.

Interestingly, this time frame has a parallel with Antichrist. According to Daniels next vision, the final seven years of this age will begin when Israel enters into a seven-year peace treaty with Antichrist. However, there is a caveat. Because the reign of Antichrist is so horrific, all flesh on the earth will be in danger of extinction. Therefore, Jesus tells us those days will be shortened:

> "Therefore when you see the 'abomination of desolation,' spoken of by Daniel the prophet, standing in the holy place" (whoever reads, let him understand), . . . 21 For then there will be great tribulation, such as has not been since the beginning of the world until this time, no, nor ever shall be. 22 And unless those days were shortened, no

flesh would be saved; but for the elect's sake those days will be shortened. —Matt. 24:15, 21-22 NKJV

In summary, when the rule of Antiochus interfered with the priestly laws of Israel, he had a little less than seven years before his death. I believe the same will be true for Antichrist.

The Temple Is Cleansed

When word of Antiochus's death reached his troops in Jerusalem, they hastily withdrew from the city knowing that Jason—the former high priest—would be coming to kill them. In fact, Jason and the traditionalists did return to Jerusalem and they cleansed the temple, built a new altar, and then resumed the daily sacrifices to God. The date of the first sacrifice in the newly cleansed temple was December 25, 165 BC—exactly three years from the date that Antiochus profaned the altar with a pig.[98]

The writings of the Maccabees chronicle the events of this time.

Satan: The Power Behind Antiochus

In his parting words, Gabriel cryptically told Daniel that the stern-faced king and master of intrigue will become strong "but not by his own power," implying that he would have a benefactor (Dan. 8:24).

In the historical record, Antiochus does not have a supporter opening his doors or watching his back. I believe that Satan—the god of this world—is the mysterious power behind this man who is successful beyond merit.

CHAPTER 24

Daniel 5:
The Miraculous Hand

Belshazzar, a grandson of Nebuchadnezzar, was the last king of the ancient Babylonian Empire.

Everyone in Babylon, including Belshazzar, knew the story of Nebuchadnezzar's pride against God and the seven years of lunacy that came upon him at the height of his power when he was driven into the wilderness to live like a beast. Even so, Belshazzar was not in the least bit inclined to fear the God who humbled his grandfather.

One fateful night in 553 BC, Belshazzar held a raucous party of idolatry, alcohol, and sex, for a thousand people that included his nobles, wives, and concubines. In the middle of the revelry, he ordered his servants to bring him the gold and silver goblets that had been looted from Solomon's temple. As the king and his entourage took the goblets filled with wine, they mocked God and gave praise to the gods of metals, wood, and stone. Then, as they were frolicking in their drunken madness, a hand suddenly appeared on the wall in front of the king and wrote a riddle: MENE, MENE, TEKEL, UPHARSIN.

Alarmed, the king's blood pressure fell dangerously, and his knees knocked uncontrollably. In utter terror, he screamed out for his soothsayers to come at once and decipher the writing; promising a reward to the one who solved the riddle.

Meanwhile, everyone in the room waited in silent terror to learn the meaning of this other-worldly omen.

When the enchanters, astrologers, and diviners were unable to interpret the strange writing, the queen mother—who had been awakened by the commotion—recommended that they summon the wise man Daniel, who had served his father and grandfather.

When Daniel arrived, he immediately understood the meaning of the omen. The king offered to give him riches and honor in exchange for his interpretation, but Daniel scoffed at the gesture and then proceeded to lay out the facts.

First of all, Daniel reminded the king of God's sovereign power over all creation and how He humbled Nebuchadnezzar for his pride (Dan. 2:21).

Then, Daniel sternly rebuked Belshazzar for his capricious dismissal of history and his arrogant mocking of God by playing sport with the temple objects. In fact, he should have bowed his knocking knees and repented to God the moment the hand appeared . . . he was without excuse!

By now, the king's attendants and guests were trembling with fear. In contrast, Daniel stood confident and regal as he proceeded to decipher the writing which was a judicial decree against Belshazzar and his kingdom (Dan. 5:18–31).

MENE MENE: God had numbered Belshazzar's kingdom, and it was finished. This numbering of days was according to God's eternal design, and it was now time for the rise of the next empire.

TEKEL: Now that the Babylonian kingdom was done, the man Belshazzar was on trial to determine his fate. God the Judge had weighed his life and deeds, and he came up short.

UPHARSIN: God had decreed that the Babylonian kingdom be divided and given to the Medes and Persians; Belshazzar was thus duly stripped of his power. Game over. It was time for the next season on God's clock.

That very night, the army of the Medes and Persians killed Belshazzar and took possession of the kingdom of Babylon.

What a night! While they were drinking and partying and carrying on like there was no tomorrow, no God, and no judgment, they unknowingly stepped into the next season on God's clock. And Jesus said, "I come at an hour that no man knows" (Matt. 24:44).

Pre-Creation God has numbered the exact days for everything under heaven (Eccles. 3:1–8). To the foolish and arrogant it appears that God acts rashly, according to whim. Nothing could be further from the truth, and this event is a warning that extends to every nation and king throughout the Gentile Age.

God has spoken loud and clear through His prophets. At the very onset of the Babylonian Empire, God gave Nebuchadnezzar a dream and revealed that he was the first king among many and that his kingdom was *temporary*.

A Prophetic Harbinger

Not only that, this event is a prophetic dress rehearsal for the final global empire ruled by Antichrist which is called "Babylon" in the book of Revelation.

In the future, we can expect another night of terror when Antichrist falls dead and his beast empire is reduced to embers on the battlefield. Surely, the bloated despot and all his international allies will be filled with fright and knocking knees when their time is up. We have been forewarned. Get ready!

Prophetic Due Diligence

God always provides extreme prophetic due diligence for the doubting and arrogant world. Scripture reminds us that God does nothing without first telling His prophets (Amos 3:7; John 15:15).

Once more, Daniel found himself at a crossroads in history. In his short life, he witnessed the fall of Israel and the rise of the

Babylonian Empire and the Gentile Age. Then, on this night, the scepter of world rule passed to the Medes and Persians!

CHAPTER 25

Daniel the Prophet
Third Vision—Daniel 9

When Daniel was about eighty-one years old, he had his third vision. It was fifteen years after his second one, and the year was 538 BC—the first year of Darius of the Medes and Persians.

By this time, Daniel had been a captive for about sixty-nine years. He had served under the Babylonian king Nebuchadnezzar, and then Cyrus the Persian. Eventually, Cyrus appointed Darius the Mede to oversee the affairs of Babylon, and this is when Daniel came under his rule.

Daniel Attacked by Jealousy

Once Darius took the throne, he formed a cabinet of 120 governors and appointed Daniel as one of three overseers. A short time later, the king recognized Daniel's exceptional qualities and decided to promote him to second-in-command over his kingdom.

Filled with jealousy over Daniel's impending promotion, the cabinet members hatched a plan to kill him. They persuaded Darius to make a decree that all worship must be directed to him for the next thirty days under penalty of death. Darius agreed, and the law was written and posted. After this, the governors broke into Daniel's home with the intention of catching him in the act of praying to God—which he did three times a day. As expected, Daniel was praying, and the governors rushed to tell Darius and demand that he enforce the death penalty per his decree.

Darius was grieved and regretted making such a law, but he relented under pressure and ordered that Daniel be thrown to the lions. Feeling tricked and angry, he stayed up all night and worried about Daniel. Finally, at the crack of dawn, he ran to the lions' den and found Daniel unharmed. It was a miracle! This proved beyond a doubt that Daniel was favored by his God and Darius was vindicated in choosing him as a coregent (Dan. 6).

As for the men who conspired to kill Daniel, they were now on the wrong side of God and Darius! The king ordered their arrest, with their families, and they were thrown to the lions who crushed their bones before they hit the ground (the wicked have no protection from the beasts of this world). After this, Daniel was promoted by Darius, without objection, and then he had his third vision.

Daniel Educated in the Scriptures

Daniel was an educated man who likely possessed copies of the writings of Moses, Isaiah, and the prophet Jeremiah.[99] In addition, Daniel was a youth in Jerusalem when Jeremiah foretold her desolation and then restoration. Knowing the Law, the prophets, and history, Daniel calculated that the seventy-year desolation of Jerusalem was coming to an end. The first raid of Jerusalem by Nebuchadnezzar was in the year 607 BC when Daniel was taken captive as a young boy. It was now 538 BC, and sixty-nine years had elapsed.

Sabbath Rest

Before Israel entered the Promised Land, Moses instructed the people to observe the appointed Sabbaths which included a rest for the land every seven years and the cancellation of all debt.

According to Moses, failure to willingly obey the Sabbaths would result in "forced Sabbaths" via conquest and slavery (Lev. 26:33–35). Either way, the law of the Sabbath was nonnegotiable. Again, God laid out the rules in advance, and the Israelites agreed to the terms.

Hundreds of years later, Jeremiah prophesied seventy years of captivity—a very specific number—because the land had been denied seventy Sabbath years of rest. Daniel was now living at the end of the season of forced captivity. The land was now rested, and the people were divested of their debts, having lost everything (2 Chr. 36:20–21).

Daniel Intercedes

Understanding the prophetic times, Daniel prepared himself to approach God in prayer and ask for the restoration of his people and Jerusalem. It is important to note that Daniel pursued the fulfillment of prophecy through prayer; he did not sit idly by.

As a show of seriousness and humility, he refrained from eating and then bowed before his God and King to confess the sins of his people and plead for mercy.

In Daniel's lengthy petition, he recounted the great history of the Exodus and the sad decline of his people into ever-increasing idolatry; and then he appealed to God's love and mercy.

As God listened to Daniel, He heard a son who implored Him to truly and deeply forgive and restore His people. Back then, most humans paid homage to distant and capricious gods, and it was rare for anyone to believe in a god of tender mercy—yet Daniel believed this was the very essence of his King.

Daniel reminded God that He had made a covenant of love with Israel. Yes, it was true that she had openly committed adultery with foreign idols right under His nose and in His house; she was now covered in shame and living as a slave. Indeed, the situation was dire, but not without hope!

God had promised a restoration, and now the nations were watching to see if He was willing or able to keep His word. In fact, God's next move would become part of the historical record for all eternity. Would the words of the prophets come to pass or not? Could God be trusted to stay faithful to Israel no matter her sins?

Daniel knew the answer. He had spent his entire life walking with a God of love and compassion, and this knowledge gave him the faith and courage to ask for *nothing less* than a shift in world politics so that Israel could go home!

God Hears Daniel

As soon as Daniel began to pray, he had God's full attention, and the angels stood by watching and listening. The deep love of Father God toward Daniel was well-known in heaven—as confirmed by the angel Gabriel. Daniel had been pulling aside to talk with God three times a day for over sixty years. Because of this, his heart was wide open toward God, and the love between them was filled with rich history. Not only that, Daniel was genuinely awed by the majesty of God his King, and he approached Him with careful reverence in order to communicate allegiance and deep joy at the privilege of serving Him.

At the sound of his prayers, a tangible swell of emotions rose from God's heart and filled heaven. It was clear to the angels that Daniel was asking for things that God wanted to give him and that he had touched a deep reservoir of desire in His heart. Yes, there was sorrow over the hard-heartedness of His people, but also joy because of children like Daniel who loved and appreciated Him.

Gabriel Is Sent

Responding with deep love, God sent Gabriel to visit Daniel and give him understanding concerning the times and seasons of Israel and, by extension, the world.

It was an honor for Gabriel to be chosen by God as the special messenger to Daniel and then to be identified by name in his writings. There are only two holy angels called out by name in the cannon of Scripture: Michael the archangel over Israel and Gabriel her special messenger.[100] Both of these are mentioned in the book of Daniel.[101]

Filled with deep affection, Gabriel rushed to Daniel who was still praying and abruptly appeared to him. Daniel immediately recognized Gabriel from his previous visit. On this occasion, his demeanor was noticeably focused and intense.

Spilling over with emotion, Gabriel took a moment to express the affection of God and told Daniel he was deeply loved and highly esteemed. Imagine for a moment the power of that greeting! Daniel lived among idol worshippers and demonic kings. *Never* in the history of the world did a demon god send messages of love and tenderness to his worshippers! In contrast, our Creator is filled with love and passion for us! His tenderness and kindness toward us are unprecedented, and He talks about it all the time in Scripture. Love is His unique and weighty signature.

Today, Daniel resides in heaven as a member of the heavenly family of saints. The glory he lives in is matchless and beyond our imagination. Even so, I am sure that he counts this greeting from the heart of God as one of his most cherished memories.

The Future of Israel and Messiah

In his opening remarks, Gabriel instructed Daniel to listen closely and understand the message of the vision. In other words, Daniel would need to actively engage his knowledge of Scripture and his skills of riddle solving in order to grasp the revelation.

According to Daniel's understanding of Jeremiah and the prophets, Israel would be restored to her home and rebuild her temple, and then Messiah would come and rule the world forevermore. Gabriel was sent to clarify the timing of these events which would happen over an extended period of time.

Gabriel's explanation of Israel's future was both expansive and brief. It spoke to the present and the future and everything in between. With broad brushstrokes, he revealed that Israel would be restored—as Jeremiah foretold and Daniel had prayed. Then, centuries later, Messiah would come and then be cut off. Finally, at the end of the age, after wickedness and backsliding had run its course, Messiah, the most holy, would be anointed as King forevermore, thus bringing to fruition and fulfillment every vision and prophecy.

Seventy Times Seven

According to Gabriel, Israel had a final unit of time called "seventy sevens" which literally equates to 7 x 70 = 490 years.

This measure of time would "finish the transgression . . . make an end of sins . . . make reconciliation for iniquity . . . bring in everlasting righteousness . . . seal up the vision and prophecy . . . and anoint the most Holy" (Dan. 9:24 KJV).

At this juncture, Israel was coming out of a season of "seventy sevens" where she had neglected to observe seventy total Sabbaths, resulting in seventy years of captivity. And now, according to Gabriel, Israel was allotted another "seventy sevens."

When Jesus walked the earth, He referenced the same calculation given by Gabriel when He commanded His disciples to forgive every trespass against them "seventy times seven." This was a clear reference to the book of Daniel and God's amazing ability to forgive Israel and by extension fallen humanity. How many times does God forgive? Seventy times seven. In other words, God's mercy toward Israel—and us—covers the entirety of this age (Matt. 18:21–23).

Seven Sevens

As Daniel listened, Gabriel organized the "seventy sevens" into three units of time. To begin with, a decree would be given, and then the Jews would return to Jerusalem and rebuild the city and the temple during a turbulent time. This season would comprise "seven sevens" or forty-nine years.

Historically, this happened shortly after this vision when Cyrus gave his decree of amnesty and the Jews returned to Jerusalem and began rebuilding. Because of opposition, their efforts took longer than expected, and the temple was finally dedicated in 515 BC, about twenty-three years after this vision.

Then, many years before and after the dedication of the temple, the scattered Jews returned home in waves. Gabriel called this season of regathering and rebuilding "seven sevens."

Sixty-Two Sevens

Gabriel then revealed that a long period of time called "sixty-two sevens" (technically 434 years) would pass, and the Anointed One—Messiah—would be cut off.

Daniel was tracking with Gabriel, and he could see the return of his people to Jerusalem and the temple rebuilt. This was perfect. After that, somewhere in the intervening years, Messiah would come to His nation and His temple. Perfect again.

But wait! Gabriel said that Messiah would be cut off at the end of this season of "sixty-two sevens." What? Why would Messiah finally come and then be cut off? Every Jew assumed that when Messiah came, all rebellion would end. Right?

Not exactly. Already in the prophetic writings, there were passages about the rejection and suffering of Messiah, but they were not understood until after His resurrection (Isa. 53:4-9).

Looking through the eyes of history, Jesus the Anointed One came to His nation at the end of this season of sixty-two sevens, and the Jewish leaders rejected Him. It is a fact of history that the Jews were expecting Messiah based on this vision, and according to their calculations, His time was imminent. Even so, they were looking for a warrior king like David who belonged exclusively to them. Instead, they got the Lamb of God who takes away the sins of the *world*—both Jew and Gentile. Because of this, they rejected Him and cut Him off.

The People of the Ruler to Come

Going further, Gabriel revealed that after Messiah was cut off—at the end of the sixty-two sevens—a certain group of people who belonged to the "ruler to come" would destroy the rebuilt city and temple. After that, a long period of wars and desolations would ensue like a flood. *This period was not given a time frame.*

As we know from history, Jesus the Messiah came to earth and was crucified (cut off) during the time that Gabriel revealed. Then, a few years later in AD 70, Titus the Roman destroyed the city of Jerusalem and her temple, thus identifying Rome as the "people group who belong to the ruler to come."

> 26 "And after the sixty-two weeks Messiah shall be cut off, but not for Himself; and the people of the prince who is to come shall destroy the city and the sanctuary. The end of it shall be with a flood, and till the end of the war, desolations are determined. —Dan. 9:26 NKJV

In the years after the destruction of Jerusalem, Imperial Rome slowly fragmented into smaller nation-states because of constant wars. As a result, power was distributed among the most beastly individuals and families who became national rulers and holders of vast wealth gained from conquest. Today many of these families continue to exert control over governments and foment wars and desolations as a means to increase their wealth and power.

After Messiah was cut off, He returned to heaven and launched His born-again Church. Since that time, we have been living in the open-ended season of wars and desolations. This parenthetical season is a time set aside for the Church to mature. Once she reaches that moment of completion, Israel will be ready for her final seven years.

Final Seven and the Abomination of Desolation

Moving on, Gabriel revealed Israel's final days as a period called "one seven" that begins when the Roman ruler to come— Antichrist—makes a treaty with Israel. Then, in the middle of the seven years, Antichrist will stop the sacrifices and offerings in the temple and claim it for his own.

> 27 he will make a treaty with the people for a period of one set of seven, but after half this time, he will put an end to the sacrifices and offerings. Then as a climax to all his terrible deeds, he will set up a sacrilegious object that causes desecration, until the end that has been decreed is poured out on this defiler."—Dan. 9:26-27 NLT

From Daniel's second vision we learned that the Jewish priesthood made a political pact with Antiochus which resulted in the desolation and desecration of the temple.

In this vision, we are talking about Antichrist and Gabriel uses the terminology "sacrilegious object that causes desecration" or in the NKJ version: "abominations that cause desolation."

By using the same terminology, Gabriel has prophetically connected the two events. Now we realize that the political agreement between national Israel and Antichrist, will be an abomination to God and it will result in desolation.

Three-and-a-Half Years

According to Gabriel, the abomination in the temple occurs at the midpoint of the final seven-year period. This leaves the Roman ruler with three-and-a-half years before the end comes.

The calculation of three-and-a-half years is exactly what Daniel was shown in his first vision when a leader arises from the fourth and final beast government and persecutes the saints for "a time, times, and half a time."

Knowing that the previous abomination of desolation was the installation of an idol altar to Zeus in the temple—the patron god of Antiochus—it follows that this final Gentile ruler will claim to be the earthly embodiment of his patron god (Satan). It is very likely that some Jews will embrace Antichrist and his claims of deity. Even so, I believe that most will reject him as they did with Antiochus and Zeus. Paul the Apostle speaks to this event:

> 3 Let no one deceive you by any means; for that Day [second coming of Jesus] will not come unless the falling away comes first, and the man of sin is revealed, the son of perdition, 4 who opposes and exalts himself above all that is called God or that is worshiped, so that he sits as God in the temple of God, showing himself that he is God.—2 Thess. 2:3-4 NKJV

Putting Daniel's first and third visions together, it follows that Antichrist will make a treaty with Israel. Then, at the three-and-a-half-year mark, he will enter a temple in Jerusalem, claiming to be the manifestation of God. In truth, Jesus Christ is God manifest. As the only begotten Son of God, He is Messiah.

When Antichrist enters the temple as "god manifest and / or messiah," he will do so as the son of Satan.

As Satan's agent, he will have three-and-a-half years (or slightly less) to persecute God's people before he is judged by the Ancient of Days and given over to a fiery destruction.

Israel's Three Distinct Periods

Many scholars have grappled with historical dates in an effort to calculate the exact moment when each unit of time begins and ends. We know that the Temple was built in the first unit of time, and Jesus came at the end of the second unit of time as foretold by Gabriel and expected by the Jewish leaders.

The third unit of seven years has not started yet. It is on-hold until the born-again Church is mature. Therefore, we are in a parenthetical season of wars and desolations.

It is my studied belief, that when the Church is ready and her work is done, we will exit the earth to be with Jesus in heaven. This might occur before or at the onset of the seven years, or sometime later (more as we continue).

No matter the exact date of our departure, the last seven years are for Israel. According to Gabriel, this short season will: finish all transgression; make an end of sins; make reconciliation for iniquity; bring in everlasting righteousness; seal up every vision and prophecy; and then anoint the most Holy (Dan. 9:24 KJV).

The Rebuilding of the Temple Begins

A year after this vision, in the seventieth year of Daniel's captivity, King Cyrus of Persia issued a decree allowing the Jews to return to Jerusalem and rebuild their city and temple. This fact is also confirmed in the archaeological find of the "Cyrus Cylinder."

It is stunning to note that the decree was given at exactly seventy years. This gives me great confidence that God has perfectly scheduled the exact date that Israel will enter her final seven-year period and become the center of world events.

CHAPTER 26

Daniel the Prophet
Fourth Vision, Part One
Daniel 10–12

Right before his death, Daniel had his fourth and final vision which took place in 534 BC—four years after the previous one—when Daniel was about eighty-five years old.

Three years prior to this vision, many Jews had returned to Jerusalem to rebuild the city and the temple when Cyrus the Persian issued a decree of amnesty that occurred after Daniel interceded.

Upon their return, they encountered resistance from the Samaritans, who feared the restoration of Jerusalem. These were a mixture of people that were captured by Assyria and then resettled in the cities that once belonged to the northern tribes of Israel (2 Kings 17:24-34, Ezra 4:1-10).

In an effort to stop the rebuilding, they sent formal complaints to Cyrus, warning that the Jews were seditious and would revolt if allowed to rebuild their temple. In this atmosphere of political intrigue, Cyrus sided with the Samaritans and instructed them to hinder the work until further notice. Because of this opposition, the Jews became discouraged and stopped building. It took fifteen years before the work on the temple was resumed and finished (see the book of Ezra).

At the time of this vision, the construction of the temple was on pause, and Daniel was still living in Babylon as an elder statesman in the Persian kingdom. According to the date he gives, he had embarked on a time of special prayer and fasting during the Passover season. It is likely that Daniel determined to petition God to break every stronghold that was hindering the completion of the temple.

The Appearance of the Deliverer Messiah

After three weeks of fasting, Daniel was standing with some men by the Tigris River—located in modern Iran near ancient Babylon—when suddenly he looked up and saw a "man" of such power and awesome glory that he uncontrollably melted to the ground. Simultaneously, his companions felt the supernatural presence and ran for their lives to hide.

Daniel had been visited by angels in the past, so he knew their appearance could be terrifying. However, this supernatural "man" was different from Gabriel and the others. He was dressed in linen—the clothing of the high priest—with a belt of the finest gold around His waist signifying wealth, glory, and royalty. His body glistened like a jewel, and His arms and feet had the appearance of gleaming brass. His face was blindingly bright like a flash of lightning, and His eyes burned like a flaming torch. When He spoke, it was like thousands of voices layered together to create a full and abundant rumble. His distinct and powerful voice was unlike anything Daniel had ever heard.

Daniel was never told the identity of this "man," but in the book of Revelation, we see Him again and He is Jesus Christ. When John the Apostle describes Jesus, He has the same attributes that Daniel observed, including the voice of many waters. Many scholars share my belief that this "man" in Daniel's vision is Jesus Christ.[102]

Think about it . . . Daniel was visited by King Messiah; the very one he had spent his life looking and longing for.[103]

When Daniel heard His voice, he instantly froze in terror. The holiness of the Majestic Messenger electrified the atmosphere, and Daniel became acutely aware of his unclean and sinful state.

The contrast between Creator and created is staggering. Imagine the day when Jesus Christ returns to rule. Every knee will bow—not because they are coerced by some warrior angel—but because of His astounding holiness. When the "Light" of the world appears in our atmosphere, all of creation will melt into the ground, all random thoughts will disappear, and every cell of our bodies will cry, "holy, holy, holy" (Isa. 45:23 and Phil. 2:9-11).

Daniel was face down on the ground and frozen in fear when a hand lifted him to his hands and knees. As he listened, the voice of majesty encouraged him: "Daniel, do not be fearful of impending horror; instead, be filled with *shalom*—a restful heart—because you are very precious and loved. Now be strengthened, listen carefully, and consider intelligently the words I am about to speak to you and stand up." Daniel stood— still trembling—but encouraged because of the kindness and love that he felt. With resolve and focus, he responded, calling Him "my Lord" (Dan. 10:10–19).

From here, the Majestic Messenger, along with other angels, began to unfold a revelation concerning the future of Israel and the continual wars surrounding her until the end of the Gentile Age.

The Backdrop of Spiritual Evil

Before launching into the future, the Majestic Messenger revealed to Daniel the spiritual rulers behind the scene of world affairs. For every territorial battle that rages in the natural, there is a corresponding battle between demon war-lords.[104]

Legally, the demons receive and hold power through fallen humans in treason. Therefore, their greatest fear is a godly saint who bows his knee in prayer to ask for mercy and justice (remember, Daniel was arrested for praying). In rank, one lowly saint has more power than all the demon hordes because we have favor with God our Father; the Omnipotent Creator.

Repentance Disarms Demon Warlords

The Majestic Messenger told Daniel that He was sent to give him understanding on the first day that he prayed, but it took three weeks to get through. During this time, the demon prince who ruled over the government of Persia stood opposed to the Messenger's passage. Evidently, the demon was justified in asserting ownership over the Persian airspace since the entire nation had pledged allegiance to idols. Furthermore, it could be argued that the Jewish people were legitimately the property of Persia because of their national rejection of God.

The resistance in the spiritual realm lasted three weeks while Daniel continued to pray, fast, and repent for the sins of his people. Finally, God sent Michael the Archangel to put an end to the confrontation.

Notice that the Persian demon firmly and legally controlled the air space and the government until Daniel's repentance prevailed with God. After that, angels were dispatched to break the demonic resistance over Persia for the sake of Israel and in response to Daniel's prayers.

If He wanted to, God could have put an end to the demon prince of Persia and sent him straight to the lake of fire. Instead, He has chosen to wait for His human children to actively engage in the disarming of principalities, and their human co-conspirators, by our petitions of fasting and prayer. I call this the honor clause.

In the Garden of Eden, God placed the government of the earth into the hands of humanity. Therefore, if we want justice, we must invoke God's participation as King and Judge. Anything less and we would be lazy couch potatoes expecting God to wait on us hand and foot.

Instead, the saints are severely pressed, harassed, tortured, and killed by constant injustice from demonic governments until we finally wake up and realize that we are God's legal team, law officers, and beloved family, and it has been granted to us to make the first move.

Jesus told the story of a woman who begged and pleaded with a worldly and crooked judge to give her justice from an adversary until finally he relented just to shut her up (Luke 18:6-8). In this parable, Jesus encouraged us to take our petitions to our righteous God who longs to adjudicate on our behalf if we would just ask. As saints, we know and abide by the laws of God, and it is our priestly and governmental duty to bring cases of injustice and wickedness into His courtroom for His ruling.

Not only that, it is our responsibility to *know the prophetic writings*, as Daniel did, and pull upon God to enact His promises at the appointed times.

Knowing the prophetic times, Daniel recognized his priestly duty. Therefore, he prepared his case to go before God and ask for the fulfillment of the prophetic promises given to Israel that were part of the public and national records. Then, in order to discharge God's ruling, Michael the Archangel was sent to break the spiritual power of the demon prince of Persia over the civil government.

Evidently, the holy angels have to exert themselves, as we do, so that we all participate in standing for righteousness and learning (in part) the price that God has paid to gain beloved children with freewill.

Michael the Guardian Prince Over Israel

In this vision, Michael the Archangel engages evil principalities in order to advance Israel's prophetic destiny among the nations. At the close of this vision, he rises to protect her survival during the reign of Antichrist.[105]

Another thing we learn is that God's holy angels have order and unity. In contrast, Satan's kingdom is filled with greed and in-fighting. At the time of this vision, Michael prevailed against the powerful demon called "the prince of Persia." However, according to the Majestic Messenger, this demon would soon be defeated by the "prince of Greece," and the power struggles would continue.

Let us pause and think on this. The Majestic Messenger (Jesus) has given us an inside glimpse of powerful demons who rule empires through the agency of fallen humans and they have been permitted to oppose God's people . . . until the saints of God bow in prayer! One man prayed, and a demon prince was overruled, and an earthly empire shifted its policy toward God's people. Seriously! It's time to pray the Scriptures and ask for the fulfillment of the prophetic promises that are waiting for us!

Leading Up to Antiochus Epiphanes

After Daniel was briefed on the spiritual backdrop of international politics, he was given a high-level overview of the remainder of Persian rule and the rise of the Greek Empire, which happened approximately 206 years later in 332 BC.

This is a long vision, and most of it concerns Greek history and how it affects the nation of Israel and the entire Middle East. The main points are told in quick brushstrokes and filled with political craft. Daniel learns that a powerful king will conquer Persia—historically this is Alexander the Great—and then his kingdom will be broken up and parceled out to the four winds of heaven, etc.

Throughout, Daniel is given various details about the constant warfare (transpiring over hundreds of years) between two Greek families that ruled the north and south. History corroborates these details that occurred within the Ptolemy kingdom based in Alexandria, Egypt—called the "South"—and the Seleucid kingdom based in Syria—called the "North."

Viewed through the lens of history, we recognize the political marriages between the Seleucid and Ptolemy families, of which the first Cleopatra is famous, and the constant warfare between them. In fact, the political narrative is so long and detailed that it begs the question: *Why?*

For starters, the generations that lived under these kings and eventually under Antiochus, were given the hope of an end date to their suffering. In addition, this prophecy gave accurate details of events hundreds of years before they transpired, resulting in astonishment among later Bible scholars. This has lifted the authority of Daniel's prophecies to the highest level. Those striving to disprove Daniel, and thereby dismiss the future that he has foretold, will never be able to overcome the fact that his book has been in the public record for over 2550 years.

Beyond that, Antiochus is a prophetic prototype for Antichrist in his belief that he is the chosen representative of his god, his obsession with war, his political alliance with the corrupt priesthood, his subsequent persecution of the Jews, and his desecration of their temple.

Finally, this entire narrative happens in the Middle East which is the epicenter of end-time events. To that point, it is significant that the Majestic Messenger (Jesus) introduced us to the demon Prince of Persia (Eastern Europe) and the demon prince of Greece (Western Europe) who are still at war with one another in their quest for global primacy.

Next Disaster: Antiochus Epiphanes

Finally, the historical narrative reaches the political career of the Greek king Antiochus Epiphanes, who came to power over Jerusalem 359 years after this vision in 175 BC.

In Daniel's second vision we are introduced to this wicked ruler. In this current vision, we learn that after much political conniving, Antiochus is on the brink of overcoming Egypt (the king of the south) when he is stopped by the "ships of the western coastland" (Dan. 11:30). This is the embarrassing incident when the Roman commander drew a line in the sand around Antiochus in front of his troops.[106]

After this, the evil ruler turns his attention to Jerusalem, marches against her, and gains access to the city with the help of Jewish traitors. Daniel is told that he vents his fury against the people and the temple, setting up the "abomination that causes desolation" so that the daily sacrifices are abolished.

> 29 "Then at the appointed time he will once again invade the south, but this time the result will be different. 30 For warships from western coastlands will scare him off, and he will withdraw and return home. But he will vent his anger against the people of the holy covenant and reward those who forsake the covenant. 31 His army will take over the Temple fortress, polluting the sanctuary, putting a stop to the daily sacrifices, and setting up the sacrilegious object that causes desecration. —Dan. 11:29-31 NLT

Abomination of Desolation

The abomination of desolation is mentioned three times in Daniel's visions.

In Daniel's second vision, he is shown a "little horn"—Antiochus Epiphanes—who comes from the Greek Empire and is allowed to prosper against Israel because of wickedness in the Jewish priesthood. This is called the "rebellion that causes desolation" (Dan. 8:12-13).

In Daniel's third vision, the final Gentile ruler—Antichrist—makes a seven-year treaty with Israel. Then at the halfway point, he violates the treaty and takes control of the temple (thus bringing desolation). We are told that these final events bring an end to iniquity and bring in everlasting righteousness (Dan. 9:24).

In this fourth and final vision, we return to Antiochus Epiphanes and all the details that lead to the abomination of desolation during his reign (Dan. 11:31).

Finally, 567 years after this vision, Jesus Christ mentions the "abomination of desolation spoken of by Daniel the prophet" when He describes the final events preceding His return (Matt. 24:15). Since Antiochus is already history, Jesus is referencing Antichrist.

Then, about forty years after the Resurrection, Titus the Roman burned the Temple in AD 70 and set up Roman regalia in the temple area after conquering Jerusalem and slaughtering as many as one million Jews (see the writings of Josephus). This certainly qualifies as an abomination of desolation and it follows after national Israel rejected Jesus the Messiah—the true temple. Even so, *Titus was not the Antichrist.*[107]

The Prince to Come: Antichrist

However, Titus was a political forerunner of Antichrist and his destruction of Jerusalem and her temple were foretold in Daniel's third vision:

> 26 "And after the sixty-two weeks Messiah shall be cut off, but not for Himself; and the people of the prince who is to come shall destroy the city and the sanctuary."—Dan. 9:26 NKJV

In the above passage "the prince who is to come" is Antichrist. When Titus destroyed the city and the sanctuary, he confirmed the Romans as "the people" who produce this final tyrant.

In summary, Jesus references Daniel to inform us of a final abomination that occurs in a Jewish temple at the end of this age. According to Daniel, this will occur under the Roman Antichrist.

In all of these visions, there is a pattern that emerges. First, the national and religious leaders of Israel are filled with compromise and corruption. Subsequently, a Gentile ruler takes control over Jerusalem and terrorizes the Jews while defiling the temple with an idol to his patron god.

In every instance, God speaks of the Gentile conquest as His method to bring wrath upon the ungodliness of His nation and purify what remains.

Corruption in the Last Temple

So, we have to wonder, what specific corruption causes the last temple to be overtaken by Antichrist? Without a doubt, the Jews who are currently involved in the third-temple project are very sincere and carefully following the ancient pattern of design, construction, and ceremonial purity.

Sincerity aside, we must remember that the Jewish "nation" is in rebellion against God by their rejection of Jesus Christ the Messiah (even so, many individual Jews are Christians). Since His resurrection, some Jewish teachers have put forth twisted interruptions of the Law of Moses, the Psalms, and the prophets, in their efforts to explain away Jesus and justify their continued search for a messiah. This erroneous path has created a jumble of mystical gibberish that has no resemblance to the Old Testament.

We should be very honest with ourselves. It is a grave error to search for a messiah that is engineered and approved by humans. In the end, it will lead to incredible deception and suffering as the man who claims to be Messiah will be Antichrist—the man who is against Christ and instead of Christ. This man will be the ultimate abomination as:

> "he sits as God in the temple of God, showing himself that he is God."—2 Thess. 2:4 NKJV

Let me quickly add that the current blindness that is over the Jewish nation will be purged through the final seven years under Antichrist and healed at the return of Jesus Christ. Meanwhile, we are commanded to pray for Israel and her peace and remember that she was created by God for His purposes.

By the way, her ultimate peace *is* the reign of Jesus Christ. So, we are actually praying for the end of this age and the destruction of all wickedness when we pray for her peace.

6 Pray for the peace of Jerusalem: "may they prosper who love you. 7 Peace be within your walls, prosperity within your palaces."—Ps. 122:6-7 NKJV

Pause to Consider Persecution

After showing Daniel a prolonged version of Greek history, the life of Antiochus, his political pact with the Jewish priesthood, his raid of Jerusalem, and the setting up of the abomination of desolation (all verifiable in history), we pause to consider the pain and suffering upon the godly. Saints are plundered, killed, or burned, causing some to stumble in their faith and the insincere to fall off. Meanwhile, the true believers become purer and wiser and do great exploits.

The persecution depicted in this vision happened under Antiochus, and according to other prophecy, it will be repeated and become more severe under Antichrist (Dan. 11:33-35; Rev. 13:5-8; 17:6). Therefore, I believe the persecution in this vison has application to both time periods; and to any and all persecution that happens under the beastly kings of the Gentile Age.

Long-Term Persecution

Persecution is a recurring theme in the visions of Daniel which reveal a prolonged and stubborn wickedness within national Israel, with very little repentance. This results in her continued suffering at the hands of outside rulers all the way to a bloody end.

Fast-forward to the book of Revelation, and we witness visions of global destruction and tyranny. The picture is so upsetting that some refuse to believe it. In fact, the world is filled with books and sermons that dismiss the book of Revelation by claiming that it has already happened or that it is fictional and not really about the last days. In both instances, great violence and twisting must be done to the Scripture in order to fit into those scenarios.

241

It reminds me of the apostle Peter who chided Jesus for saying that He would be hated and killed by the elders in Jerusalem. On that occasion, Jesus responded swiftly and rebuked Peter by calling him Satan. Jesus expected persecution, and He taught His disciples to expect the same (Matt. 16:21-23).

King of the North Character Sketch

After looking at persecution, we are given a character sketch of the king of the north who is presumably Antiochus. Seething with rage and hatred, he considers himself greater than God and he serves a "god of war" which implies that he worships Satan who is in the business of stealing, killing, and destroying (Dan. 11:37–38). In addition, he has wealth and power, rules over many, divides the land at whim, and is vacant of familial affections due to his extreme self-worship (Dan. 11:36-39).

Obviously, this character sketch is applicable to Antiochus, but it also extends to Antichrist. In fact, it could apply to most tyrants throughout the ages.

It seems that the Majestic Messenger (Jesus) wants to make sure we have a good look at the evil face of Antiochus and his successor Antichrist. These men are world leaders who are also sons of Satan and bearers of his image.

Future Middle Eastern War

After looking at the historical battles between the Greek kings of the north and south, the persecution of Israel, and then a character sketch of the king of the north, this vision shifts to a war that cannot be verified in history.

What just happened? We thought we were talking about Antiochus "the king of the north" when suddenly we encounter this unknown war.[108] Over the years, this juncture has puzzled Bible scholars, and many agree that a transition has occurred. Having all of Scripture, as well as the historical record, we realize that this war is still in the future and that means the identity of the king has changed.

To Daniel, the king probably appeared to be the same man. To God, these men would be like-minded rulers, who are both under the sway of the demon Prince of Greece.

As we have seen, it is common in Scripture for a prophetic word to span the generations. Often, a message is directed to a contemporary person or nation, while at the same time it will be utterly fulfilled at the end of this age. For instance, the prophet Isaiah gave a message to the ancient king of Babylon that extends to the final king of Babylon—Antichrist—and also cryptically addresses Satan who is the spiritual king of Babylon (Isa. 14).

Another example is the prophecy against the merchant city of Tyre, her prince, and her king. In this prophesy, we understand that God is speaking to an ancient city and her rulers, while also speaking to Antichrist and Satan (Ezek. 26—28).

Turning Point in World Affairs

When we arrive at this "unknown war," the northern Greek king sets out to attack the southern Greek king of Egypt and along the way he invades a vast portion of the Middle East and "passes" through Israel. After this, he is called to task by northern and eastern powers before he dies suddenly on the battle field (Antiochus died at home of an illness). So, who is this person?

Some Bible commentators propose that the northern king is Antichrist and he starts this war and then dies on the battle field. If this is true, the battle before us is Armageddon that ends when God pours out His climactic wrath right before Jesus returns.

One difficulty with this interpretation is that this battle is directed toward Israel's neighbors and not Israel. As we know, the focus of Armageddon is an attack on Israel.

In my research, there lacks broad agreement among scholars. Therefore, I remain teachable and admit that I don't know for sure.

Having said that, I have a theory that this northern king is not Antichrist. If my theory is correct, this particular king and this battle must occur before the appearance of Antichrist and as a run-up to his reign.

To that point, the largest volume of this vision concerns a string of battles that occur within the Seleucus and Ptolemy kingdoms over a period of hundreds of years. All of these battles affect Israel and therefore they are all "precursors" or "run-ups" to the final battle of Armageddon.

I believe God has emphasized these ancient battles between the north and south Greek kings because their modern descendants will play a major role in the final hours of this age.

In fact, it is highly possible that Antichrist will rise from the lands of Antiochus which became a territory of Rome. In several prophetic Scriptures, Antichrist is alluded to as the "Assyrian," and Assyria is called the home of Nimrod. Today Assyria would include parts of Iraq, Iran, Syria, and Turkey; all within the realm ruled by Antiochus. And, all of these nations were absorbed by Imperial Rome (Mic. 5:5-6; Isa. 10:24; Isa. 14:24-27).

To sum this up, I speculate that this northern king is a modern ruler that resides around Syria and he embarks on a war that levels the Middle East and sets the stage for international conflict. Because of this war, global power will become consolidated, thus allowing the reemergence of Rome. Then, once the seat of Roman power is ready, Antichrist will take over as the world leader. More as we continue . . .

Time of the End

When this vision shifts to the "unknown war," we enter "the time of the end" (Dan. 11:40). This detail definitely places this war after the resurrection of Jesus Christ and therefore after the reign of Antiochus.

Technically, the "time of the end" or the "last days" are catch-all phrases in Scripture that refer to the turning point in history when Jesus the Rock struck the feet of the kingdoms of man with His life and resurrection.[109]

That event gave birth to His born-again Church, opened up salvation for all people, and commenced the "undefined" season of wars and calamities that lead to the maturity of the Church and the ripeness of wickedness (Dan. 9:26; Matt. 24:1-31).

Day of the Lord

Beyond the open-ended "time of the end and / or last days," there is a time called "the day of the Lord."[110]

The "day of the Lord" happens during the last seven years of this age. More specifically, it happens after Antichrist takes over the temple. Therefore, it will happen sometime during the last three-and-one-half-years.

Paul the Apostle speaks of the "day of the Lord" and connects it to Antichrist and the final judgment of fallen mankind. In addition, he tells us that it does not occur until the restraining power of God is removed which might be a reference to the removal of the born-again Church:

> 3 For that day [day of the Lord] will not come until two things happen: first, there will be a time of great rebellion against God, and then the man of rebellion will come-the son of hell. 4 He will defy every god there is and tear down every other object of adoration and worship. He will go in and sit as God in the temple of God, claiming that he himself is God.

> 7 . . . [Antichrist] will not come until the one who is holding him back steps out of the way . . .

> 9 This man of sin will come as Satan's tool, full of satanic power, and will trick everyone with strange

demonstrations, and will do great miracles. —2 Thess. 3-4, 7, 9 TLB

Nations Affected by This War

Now . . . back to our future war. According to this vision, the war is started when Egypt (the king of the south) makes the first move toward battle, thus provoking the king of the north to launch out in full military regalia. This is not a small skirmish where a few troops are sent in. This is full-blown war with a massive army, military vehicles, and battleships.

We are told that many countries are invaded along on the way to Egypt. This would presumably include the Mediterranean coast, the Judean coastline (Palestine), the West Bank, and the Gaza Strip. In addition, Egypt, Libya, and Sudan are specifically called out and overtaken (Dan. 11:40-45). [111]

For some reason, the northern king does not invade Edom, Moab, and Ammon—located today in the territories of Jordan and Saudi Arabia. Scripturally, these nations belong to the descendants of Esau (Jacob's twin brother). Historically they were hostile to Israel, and they aided Babylon and Antiochus in campaigns against her (see Obad).[112]

Perhaps they are not invaded because they are loyalist to the northern king and his agenda? Or, if we consider modern political alliances, they may be protected by the U.S. who currently uses these nations to station military assets. Or, as an option, they may not be in agreement with the anti-Israel forces of this Syrian king.

Israel's Ancient Enemies are Judged First

The nations affected by this military invasion just happen to be Israel's Middle Eastern neighbors, who in ancient times were warned through the prophets that God would someday visit them with judgment in proportion to their treatment of Israel (Jer. 25:15-29). This war brings to pass many of these prophesies.

I believe this war will ignite a renewed interest in biblical prophecy because it will be an international spectacle that shines a gigantic spotlight on the veracity of Scripture. Also, it will put every nation on notice that we have crossed a prophetic threshold and entered the most critical season of nation reckoning in history.

Meanwhile, the saints worldwide are and will be active preaching the gospel of Jesus Christ, while explaining the times we live in with great clarity and authority.

Israel

In passing, we are told that the beautiful land—Israel—is invaded, but nothing else. This indicates to me that the judgment of Israel's ancient enemies is the main focus of this war.

According to Scripture, Israel remains as a distinct nation all the way to the second coming of Jesus Christ. Therefore, we know she survives the war, even though she suffers an invasion. Perhaps this is when her walls of protection are leveled (see chapter 18).

Alarming Reports from the East and North

After successfully overrunning the Middle East from Syria down to Egypt, Libya, and the Sudan, the king of the north is stationed with his army somewhere in the mountains of modern Palestine. At this juncture, he receives alarming reports from the east and the north that send him into a suicidal rage of destruction. Probably, he discharges the remainder of his military arsenal as he goes to his death.

> 44 But news from the east and the north shall trouble him; therefore, he shall go out with great fury to destroy and annihilate many. 45 And he shall plant the tents of his palace between the seas and the glorious holy mountain; yet he shall come to his end, and no one will help him. —Dan. 11:44-45 NKJV

Most likely, the east and north powers have called for his surrender. Evidently, he is forsaken by the international community because he comes to his death with no one to help.

What modern countries in the east and north could pose such danger to this modern northern king who has just invaded the Middle East with seemingly no opposition from the world's greatest empires?

If we keep Israel as our compass, the east would be China or possibly India. The north would be Turkey and / or Russia.

It is interesting that these superpowers wait until he has successfully conquered a large portion of the Middle East and North Africa before they call for his surrender. Perhaps they covertly supported his campaign to conquer these nations, and now that he has succeeded, they are ready to dispose of him and take possession of his conquests.

Prophetic Harbinger

I believe this war occurs in the epicenter of the Middle East as a fulfillment of prophecy, and a harbinger of things to come. As such, it is a catalyst that ignites rings of war that radiate outward until all nations are visited with blessings or judgments that correspond to their actions toward God and His people.

Using the history of Israel as our pattern, nations will experience calamities, pestilences, increased taxation, loss of sovereignty, slavery, famine, and finally war on their soil if they seek to annihilate Israel, nationalize demonic religions, and codify laws that deny the liberties of the saints. On the other hand, they will be visited with blessings if they honor God.

By the way, every nation has the opportunity to repent of crimes against God and make changes so that they receive mercy in the midst of reaping what they have sown. That door is always open.

In addition, there are godly people in every nation that do not agree with the policies and actions of their rulers; and they actively grieve, pray, and speak out. They are not under judgment as individuals. Even so, Scripture is clear that nations as a unit are judged. Just like ancient Israel, God judged her as a unit, but first He marked and pulled out a remnant (like Daniel and Ezekiel) and He protected Jeremiah during the siege of the city.

Extinction Level Persecution Leads to Resurrection

After this war, and the death of the king of the north, the vision abruptly shifts and a summary is given of the final seven years of this age when Michael the Archangel rises to fight for Israel as she enters the greatest anguish and peril in her history. After which, there is a resurrection of the godly and the wicked:

> "At that time Michael, the mighty angelic prince who stands guard over your nation, will stand up [and fight for you in heaven against satanic forces], and there will be a time of anguish for the Jews greater than any previous suffering in Jewish history. And yet every one of your people whose names are written in the Book will endure it. And many of those whose bodies lie dead and buried will rise up, some to everlasting life and some to shame and everlasting contempt." —Dan. 12:1-2 TLB

Keep in mind, this prophecy is directed to the nation of Israel who will be the center of international events in the final seven years of this age. Also, it is important to note, that many Jews come to faith in Jesus Christ before and during this period because their names are in the book of life which is only possible by faith in Jesus the Messiah.

Jesus also referenced this vision and called this time of Israel's suffering the "great tribulation" that begins when Antichrist sets up the abomination of desolation in the temple. In addition, Jesus also mentions the danger of extinction that results in a shortening of time. Finally, after all this, Jesus will return to gather the elect from the four corners of the earth.

15 ". . .when you see the 'abomination of desolation,' spoken of by Daniel the prophet, standing in the holy place . . . 21 for then there will be great tribulation, such as has not been since the beginning of the world until this time, no, nor ever shall be. And unless those days were shortened, no flesh would be saved; but for the elect's sake those days will be shortened.

29 Immediately after the tribulation of those days the sun will be darkened, and the moon will not give its light; the stars will fall from heaven, and the powers of the heavens will be shaken. 30 Then the sign of the Son of Man will appear in heaven, and then all the tribes of the earth will mourn, and they will see the Son of Man coming on the clouds of heaven with power and great glory. 31 And He will send His angels with a great sound of a trumpet, and they will gather together His elect from the four winds, from one end of heaven to the other."—Matt. 24:15, 21, 29-31 NKJV

Now let's go to the book of Revelation, where more details emerge. John the Apostle learns that Antichrist and his kingdom are destroyed by the bowls of God's wrath and Satan is bound for a thousand years (Rev. 20:2-3). After this, Jesus returns and the righteous ones who have died under Antichrist will be *"resurrected"* and reign with Him for a thousand years (Rev. 20:4-5).

Then, at the end of the thousand-year reign of Jesus and His righteous saints, Satan will be allowed to tempt mankind one last time before being thrown into the lake of fire for all eternity (Rev. 20:7-8).

Finally, after all this has transpired, the ungodly will be *"resurrected"* from all of human history and they will be judged (Rev. 21:11-15). Notice that the resurrection of the godly and the ungodly are two separate events, and they are over a thousand years apart!

This detail alone tells us that the events portrayed in the final summary of Daniel's vision will happen over an extended period of time.

Putting together Daniel's visions, the words of Jesus, and the book of Revelation, here is a proposed sequence of events:

1. The modern king of the North (Syria) invades the Middle East and passes through Israel; possibly leveling her walls. The kings of the north and east call for his surrender and he goes on a murderous campaign before he is killed.

2. There is an unidentified period of time that elapses during which various Roman nation-states coalesce to become the final world empire. During this time, there is war, tyranny, and persecution against Christians and Jews.

3. Eventually, Antichrist is made the leader of this final empire and he makes a seven-year treaty with Israel.

4. Michael the archangel stands to defend Israel and assure her national survival and destiny through these final seven years of the greatest tribulation.

5. Somewhere before or during the last seven years under Antichrist, the born-again Church is taken to heaven (often called the rapture). I believe this is what is meant by the "removal of the restraining power" (2 Thess. 3:7). This will be covered more in the next chapter.

6. At the half way point of the seven years, Antichrist sits on a throne in the temple, and claims to be the manifestation of God. However, his god is Satan. This is the final abomination of desolation.

7. The "Great Tribulation" ensues under Antichrist, who goes on a killing spree and all life on earth is in danger of extinction.

8. Now that man-made government in collusion with Satan is on the verge of killing all life on the planet, God pours

out His climactic bowls of wrath upon Antichrist and his beastly kingdom.

9. At the end of the final three-and-one-half years, perhaps shorter in God's mercy, all the powers of evil will be broken and destroyed.

10. After this, Jesus will return in the clouds and gather His elect who have died under Antichrist (Rev. 20:4-6).

11. Jesus will set up His kingdom from Jerusalem and His born-again saints (Jew and Gentile) will rule with Him for a thousand years. In fact, His twelve disciples will sit on twelve thrones to rule the twelve tribes of Israel according to the promise of Jesus (Matt. 19:28).

12. After a thousand years, Satan will be released for a short season and allowed to tempt mankind one last time (Rev. 20:7-10).

13. After this, Satan, will be thrown into the lake of fire for all eternity.

14. Finally, any human who has not yet been resurrected, will be resurrected and judged. Those who are not in the book of life, will be sent to the lake of fire for all eternity (Rev. 20:11-15).

Summary

In summary, this vision is a long history of the Greek empire and the career of Antiochus—the northern king of Syria. Once we get to his life, we do a review of his evil ego, the compromise in the Jewish priesthood, the abomination of desolation, and the persecution of the saints. All of this speaks to the career of Antiochus, while at the same time foreshadowing Antichrist.

After this, we mysteriously advance to the future Middle Eastern war that is started by a northern / Syrian king and this sets the stage for the greatest persecution to ever occur and then the resurrection of the godly who were killed by Antichrist.

Finally, a thousand years later, the ungodly are pulled from their graves to stand before God at the final judgment.

Timing

At the very close of this vision, Daniel is struggling with all the details and wondering about timing. An angel tells him to seal the book (vision) until the time of the end when knowledge will be increased and many of the righteous will have wisdom and understanding.

After this, the angel raises his right hand to heaven and swears upon God who lives forever and forever that from the time of the final abomination of desolation, to the end, there will be one thousand two hundred and ninety days—three and half years (Dan. 12:7-11). Remember, this is the same time frame that Gabriel gave Daniel for the second half of Israel's final seven years (Dan. 9:27). Therefore, this is a reiteration of the facts; so that the matter is clear and settled.

Daniel and Revelation Together

Now flash forward to the book of Revelation, and a magnificent angel steps onto the planet with a little book in his hand and roars with the force of a lion.[113]

After this, he raises his right hand to heaven and swears by Him who lives forever and ever (the same thing the angel just did with Daniel). Then, he tells John, that when the *seventh angel of Revelation sounds the seventh trumpet,* it will end all delays and the mystery of God that He gave to His prophets will be finished (Rev. 10:5).

> 1 I saw still another mighty angel coming down from heaven . . . 2 He had a little book open in his hand. And he set his right foot on the sea and his left foot on the land, 3 and cried with a loud voice, as when a lion roars . . .
>
> 6 . . . and swore by Him who lives forever and ever . . . that there should be delay no longer, 7 but in the days of the sounding of the seventh angel, when he is about to sound, the mystery of God would be finished, as He declared to His servants the prophets. 8 Then the voice which I heard

from heaven spoke to me again and said, "Go, take the little book which is open in the hand of the angel who stands on the sea and on the earth." . . . 10 Then I took the little book out of the angel's hand and ate it, and it was as sweet as honey in my mouth. But when I had eaten it, my stomach became bitter. 11 And he said to me, "You must prophesy again about many peoples, nations, tongues, and kings."—Rev. 10:1-3, 6, 7, 10-11 NLT

The raising of the hands and swearing by God connects these two visions and it links the final abomination of desolation in Daniel's vision with the *seventh trumpet in John's vision.* By the way, the seventh trumpet releases the "bowls" of wrath.

After this, John is instructed to eat the little book from the hand of the angel and then prophesy to the nations. As commanded, John ate the little book and then delivered the message of its contents which unfolded with the seventh and last trumpet.

I propose that this little book represented the visions of Daniel that were over 550 years old in John's day.

When we understand that Daniel's visions are built upon the prophetic foundations laid by Adam, Enoch, Moses, and all the prophets, we are able to recognize the book of Revelation as the "capstone" that crowns the prophetic edifice called the Bible.

For two thousand years, John has been prophesying to the entire world through the book of Revelation. I believe that during the great tribulation, John's vision will be studied by sincere Jews who will connect it to Daniel and the other prophets. This will produce a wave of fear, sobriety, and repentance when they realize that Jesus Christ is Messiah (Rev. 10:1-11).

The War that Restarts Rome

Now some final thoughts on the pivotal Middle Eastern war. To properly understand it, we look back to Nimrod's occultic dream of world dominion that was put on hold at the tower of

Babel. After Israel achieved her maturity, the dream was restarted under Nebuchadnezzar, the head of gold, and the first of four empires. Then, at the resurrection of Jesus, the aspirations of Imperial Rome, the fourth and final empire, were put on pause so that the Church could be born and mature.

Nimrods Babylon never went away; it was paused. Nebuchadnezzar's world empire of treason never ended—it was simply paused at the resurrection. Now, with this war, I believe the kingdoms of this world are taken off of pause so that Rome can regain her power and military might. Once sufficiently energized, she will finish the aspirations of Nimrod by casting her dragnet over all the earths' inhabitants so that men are controlled and killed at the whim of Antichrist and his collaborators who take their orders from Satan.

Antiochus and Antichrist

Before we move on, it is important to remember that in Daniel's visions, we go back and forth between Antiochus and Antichrist, and sometimes it can get confusing because they have similar characteristics. I believe God has purposely blurred the lines so that we understand they are prophetically related. Antiochus is a prototype of evil rulers who terrorize God's people. Also, he provides us with a historical template for Antichrist who will rise from the ancient lands of the Babylonian Empire, which became the Medo-Persian, and then the Greek, and finally the Roman Empire.

It is important to note that the national boundaries are also blurred because all these kingdoms folded into one another to become Imperial Rome. This leaves room for the final Babylonian government to be composed of assorted modern nations and for Antichrist to arise from any number of places.

Prophetic Scripture Crosses the Chasm of Time

Another very important aspect of this vision (and all of biblical prophecy) is that God masterfully weaves together the storyline of multiple generations and highlights certain events and people in order to give us a big picture understanding. This is a key feature of prophecy.

God easily crosses the chasm of time with His all-encompassing messages, forcing us to see the panorama of history. When He speaks, He is a wonder to behold. He lives in the now-moment and at every point in eternity. Therefore, He can span the ages and blend them together in His narrative like no one else.

Our most honest response to His Majesty, is to allow Him to carry us across the ages and breathe in the rarefied air of His omniscience.

CHAPTER 27

Daniel the Prophet
Fourth Vision, Part Two
Daniel 10-12

The Stage Is Set

The war in this vision could unfold *right now!*

In this last chapter I will combine the many details of Daniel's prophecies, and everything we have learned, and venture out to propose a possible scenario of events that begin with this future war.

Keep in mind, that I am simply a student of the Bible and these are my opinions and personal insights based on a lifetime of study (and subject to change as I grow in grace). Among excellent Bible scholars there are differing opinions so it's crucial to stay humble and teachable.

King Vile

When Daniels vision shifts, the king of the north starts a war in the Middle East. Earlier in the vision, the Majestic Messenger called him a vile person (Dan. 11:21). We will call him King Vile.

As King of the north, I will assume that Antiochus and King Vile share some of the same background. Antiochus was born a Greek, was raised in Rome, and then ruled over the Middle East. Historically, he had palaces in Antioch and Babylon which are modern Syria and Iraq. His vast kingdom included what is today Syria, Turkey, Pakistan, Iraq, Iran, and Afghanistan. Over time, he subjugated Palestine, Israel, and parts of Egypt.

King Vile is no wimp. I believe his goal is to control the flow of international power and commerce in the Middle East. He is arrogant and well-funded. When he sits at the table with regional powers to negotiate their surrender, he has a huge bank account and a powerful military to back him up because he "prospers and frightens the surrounding nations with his ability to make war" (Dan. 11:36; Dan. 8:24).

Demon Warfare

At the onset of Daniels vision, the prince of Persia was the ruling demonic principality who is followed by the prince of Greece. The Majestic Messenger brought this to our attention for a reason. I believe these two demons are still at war with each other as they seek to rule the ancient Persian (East) and Greek (West) Empires.

Modern leaders, including King Vile, are simply pawns in the hands of these demon warlords whose ancient rivalry has filled the Middle East with bloodshed.

On that note, there is a real and current geopolitical battle for the Middle East between eastern and western world powers. It seems obvious to me that this divide corresponds to these two demon princes.

Modern Scenario

Today the superpowers of Russia, China, Western Europe, and the U.S. are vying for strategic access and control over the waterways surrounding the Middle East. These include the Mediterranean Sea, the Suez Canal, the Red Sea, and the Black Sea.

Also, the Middle East sits between east and west powers, has vast wastelands, and is filled with oil and natural resources. As a whole, she lacks the military prowess of a superpower and this makes her vulnerable.

Meanwhile, the mega-empires of the east and west are racing against each other in their quest for global supremacy. With great vigor, they are securing allies and subduing opposition while they flex their military muscles.

And what better place for a military show-down than the "wretched" Middle East that none of them care about except that it serves their purposes? Frankly, from a tyrant's perspective, this land mass is perfect for war.

Looking at this strategically, it makes sense that the super-powers would stage their conflicts in this middle ground and thereby keep the collateral damage away from their homelands. We have to wonder if the Middle East has already been designated by the global powers as the "theater of war" for the coming showdown between east and west.

In Daniel's vison, and also Ezekiel's vision of Gog and Magog, the wars are fought in and around Israel who sits in the center of the Middle East. Also, in the Book of Revelation, Armageddon occurs in the valley of Megiddo which is located in the Gaza Strip below Lebanon (Rev. 16:16). God told us about these final battles over 2500 years ago; long before we had any knowledge of the geo-political realities of today.

Not only that, the Majestic Messenger informed us that two demon princes—east and west—are battling over this stretch of land. In the end, I believe that one of them will prevail as the prince (under Satan) over the final empire called Babylon the great.

Keep in mind, the Roman Empire ruled over both regions. Therefore, at the end of the day, Rome is still the final beast no matter which demon prince prevails.

Scorched Earth War

I theorize that Daniel's future war may be a covert operation and a scorched earth campaign to clear the land of menacing opposition (in the minds of tyrants).

Remember when ancient Jerusalem revolted against Antiochus and ousted Menelaus his appointed tax collector? She made herself a nuisance and was promptly pounded into the sand. Same scenario here. The regional leaders along the Mediterranean Sea have become an unmanageable mess to the world powers and they are too poor to render any tax value.

I believe the only reason these nations are still standing is the providence and timing of God, and the inconvenient presence of Israel who sits in the middle of everything with her nuclear capabilities, military vigilance, and monetary strength. Clearly, the superpowers would welcome a war that weakened or destroyed the regional powers.

So, who will take the first step and start a war in this region? Obviously, the superpowers cannot be overtly involved, which would lead them to use a proxy to do their dirty work.

Against this backdrop, perhaps a superpower behind the scene persuades King Vile to invade Egypt—the provoker of the war—and the surrounding nation's which include Israel.

> "At the time of the end the king of the South shall attack him; and the king of the North shall come against him like a whirlwind, with chariots, horsemen, and with many ships; and he shall enter the countries, overwhelm them, and pass through. 41 He shall also enter the Glorious Land [Israel], and many countries shall be overthrown; but these shall escape from his hand: Edom, Moab, and the prominent people of Ammon. 42 He shall stretch out his hand against the countries, and the land of Egypt shall not escape. 43 He shall have power over the treasures of gold and silver, and over all the precious things of Egypt; also the Libyans and Ethiopians shall follow at his heels. —Dan. 11:40-44 NKJV

The war in this vision overwhelms the Middle East. After this, King Vile is no longer needed. At this point, he receives an alarming message from the north and east—possibly Turkey, Russia, and China. I believe they call for his surrender, and he realizes he has been a pawn in the hands of malevolent and powerful greed.

With great fury, King Vile erupts in a suicidal storm of carnage and collateral damage between two seas (probably the Mediterranean Sea and the Sea of Galilee).[114] Most likely, this elicits an international response so that he and his troops are handily reduced to oil spots on the field of battle.

At once, the superpowers of the world convene to draft a plan of restoration and international governance in this war-torn region. I believe this effort of global cooperation will form the outlines from which a revived Rome will coalesce.

United Nations

Backing up, we can see that the stage was set for the reemergence of Rome when the United Nations was formed in 1945, just before the rebirth of Israel in 1948.

Through the United Nations, rulers now jostle among themselves in their council meetings. Those nations who possess staggering weapons of mass destruction, tout their military prowess as they seek allies to join them. In this cauldron of persuasion, serious decisions are being made with serious consequences.

We are in the age of governmental maturity and ultimate accountability and the stakes are eternal. As rulers fight to gain and hold power, God has placed Israel—a sign and a wonder—in the middle of the table. Her national rebirth represents the fulfillment of multitudes of ancient prophesies and it serves as a provocation from God. Who among the nations will dare to bet against His Majesty?

Sheep and Goat Nations

During this time of war and global posturing in the Middle East, nations will be forced to take sides. Will they align with wicked schemes to annihilate national Israel as an act of hatred toward God? Or, will they enact unjust laws against the saints who shine the light of truth upon their evil? Will they align with East or West superpowers? Will they be sheep or goat nations? Each nation is now choosing its place in the final battles of this age.

It is important to note that when Jesus returns, there will be sheep nations. This indicates there will be resistance to Antichrist and his government.

> 31 "When the Son of Man comes in His glory, and all the holy angels with Him, then He will sit on the throne of His glory. 32 All the **nations** will be gathered before Him, and He will separate them one from another, as a shepherd divides his sheep from the goats. 33 And He will set the sheep on His right hand, but the goats on the left."—Matt. 25:31–33 NKJV (emphasis mine)

In this war, Israel is invaded. Any nation involved directly or covertly—by suppling money, arms, and intelligence—is guilty of war crimes against God. It matters not that national Israel is in rebellion against Messiah. She is a litmus test nonetheless because God has set her apart and warned the nations not to abusively touch her.

In fact, God has been very open about Israel's penchant for occultic deception and His many cleansing judgments upon her. They serve as educational fodder for all nations. Wherever evil is located, it will be dealt with.

> 24 Who gave Jacob for plunder, and Israel to the robbers? Was it not the Lord, He against whom we have sinned? For they would not walk in His ways, nor were they obedient to His law. 25 Therefore He has poured on him the fury of His

anger and the strength of battle; it has set him on fire all around . . . —Isa. 42:24-25 NKJV

6 For You have forsaken Your people, the house of Jacob, because they are filled with eastern ways; they are soothsayers like the Philistines . . . 8 Their land is also full of idols; they worship the work of their own hands . . .

11 The lofty looks of man shall be humbled, the haughtiness of men shall be bowed down, and the Lord alone shall be exalted in that day. 12 For the **day of the Lord** of hosts shall come upon everything proud and lofty, upon everything lifted up—and it shall be brought low . . . —Isa. 2:6, 8, 11-12 NKJV (emphasis mine)

Harbinger of Things to Come

The Middle Eastern war ends when King Vile is betrayed by the global superpowers that exploited and then sacrificed him without blinking. I believe this is a harbinger of things to come.

After this war, the same playbook will be used by the goat nations as they form tighter circles of power, and exert stronger waves of wars, in their quest to conquer the world. This will be a time of increasing conflict and distress that could last for years or decades before Antichrist emerges. As Gabriel and Jesus said, this is (and has been) an indeterminate season of wars and desolations (Dan. 9:26; Matt. 24:6).

As the goat nations rise in power, the earth will languish under the dictatorial abuse of intrusive technologies. Then, at some point, Antichrist will rise as the leader over the most powerful empire in world history after overthrowing three others in his lunge for the throne (Dan. 7:19-20).

23 Then he said to me, "This fourth beast is the fourth world power that will rule the earth. It will be different from all the others. It will devour the whole world, trampling and crushing everything in its path. 24 Its ten horns are ten kings who will rule that empire. Then another king will arise, different from the other ten, who will

subdue three of them. 25 He will defy the Most High and oppress the holy people of the Most High. He will try to change their sacred festivals and laws, and they will be placed under his control for a time, times, and half a time. —Dan. 7:23-25 NLT

Notice that the final beast empire rules and crushes the world *before* Antichrist rises. This indicates a buildup of tyranny and persecution before his arrival.

When Antichrist finally emerges, he takes down three leaders and / or nations. This underscores the fact that Satan has a fragile hold on humanity. Even the nations aligned with him are fickle.

As a shrewd tyrant with thousands of years of job experience, I have no doubt that Satan is currently grooming many possible contenders for "Antichrist." I can imagine how difficult it is for him to herd humans. Any number of things can happen, including losing them to Jesus Christ.

When God finally allows the Roman beast to fully rise, and Satan gets his opportunity to install his human mouthpiece, he knows he has seven short years before he is arrested and put in prison. With time ticking away, he will aggressively rearrange the leaders within the beast conglomerate so that the ranks are cleansed of anyone who is slightly inconvenient. This small season of seven years will be pure terror.[115]

> 12 . . . Woe to the inhabitants of the earth and the sea! For the devil has come down to you, having great wrath, because he knows that he has a short time."—Rev. 12:12 NKJV

The Saints of God

So far in this vision, we have learned about a future Middle East war that I believe results in international alliances that lead to a revived Roman government, and a throne for Antichrist.

Where are the born-again saints in all of this?

Before the Middle East war, we were told that the people who know their God will be strong and do great exploits during the times of persecution (Dan. 11:32).

The immediate application of that promise was to the righteous Jews under Antiochus. The final application is to those who come to Jesus the Messiah under Antichrist (Jews and Gentiles).

Beyond that, this has application to the born-again saints who have suffered through the ages at the hands of wicked leaders, both civil and religious. This harassment extends into modern times and it is growing exponentially as we draw closer to the end of this age.

How do we overcome? How do we respond? We live in radical consecration and obedience to God and step into the marketplace with faith and courage. In other words, we overcome by the blood of the Lamb and we respond with the testimony of our lives (Rev. 12:11).

Our posture of love and obedience is so powerful that it clarifies the air around us and evil mischief is brought under the light of judgment. Think of Jesus stepping into the room and demons shrieking, or Jesus walking along the sea shore when a pack of demons named legion beg not to be thrown into the abyss (Luke 4:33-34 and Mark 5:1-20).

When light enters, the darkness runs, and people in bondage get an invitation to repent . . . or rage.

Saints in Heaven and Earth

Now let's get more specific . . . where are the born-again saints during the time of Antichrist and the last seven years of this age?

In Daniel's first vision, a group of saints in heaven watch the raging of Antichrist. These *saints* are in the courtroom with the Ancient of Days while Antichrist is on the earth killing the *saints*, and bellowing threats against God (Dan. 7). The fact that Antichrist is raging against God, indicates he has already taken over the temple. The fact that he is just about to get thrown into the lake of fire, indicates that his army is stationed on the plains of Megiddo at the battle of Armageddon.

From this vision, we see *two groups of "saints"* during the final antics of Antichrist: those in heaven and those on the earth. I propose that the heavenly group is the born-again Church that is taken to heaven before the bowls of wrath are poured on Antichrist and his army of treason. I believe the second group of saints, are those Gentiles and Jews who repent when they realize they are left behind to endure the rage of Satan because they rejected the rule of Messiah.

This was prophetically foreshadowed by Enoch who was removed to heaven after he finished warning of God's wrath upon ungodliness. During that judgment, Noah and his family were on the earth and safely tucked in the ark. In another example, the remnant Jews were marked by God and then forcibly removed from Jerusalem and relocated to Babylon before the city was burned down—but not before they endured foreign occupation and the plundering of their wealth. In this instance, Jeremiah the prophet was in the city as a prisoner and half starved, but he survived the destruction. In both of these instances, some are removed, and some are protected.

In the case of Sodom and Gomorrah, Lot and his family were miraculously spared from the wrath of God when they were removed from the city. But not before a sexually crazed mob rushed upon their home with the intent of ravaging the men.

Let's be honest. We will face danger, persecution, and sometimes death from the wicked. Even so, we will never be the direct object of the wrath of God during judgement. However, if we are in the vicinity when His wrath comes, we will be affected.

When will the Saints be Removed to Heaven?

When do the born-again saints get taken to heaven? Is it right before or at the moment that Antichrist makes his seven-year treaty with Israel? Is it at the half way point when he sets up the idol of abomination and openly declares war on the saints? Or, is it right before God pours out His bowls of wrath at the seventh trumpet?

I personally lean toward the removal of the saints before the wrath of God is released. It could also happen at the start of the seven years as some believe (I'm all for that). Either way, according to Daniels third vision of the seventy weeks, the final week is for Israel. They will be the focus. That seven years will bring their national transgressions to an end and finish every vision and prophesy (Dan. 9:24). Beyond that, it will bring a worldwide end to transgressions.

In our current parenthetical season, the maturity of the Church is the focus. Once she has matured, and the final seven years begin, there is no reason for her to be here. Unless . . . God has decided to make the Church a prophetic voice of warning against Antichrist, before God releases His wrath. Whether at the beginning, the middle, or the end of the last seven years, I believe the Church will definitely be removed before the bowls of wrath.

Harvest Time and the Saints

Speaking to the removal of the saints, Jesus referred to the end of this age as a great harvest of the crop that He has planted (Matt. 13:24-30).

In the parable, Jesus plants His crop, and then Satan secretly comes in and plants tares. Even so, Jesus allows both to grow together to ensure the full maturation of *His crop*. Finally, the harvest comes when *His crop* is ripe. After that, the tares are gathered and burned.

From this we learn that the saints are the important ones. No farmer waits for tares to mature as his signal for harvest. Likewise, with God. When His people are fully mature—in holiness, love, and authority—He will harvest us. There will be no more delay. The mature and holy saints will not be left to deteriorate in the fields or be burned by the fire of wrath.

Instead, at our maturity, the beautiful fruit of our lives will be on full display in the earth, before our removal to heaven.

Therefore, this current season of "indeterminate time" is for the born-again saints to mature. Once we have crossed that threshold, the end-time harvest begins. In this parable, Jesus reveals the fate of the wheat and the tares:

> 30 "Let both grow together until the harvest and at the time of harvest I will say to the reapers, "First gather together the tares and bind them in bundles to burn them, but gather the wheat into my barn.""—Matt. 13:30 NKJV

In a companion passage, in the book of Revelation, Jesus reaps His harvest and then an angel gathers the remaining grapes and throws them into the winepress of God's wrath.[116]

Clearly, the saints are treated differently and have a different outcome than the tares. This is illustrated in the following passage:

> 14 Then I looked, and behold, a white cloud, and on the cloud sat One like the Son of Man, having on His head a golden crown, and in His hand a sharp sickle. 15 And another angel came out of the temple, crying with a loud voice to Him who sat on the cloud, "Thrust in Your sickle and reap, for the time has come for You to reap, for the harvest of the earth is ripe." 16 So He who sat on the cloud thrust in His sickle on the earth, and the earth was reaped.

> 17 Then another angel came out of the temple which is in heaven, he also having a sharp sickle. 18 And another angel came out from the altar, who had power over fire, and he cried with a loud cry to him who had the sharp sickle, saying, "Thrust in your sharp sickle and gather the clusters of the vine of the earth, for her grapes are fully ripe." 19 So the angel thrust his sickle into the earth and gathered the vine of the earth, and threw it into the great winepress of the wrath of God.—Rev. 14:14-19 NKJV

The Recipients of God's Climactic Wrath

In the above passage, the tares are burned with fire after the wheat has been harvested by Jesus. This indicates that the saints are not on the earth for the fire—called wrath—that destroys the tares.

Wrath is not persecution. Persecution is the result of sinful man warring against God and His people. Wrath is God's judgment that comes directly from Him and rushes upon any and all sin that is not under the blood of Jesus.

Scripture is clear that God's fiery wrath is reserved for and directed against all ungodliness. By all standards of sound biblical doctrine, the wrath of God cannot consume Jesus Christ and His saints, because He is holy, and so are we. Wrath has no jurisdiction over holiness. It can only consume sin. The Bible tells us:

> 7 But the heavens [our atmosphere] and the earth that now exist are being preserved by the same command of God, in order to be destroyed by fire. They are being kept for the day when godless people will be judged and destroyed. —2 Peter 3:7 TEV

> 9 For God did not appoint us to wrath, but to obtain salvation through our Lord Jesus Christ . . . —1 Thess. 5:9 NKJV

Sowing and Reaping—the Honor Clause

Even though the saints are not the object of God's wrath, they are subject to sowing and reaping. By virtue of living in the last days, every person will experience the end results of the maturity of God's kingdom and the kingdom of treason.

The citizens of God's holy nation will reap an anointing of glory, authority, and supernatural signs and wonders. At the same time, they will also reap the mature fruit of the earthly governments that they inhabit.

Conversely, the ungodly will reap a crop of confusion and misery with no power to help themselves; while they also reap the mature fruit of the earthly governments that they inhabit

I call this the honor clause. God has assigned dominion to mankind and our maturity requires that we fully reap what we have sown. Otherwise, the righteous could argue that God never gave them an opportunity—as a holy nation—to walk in the anointing of the Kingdom of God with authority and power during the darkest period of human history. We would be left wondering what happened to these promises:

> "Darkness as black as night covers all the nations of the earth, but the glory of the LORD rises and appears over you."—Isa. 60:2 NLT

> . . .but the people who know their God shall be strong, and carry out great exploits. 33 And those of the people who understand shall instruct many; yet for many days they shall fall by sword and flame, by captivity and plundering. —Dan. 11:32 NKJV

The saints will reap a powerful anointing and we will have our day of great exploits.

Likewise, the wicked will also reap a full harvest. They will never be able to accuse God of denying them the opportunity to "prove" the bliss of living life apart from God and being allowed to raise up a rival system of government.

Armageddon

The final seven years will end with the battle of Armageddon. This is when the last drop of God's wrath is poured out of "bowls" upon those people and nations who take their stand against God (Rev. 16:16-21).

> 16 And the demonic spirits gathered all the rulers and their armies to a place with the Hebrew name Armageddon.

17 Then the seventh angel poured out his bowl into the air. And a mighty shout came from the throne in the Temple, saying, "It is finished!" . . . 19 . . . So, God remembered all of Babylon's sins, and he made her drink the cup that was filled with the wine of his fierce wrath. —Rev. 16:16-17,19 b NLT

Zechariah the prophet speaks to this battle against Jerusalem and God's intervention to save her and end all treason. It is stunning to note that the "plague" that comes upon the enemies of God sounds like nuclear war. Something to consider . . .

Below are excerpts that I have arranged for ease of understanding. Please note that this prophetic utterance speaks to many things that we have covered. Please read it all.

12:2 "Behold, I will make Jerusalem a cup of drunkenness to all the surrounding peoples, when they lay siege against Judah and Jerusalem.

12:8 In that day the LORD will defend the inhabitants of Jerusalem . . . 9 It shall be in that day that I will seek to destroy all the nations that come against Jerusalem.

12:10 "And I will pour on the house of David and on the inhabitants of Jerusalem the Spirit of grace and supplication; then they will look on Me [Jesus] whom they pierced. Yes, they will mourn for Him as one mourns for his only son, and grieve for Him as one grieves for a firstborn.

14:5 . . . Thus the LORD my God will come, and all the saints with You.

14:9 And the LORD shall be King over all the earth. In that day it shall be—"The LORD is one," and His name one.

14:10 . . . Jerusalem shall be raised up and inhabited in her place . . . 11 The people shall dwell in it; and no longer shall there be utter destruction, but Jerusalem shall be safely inhabited.

14:12 And this shall be the plague with which the LORD will strike all the people who fought against Jerusalem: their flesh shall dissolve while they stand on their feet, their eyes shall dissolve in their sockets, and their tongues shall dissolve in their mouths . . . 15 Such also shall be the plague on the horse and the mule, on the camel and the donkey, and on all the cattle that will be in those camps. So shall this plague be.

14:16 1 And it shall come to pass that everyone who is left of all the nations which came against Jerusalem shall go up from year to year to worship the King, the LORD of hosts, and to keep the Feast of Tabernacles. —Zech. chapters 12-14 NKJV (emphasis mine)

Antichrist Dies, Satan is Bound

In Daniels first vision, the saints are in heaven with the Ancient of Days when He passes judgment on Antichrist and destroys him with fire.

In the book of Revelation, more details emerge and we learn that Antichrist has gathered his army against Jerusalem in the Battle of Armageddon, when he is captured and thrown into the lake of fire with his side-kick the false prophet. Meanwhile, his army is killed with the sword that proceeds from the mouth of Jesus Christ.

19 And I saw the beast, the kings of the earth, and their armies, gathered together to make war against Him who sat on the horse and against His army [Jesus Christ]. 20 Then the beast was captured, and with him the false prophet who worked signs in his presence, by which he deceived those who received the mark of the beast and those who worshiped his image. **These two were cast alive into the lake of fire burning with brimstone.** 21 And the rest were killed with the sword which proceeded from the mouth of Him [Jesus] who sat on the horse . . . —Rev 19:19-21 NKJV (emphasis mine)

Scripturally, Jesus Christ is the Word of God and the Word of God is a sword (John 1:1; and Eph. 6:17). In addition, the Church is commanded to take up the sword of the Spirit and speak as speaking God's very own words.

Therefore, the wicked army is destroyed by the Word of God that has gone forth from the mouth of His prophets and saints, since the Garden of Eden, declaring the end from the beginning and standing as a witness and a judge. Because the fullness of time has come, the prophetic Word of God concerning the "day of the Lord" comes to pass.

The Drama Unfolds

Our journey has taken us from the soon-coming Middle East war, to the realignment of nations, the rise of a global empire after the order of Rome, the enthronement of Antichrist, his seven year peace treaty with Israel, his takeover of the temple—the abomination of desolation—at the three-and-one-half year mark, the removal of the Church somewhere during this time, and finally the last stand of Satan and Antichrist at the war of Armageddon. Now let's imagine the scene before us . . .

Antichrist has gathered the kings of the earth to the plains of Megiddo in order to destroy Jerusalem and by extension the prophesied earthly headquarters of Jesus Christ the Messiah. Somehow, the Jews have secured the city and Antichrist is blocked from entering.

After suffering abuse from Antichrist for almost seven years, and then watching him take control of the temple at the half-way point of his peace treaty, perhaps the Jews have erupted in a civil war and are fighting to regain and purify their temple. By now, Antichrist has declared himself the earthly representative of his god—Satan—and ceremonially defiled the holy of holies with a satanic throne.

At this point, many Jews have been killed, and many are coming out of a deep fog of deception. No doubt, thousands have read Daniel and the book of Revelation, and any other book they can find to explain the unfolding apocalypse . . .

By this late hour, the new world order is in full swing. Having weapons of mass destruction, and a global web of technology, Antichrist has devoured the economies of the world like a table of tasty morsels and left the nations trembling with fright.

Satan Revealed

At the half-way point of the last seven years, Satan finally stepped out of the dark shadows of occultic secrecy, and onto the world stage when he sat in the temple claiming to be God through his proxy Antichrist (2 Thess. 2:6-8).

We can imagine the spectacular show of spiritual power at that ominous event. It will be a highly choreographed spectacle of signs and wonders meant to wow the masses to their knees in worship. I have no doubt, that on that day, Satan will step into the body of Antichrist and look into the cameras of the world and deliver the most intoxicating speech to ever come from the lips of a demon possessed man. I can hear the people say "surely god speaks through him!" The speech will be a revelation. I speculate that the world will be told that Satan—or his less frightful name of Lucifer—is the rightful God who has struggled throughout the ages to tell his story and gain the worship and respect due him.

The crowds will be eating out of his hands like a dog. Immediately afterwards, they will throng to take his mark upon their bodies as a sign of allegiance to his lordship.

After securing his followers, Satan through Antichrist, will order the genocide of those without his mark. There will be pockets of resistance among groups and nations; including a great number of Jews. Many who turn to God and accept Jesus Christ, will be martyred.

Sometime before, or in the midst of this murderous campaign, the Church will be removed as God prepares to pour out His bowls of wrath. Finally, the surviving Jews who oppose

Antichrist, will somehow succeed in cutting off his access to the city. Filled with rage, Satan through Antichrist will marshal the nations of the earth to the plains of Megiddo.

In the recesses of his dark soul, Satan will be racked with rage knowing that the time is drawing near for his grand humiliation in front of the world, and his imprisonment for a thousand years. Determined to control the narrative, he will likely cast himself as the suffering "God," fighting for his throne. This will cleverly set the stage for his next act, when he is allowed one last opportunity to recruit worshipers after the millennial reign of Christ (Rev. 20:7).

With his troops marshalled in the valley of Megiddo, Satan, through Antichrist, will stir the hatred of his followers by cursing God and His saints, and bragging of his supposed supremacy.

As if taken from the pages of time, we can hear the Assyrian king Sennacherib, as he boasts of his power over the God of Israel:

> 33 Has any of the gods of the nations at all delivered its land from the hand of the king of Assyria? . . . 35 Who among all the gods of the lands have delivered their countries from my hand, that the LORD should deliver Jerusalem from my hand?'—2 Kings 18:33, 35 NKJV

The Ancient of Days and Judgment

Meanwhile, in the Kingdom of heaven, the citizens have assembled in the throne room of the Ancient of Days. Waiting in silent and reverent awe, they watch as the judgment books are opened to determine the fate of the arrogant little horn and his Babylonian government. When the gavel of justice falls, a guilty verdict is rendered. Immediately, Antichrist, the false prophet, and Satan, are bound and escorted to the courtroom to receive their sentences.

Bristling with fear, they will crouch before the Ancient of Days as He sits with His holy saints and angels. Looking nervously upon our matchless and resplendent God, and the sea of holy faces, Antichrist will realize that he overestimated his appearance, importance, and power. But it will be too late, because his name will not be found in the book of life. Then, with grand efficiency, he and the false prophet will be disposed of in the lake of fire, and Satan will be bound for a thousand years.

Back on the earth, the army surrounding Jerusalem, has melted on the battlefield from an inferno of fire called the bowls of the wrath of God. Standing at a distance, the surviving nations are trembling uncontrollably as they watch the smoke of her burning. Every person small and great, will be in shock and struggling to survive the ecological and genocidal apocalypse that has been the past seven years.

Languishing and broken, the surviving Jews will cry out to God and beg for His help and mercy.

> 37 "O Jerusalem, Jerusalem, the one who kills the prophets and stones those who are sent to her! How often I wanted to gather your children together, as a hen gathers her chicks under her wings, but you were not willing! 38 See! Your house is left to you desolate; *39 for I say to you, you shall see Me no more till you say, 'Blessed is He who comes in the name of the Lord!'*—Matt. 23:37-39 NKJV (italics mine)

King Messiah

In heaven, at this epic moment, Jesus Christ the Messiah will be ushered before His Father, the Ancient of Days, to receive the scepter of the earth. With great joy, the Father will crown His Son, and send Him forth with His holy saints and angels to take dominion over the earth (Dan. 7:13-14).

At once, a deep and ancient cry will pour forth from the bosom of the saints who have held this moment in their hearts for thousands of years through perils, pains, and persecution. They will sing a new song that only they can know and learn. This song will be born in the secret place of love and communion, and in the marketplace of rejection, and martyrdom (Rev. 5:14).

It will take a moment . . . perhaps longer . . . for the welled-up emotions to be fully released and the tears to fall. Shut off from the world and tucked safely in the arms of Messiah, His Bride will find healing and strength in the reward of her faith: a face-to-face eternity with the One she has yearned for since time began.

From this chamber of paradise and empowerment, Messiah will rise with His Bride and return to the earth. In response to His coming, the skies will roll back with a thunderous roar of reverence, and the sun will stand still. The waves of the sea will fall silent, and the animals will bow in grateful submission. After laying in the darkness of a satanically controlled nightmare, the earth and all her inhabitants will see the blinding light of Messiah approaching with myriads of saints and angels, and trumpets blaring (just as Enoch prophesied).

Everywhere, hearts will explode, and tears will fall as every creature small and great, bows low to the ground to honor her God and her King.

In that moment, when Jesus enters Jerusalem to establish His kingdom, the surviving Israelites will look upon the One they crucified, and their hearts will melt into a river of tears and stabbing sorrow.

Looking on, the nations will stand in silent awe as they witness the tender mercy of Messiah toward his Jewish brethren who rejected Him.

Despite this crime, the prayer of Jesus at the Cross will whisper through the ages "Father forgive them for they know not what they do." Stunned and mute, the nations will marvel as they witness Love personified. Opening His arms of healing, and gathering His brethren as a hen gathers her chicks, Jesus the Messiah will embrace His remnant brothers and the old order will pass away (Zech. 12:10; Rev. 1:7).

18 Where is another God like you, who pardons the sins of the survivors among his people? You cannot stay angry with your people, for you love to be merciful. 19 Once again you will have compassion on us. You will tread our sins beneath your feet; you will throw them into the depths of the ocean! 20 You will bless us as you promised Jacob long ago. You will set your love upon us, as you promised our father Abraham! —Micah 7:15-20 TLB

Why Do the Nations Rage?

As the nation's rage against God and His people, they conveniently and perilously forget that God sits in heaven upon His throne watching them and placing every careless word and deed in His bowls of wrath for the final fire (1 Cor. 3:12–15).

At this very moment, every person and all nations are in the valley of decision. Events are transpiring—in rapid succession—that require us to choose sides in this epic drama. This is not an age for the immature (as Jesus said, "woe to those with child"). As a collective, mankind has entered the last hours of his prophetic six days of work and very soon he will stand before his Creator to give an account of his life.

The historical record of Scripture informs us concerning our first act of treason with Satan and its outgrowth in our lives and in the governments we have formed. We now stand at the threshold of the "day of the Lord," armed with prophetic revelation that is irrefutable, provocative, and confident.

In this moment of time, the truth of Scripture will produce profound peace or gripping rage depending on your relationship with God the Father, His Son Jesus Christ, and Holy Spirit. Be brave. Be sober. Be honest. Be humble. Choose life.

What fools the nations are to rage against the Lord! How strange that men should try to outwit God! For a summit conference of the nations has been called to plot against the Lord and his Messiah, Christ the King. "Come, let us break His chains," they say, "and free ourselves from all this slavery to God."

278

But God in heaven merely laughs! He is amused by all their puny plans. And then in fierce fury He rebukes them and fills them with fear. For the Lord declares, "This is the King of my choice, and I have enthroned him in Jerusalem, my holy city."

His chosen one [Jesus] replies, "I will reveal the everlasting purposes of God, for the Lord has said to Me, 'You are my Son. This is your Coronation Day. Today I am giving you your glory. Only ask and I will give you all the nations of the world. Rule them with an iron rod; smash them like clay pots!'"

O kings and rulers of the earth, listen while there is time. Serve the Lord with reverent fear; rejoice with trembling. Fall down before his Son and kiss His feet before His anger is roused and you perish. I am warning you—His wrath will soon begin. But oh, the joys of those who put their trust in Him! —Ps. 2, TLB

Reference:
Timeline of Events

Event	Date BC	Years Elapsed	References
Creation per Ussher	4004		Gen. 1:1
Enoch is born—seventh from Adam	3382	622	Gen. 5:18
Methuselah—born to Enoch when he was 65	3317	687	Gen. 5:21
Lamech—born to Methuselah when he was 187	3130	874	Gen. 5:25
Adam died, age 930	3074	930	Gen. 5:5; Ussher paragraph 21
Enoch disappears into heaven, age 365	3017	987	Gen. 5:23–24; Heb. 11:5; Ussher paragraph 22
Noah is born to Lamech when he was 182	2948	1056	Gen. 5:29; Ussher paragraph 24
Lamech, the father of Noah, dies at the age of 777	2353	1651	Gen. 5:31; Ussher paragraph 32
Noah enters the ark at age 600; the flood comes	2349	1655	Gen. 7:1–10; Matt. 24:38; Ussher paragraphs 34-39
Nimrod and the Tower of Babel incident	2242	1762	Gen. 11:1-9; Ussher paragraph 49
Noah dies at the age of 950; living 350 years after the Flood	1998	2006	Gen. 9:28–29; Ussher paragraph 63
Abraham Born	1996	2008	Gen. 11:10-35; Gen. 12:1,4; Acts 7:4; Ussher paragraph 64
Abraham 75 years, called by God	1921	2083	Gen. 15:7; Ussher paragraphs 72-73
Abraham offers up Isaac and God stops him and supplies the sacrifice	1871	2133	Gen. 22:1-19; Ussher reference: Josephus, Antiq., 1.1.c.13.s.3. (227) 4:113; Ussher paragraph 91
The Exodus from Egypt	1491	2513	Exod. 12:29-42—430 years since the call of Abraham; Ussher paragraph 192
King David sacrifices at the spot where the destroying angel stops	1017	2987	2 Sam. 24:1-25; 1 Chr. 21:1-30; Ussher paragraphs 453-454
The death of King David	1015	2989	1 Kings 2:1-12; Ussher paragraph 460
Solomon lays the foundation stone for the temple	1012	2992	1 Kings 6:37; Ussher paragraphs 466, 468-471
Solomon dedicates the temple	1004	3000	1 Kings 8:1-66; 2 Chr. 5:1-14; Ussher paragraph 469-471
King Solomon dies, his son Rehoboam becomes king; the northern tribes break	975	3029	1 Kings 11:42; 2 Chr. 9:30 and 12; 1 Kings 14; Ussher paragraph 477

away			
Unnamed prophet rebukes king Jeroboam (Northern tribe) and foretells God's judgement through Josiah	975	3029 3030	1 Kings 12:32; 13:1-24; 2 Kings 23:15-20; Ussher paragraphs 481-482
Ahab becomes king of the northern tribes and reigns 22 years	918	3086	1 Kings 16: 29-34; Ussher paragraph 507
Elijah is taken to heaven in a fiery chariot	896	3108	2 Kings 2:1-25; Ussher paragraph 524
The Northern Kingdom of Israel is taken captive by Assyria and removed from the land	721	3283	I Chr. 5:26; 2 Kings 17:6, 23; Ussher paragraph 634
King Hezekiah receives visitors from Babylon	713	3291	Isa. 39:6; Ussher paragraphs 651-652
Josiah, becomes king of Judah at 8 yrs. old	641	3363	2 Kings 22:1; 2 Chr. 34:1; Ussher paragraph 719
King Josiah began to cleanse the land of idolatry, destroy the altars, and burn the bones of false priests	630	3374	2 Chr. 34:3-7; 2 Kings 23:15-18; Ussher paragraph 737
Jeremiah called to be a prophet	629	3375	Jer. 1:2-17 Ussher paragraph 738
Josiah calls the nation to a Passover feast	624	3380	2 Kings 23:21-23; 2 Chr. 35:1-19; Ussher paragraph 744
Josiah killed in battle by Pharaoh Necho in the valley of Megiddo	610	3394	2 Kings 23:29-30; Ussher paragraph 755
The Jews appoint Jehoahaz, Josiah's youngest son as king and he is deposed after 3 months	610	3394	2 Kings 23: 29-35; 2 Chr. 36:1; Ussher paragraph 760
Jehoiakim (older brother of Jehoahaz) made king by Pharaoh Necho	610	3394	2 Kings 23: 29-35; 2 Chr. 36:1; Ussher paragraph 761
Babylon raids Jerusalem first time and leaves Jehoiakim as vassal king. Daniel is taken captive; estimated age: between 12-15 years old	607	3397	Dan. 1:2; 2 Kings 24; 2 Chr. 36:5-8; Jer. 25; Ussher paragraphs 774-777
Nebuchadnezzar dreams of giant metal image	604	3400 - 3401	Dan. 2:1-49; Ussher paragraph 787
Babylon raids Jerusalem a second time; takes Ezekiel captive; kills king Jehoiakim; installs his son Jehoiachin, who reigns three months	599	3405	Ezek. 1:2-3; Jer.22:18-23; ;2 Kings 24; 2 Chr. 36; Ussher paragraphs 797-798
Zedekiah—son of Josiah—is made vassal king and rules 11 years. He is the last king of Judea	599	3405	Jer. 37:1; 2 Kings 24:17; Jer. 52:1-11; Ussher paragraphs 806-807
Ezekiel's first vision: his calling	595	3409	Ezek. 1-7; Ussher paragraphs 822-823
Ezekiel's second vision: God departs from Jerusalem	594	3410	Ezek. 8-11; Ussher paragraph 526
Babylonian army surrounds Jerusalem and stays for 19 months	590	3414	2 Kings 25: Jer. 39; Ussher paragraphs 832-833
Nebuchadnezzar King of Babylon burns Jerusalem, third raid	588	3416	2 Kings 25:8-10; Ussher paragraph 851
Messengers arrive in Babylon with news of the burning of Jerusalem	587	3417	Ezek. 33:21-29; Ussher paragraph 560
Ezekiel's temple vision	575	3429	Ezek.; 40—48; Ussher

			paragraph 874
Nebuchadnezzar dreams of large tree that is cut down	570	3434	Dan. 4:1-37; Ussher paragraph 882
Daniel's first vision. Assuming he was taken captive at 12, he is 64 years old	555	3449	Dan. 7: 1-28; Ussher paragraph 914
Daniel's second vision. Assumed age: 66 years	553	3451	Dan. 8; Ussher paragraph 916
Daniel interrupts the writing on the wall for king Belshazzar	538	3466	Dan. 5:1-31; Ussher paragraphs 938-939
Medio-Persian Empire overtakes Babylon and kills Belshazzar	538	3466	Dan. 5:1-31; Ussher: paragraph: 938-939
Daniel's third vision. Assumed age: 81 years	538	3466 3467	Dan. 9; Ussher paragraph 947
The Judean remnant returns from Babylonian captivity	537 - 536	3467- 3468	2 Chr. 36:22; Ezra 1; Ussher paragraphs 950-952
The foundation of the second temple was laid, old men cried	535	3469	Ezra 3:10-13; Ussher paragraph 954
Daniel's fourth and final vision. Assumed age: 85 years	534	3470	Dan. +10—12; Ussher paragraph 957
The second temple completed and dedicated	515	3489	Ezra 6:15-18; Ussher paragraph 1033-1034
Malachi the prophet mentions Elijah who will come before Messiah	416	3588	Mal. 4:5-6; Luke 1:17; Matt. 11:14; Ussher paragraph 1306
Alexander the Great marches into Jerusalem to take control and defeats Darius a short time later	332- 330	3672 3774	Ussher paragraphs: 1815, 1888; 1946
Alexander dies in Babylon after a massive idol ritual and drunken feast	323	3681	Ussher paragraphs: 2353-2355
Antiochus Epiphanes the Greek, begins his reign over Jerusalem	175	3829	Ussher: paragraphs: 3203-3222
Antiochus defiles the temple with pigs blood and forbids Jewish customs by pain of death	167	3837	Ussher paragraphs: 3348, 3351
Antiochus dies a miserable death	164	3840	Ussher paragraphs: 3427-3430
Battle of Corinth; Rome is established as the fourth empire	146	3858	Ussher: paragraph: 3628
Herod begins to refurbish temple	17	3987	John 2:20; Ussher paragraph 5944
Jesus Christ is born in Bethlehem (varies by a few years among differing scholars)	4	4000	Matt. 1:25; Luke 2:7; Ussher paragraphs 6059-6061
Herod dies (date varies by a few years among differing scholars)	5-4	4001	Matt. 2:19-20; Ussher paragraph 6082
Jesus is baptized by John and filled with the Holy Spirit	AD 27	4030	Matt. 3:14-17; Luke 3:23; Ussher paragraphs 6289-6292
Jesus attends the Passover and goes into the temple and drives the money changers out	AD 30	4033 4034	John 2:13-22; Ussher paragraph 6305
Titus the Roman burns Jerusalem and destroys the second temple	AD 70	4074	Ussher paragraphs: 6968-6981

ABOUT THE AUTHOR

Debra Ortiz is an accomplished writer and speaker with a unique ability to sift through the noise of opinions and philosophies while anchoring us to our biblical roots. With a no-nonsense style, she tackles life's most pressing questions: Who are we? Why are we here? And why does it all matter?

Surrounded by an awesome family, Debra is an ordained minister with a ministry degree of Master of Theology. Her books include Epic Earth; and Epic Woman: The Creation of Gender.

For more information, or to order more books, visit her website at www.epicearthbook.com. In addition, Epic Earth and Epic Woman are available on Kindle at www.amazon.com.

END NOTES

Notes

1 All dates are derived from Reverend James Ussher's, The Annals of the World (Green Forest, AR: Master Books, 2007), first published in England in 1658. Ussher, later the Archbishop of Armagh and Primate of Ireland, entered Trinity College at age thirteen and received his master's degree at age eighteen. He was ordained as a deacon and priest in the Anglican Church at the age of twenty. In 1625, he held the highest position of Archbishop of Armagh. Ussher received his Doctor of Divinity at age twenty-six, was twice appointed vice-chancellor of Trinity College, and was an expert in Semitic languages. He is buried in Westminster Abby.

AD 1658 / 5662 years since Creation; James Ussher's Annals of the World is published

2 AD 400/ 4404 years since Creation

The Library of Alexandria vanishes; scholars are undecided on the exact date.

Encyclopædia Britannica Online, s. v. "Library of Alexandria," accessed March 21, 2016; https://www.britannica.com/topic/Library-of-Alexandria. See also J. Harold Ellens' article "The Ancient Library of Alexandria," originally appearing in the February 1997 issue of Bible Review: https://www.biblicalarchaeology.org/daily/biblical-sites-places/biblical-archaeology-places/the-ancient-library-of-alexandria/

3 Jerusalem came under foreign domination in the days of Jeremiah the prophet. In the year 610 BC, Pharaoh Necho, King of Egypt, killed the Jewish king, Josiah, in battle and then took dominion over Israel. From that point forward, the Israeli people and their city Jerusalem ceased to be a sovereign nation until

modern history.

In Luke 21, Jesus spoke of Jerusalem as being under Gentile rule until those times are complete:

> "And they [the Jewish people] will fall by the edge of the sword, and be led away captive into all nations. And Jerusalem will be trampled by Gentiles until the times of the Gentiles are fulfilled."—Luke 21:24

4 AD 1948 / 5952 years since Creation; Israel declares independence and reclaims ancient homeland on May 14, 1948.

5 AD 1967 / 5971 years since Creation; Israeli army converges on the Western Wailing Wall on June 7, 1967.

6 AD 1980 / 5984 years since Creation; The Israeli government proclaims that "Jerusalem, complete and united, is the capital of Israel.

7 Moses warned the Israelites before they entered the Promised Land not to turn away from God or they would lose their land (Deut. 30:1–10).

8 Jer. 52:1–30 tells the story of the Babylonian attack on Jerusalem.

Ezek. 23:36-39. In Ezekiel, God talks about how His people lusted after the Babylonians, sacrificed their children in fire, and then entered His sanctuary with blood on their hands.

9 Those who are willing:

> "For 'whoever calls on the name of the LORD shall be saved.'" Rom. 10:13

> "You search the Scriptures, for in them you think you have eternal life; and these are they which testify of Me. But you are not willing to come to Me that you may have life."—John 5:39–40

The work of salvation and redemption was done pre-Creation: Eph. 1:3-6

Jesus the lamb who was slain before the foundation of the

world: Rev. 13:8

10 See Authors other books for more on this subject: Epic Earth and Epic Woman.

11 Hades: There are varying opinions among scholars but generally it is agreed that Hades is a holding area for the dead and not the final location of hell for the unrighteous and heaven for the righteous (Rev. 20:14—death and hades are eventually are thrown into the lake of fire and therefore are separate from the lake of fire). Jesus told a parable about Abraham and Lazarus (Old Testament period before the finished work of Jesus at the Cross) and they were in Hades but in separate areas. Abraham was in an area of comfort and Lazarus an area of torment (Luke 16:19-31). After His crucifixion, Jesus (while in His spirit and anointed by Holy Spirit) went to Hades and preached (1 Peter 3:19). The word used denotes that He proclaimed truth. Surely, He gave witness to His identity as the Lamb of God who takes away the sins of the world and that He was on His way to heaven thus opening the door of salvation for those who repent and call upon His name. Then, after preaching in hades, He resurrected in bodily form. After this, many saints who died before, came out of their graves and were taken to heaven (Matt. 27:51). All of this may indicate that the saints who die after the resurrection of Jesus go directly to heaven since Jesus has now made a way for us.

Jesus overcame the power of death and it no longer has a sting. He also has the keys to death and hades (1 Cor. 15:5; Hos. 13:14; Rev. 1:18). In summary, the sin of man in the Garden resulted in the death of man and the only way back to life and into God's home in heaven is through the Lamb of God. Jesus therefore, annulled the death penalty and by that He took away the "sting"—the terror—of death. He has the keys and therefore He alone can unlock us from the effects of death and deliver us into eternal life.

12 See the following entries on Polytheism:

From John McClintock and James Strong, Cyclopedia of Biblical, Theological, and Ecclesiastical Literature (Grand Rapids, MI, Baker, 1981):

(1.) To a great extent, polytheism at its foundation is the worship of nature, i.e. of objects in nature which strike the attention of man, and are important aids to his well-being in the world.

(2.) These objects are conceived of as living existences, and as having, together with superhuman power, the feelings and the will of men.

(3.) In the course of time, the living thing or god in the natural object becomes detached from it, is conceived of as an agent in human affairs, and may greatly enlarge its sphere of operations.

(4.) This process changes the attributes and functions of the divinities. In this way, or by the mythological processes, the religions of heathenism may for some time be in a constant flux, and this will last as long as faith in the gods and the mythological spirit lasts.

(5.) Among the changes may be mentioned the following: the god of a clan or district becomes the god of a race; foreign gods are introduced; the same divinity, through the help of a new name, becomes a new personality by the side perhaps of the old one; old divinities drop out of worship; the relative importance of different gods may change . . .

13 See the author's first book Epic Earth, pp. 117–119; see also Gen. 3:14–15 for the judgment upon Satan and Isa. 14: 3-21 for a prophetic depiction of Satan and his impotence.

14 In Job 38:4–7, God speaks of Creation and how the angels were present at the laying of the foundation of the earth. This implies and confirms that they are older than humanity.

Also, we know the angels were given choice because we are

told that Satan was cast out of heaven along with the angels who followed him in rebellion against God: "And war broke out in heaven: Michael and his angels fought with the dragon; and the dragon and his angels fought, but they did not prevail, nor was a place found for them in heaven any longer. So the great dragon was cast out, that serpent of old, called the Devil and Satan, who deceives the whole world; he was cast to the earth, and his angels were cast out with him" (Rev. 12:7–9).

15 Man's carnal nature must be brought under control. See Rom. 1:18–32; Ps. 53:1–3; 1 John 2:15–17; 2 Peter 2:19; John 8:34–35.

16 See authors book: "Epic Woman" for a more in-depth look at the love of family and its role in teaching us about who we are created to be.

17 Those who give themselves to perversion are under Satan: See 1 John 3:8–10; 1 John 5:19; Prov. 5:22–23; John 8:34, 44; Acts 13:10; 2 Tim. 2:26; James 3:14–16.

18 See Gen. 5:21–24; Luke 3:36-37; Heb. 11:5; Jude 14–15.

19 METHUSELAH: From A.R. Fausset, Fausset's Bible Dictionary; In PC Study Bible: Advanced Reference Library (Seattle, WA: Biblesoft, 2002):

"METHUSELAH: 'He dies and it (the flood) is sent.' A name given prophetically by Enoch, or given after the event. Phoenician inscriptions use methu = betha = a man. The man who lived the longest—969 years. He died in the year of the flood, possibly by it . . . "

20 An excellent resource for study of the Old Testament appearances of Jesus Christ is the book "The Unseen Realm" by Michael S. Heiser.

21 Jesus Christ is God and Creator of creation: see John 1:1–14 and Rev. 1:5; God gives the first prophetic word about the Deliverer in Gen. 3:15.

22 The Word of God is eternal: See Isa. 40:8; 55:11; Matt.

5:17–18; 24:35; Luke 24:44; Rev. 22:19.

23 The earth ends with fire: 2 Thess. 1:7–10; 2 Pet. 3:4–7; 2 Peter 3:10–12; Rev. 16:8–9.

24 The saints are taken to Heaven before the final judgement: See Matt. 16:27; Jude 14; Col. 3:4; 1 Thess. 4:15-18; 2 Thess. 2:1–4; Rev. 1:7; 19:11–16.

25 From Carl Friedrich Keil and Franz Delitzsch, Commentary on the Old Testament (Peabody, MA: Hendrickson, 1996).Gen. 5:29–30; 5:3–32.

> Noah: nowach, from nuwach, "to rest" and heeniyach, "to bring rest," is explained by nicham, "to comfort," in the sense of helpful and remedial consolation. Lamech not only felt the burden of his work upon the ground which God had cursed, but looked forward with a prophetic presentiment to the time when the existing misery and corruption would terminate, and a change for the better, a redemption from the curse, would come. This presentiment assumed the form of hope when his son was born; he therefore gave expression to it in his name (Gen. 9:8–17).

26 Noah: From Adam Clarke's Commentary; In PC Study Bible: Advanced Reference Library (Seattle, WA: Biblesoft, 2002).Gen. 6:3:

> "God delights in mercy, and therefore a gracious warning is given. Even at this time the earth was ripe for destruction, but God promised them one hundred and twenty years' respite: if they repented in that interim, well; if not, they should be destroyed by a flood."

Scriptures about Noah: Gen. 6:9–10; Gen. 7:6; Gen. 9:28–29

27 James Ussher places the date of Methuselah's death at 2349 BC. Per Ussher, Noah entered the Ark in the same year (Sunday, November 30, 2349 BC). Gen. 5:21–32 gives the genealogy of Enoch, Methuselah, Lamech, and Noah. Genesis 7 tells of Noah entering the Ark.

28 The exact dates of Nimrod and his building projects is a point of scholarly debate. In this book, I am using the dates put forth by Ussher, which may vary from other excellent sources.

29 For a discussion on archeology and Flood legends see: https://answersingenesis.org/the-flood/flood-legends/

30 Nimrod, a descendant of Ham, founded Babylon; Mizraim, another of his descendants, established the kingdom of Egypt. Both Egypt and Babylon eventually became subject to the Persians, who descended from Shem, and afterward to the Greeks and Romans, who were the children of Japheth (Gen. 10:1–20; Gen. 9:18).

Mic. 5:6 records that Assyria is the land of Nimrod. All of these peoples were deeply occultic.

31 Isa. 11:11: (2) (from Barnes' Notes, Electronic Database Copyright © 1997, 2003 by Biblesoft, Inc. All rights reserved.)

> Most generally the name Assyria means the "kingdom of Assyria" including Babylonia and Mesopotamia, and extending to the Euphrates. Isa. 7:20; 8:7.

> (3) After the overthrow of the Assyrian empire, the name continued to be applied to those countries which were formerly held under its dominion-including Babylonia (2 Kings 23:29; Jer. 2:18), Persia (Ezra 6:22), and Syria. - "Robinson; Calmet."

32 Nimrod: From Keil and Delitzsch Commentary on the Old Testament: New Updated Edition, Electronic Database. Copyright © 1996 by Hendrickson Publishers, Inc. All rights reserved.) See commentary on Gen. 10:6-20.

33 Nimrod: From Adam Clarke, Commentary on the Bible; In PC Study Bible: Advanced Reference Library (Seattle, WA: Biblesoft, 2002):

> Gen.10:8 [Nimrod]: Of this person little is known, as he is not mentioned except here and in 1 Chronicles 1:10, which is evidently a copy of the text in Genesis. He is called a

mighty hunter before the Lord, and from Genesis 10:10, we learn that he founded a kingdom which included the cities Babel, Erech, Accad, and Calneh in the land of Shinar. Though the words are not definite, it is very likely he was a very bad man. His name Nimrod may come from maarad, "he rebelled"; and the Targum, in 1 Chronicles 1:10, says, "Nimrod began to be a mighty man." The Jerusalem Targum says, "He was mighty in hunting (or in prey) and in sin before God, for he was a hunter of the children of men in their languages, and he said unto them, depart from the religion of Shem, and cleave to the institutes of Nimrod." The Targum of Jonathan ben Uzziel says, "From the foundation of the world none was ever found like Nimrod, powerful in hunting, and in rebellions against the Lord." The Syriac calls him a warlike giant. The word tsayid, which we render "hunter," signifies prey; and is applied in the Scriptures to the hunting of men by persecution, oppression, and tyranny.

Hence, it is likely that Nimrod, having acquired power, used it in tyranny and oppression, and by rapine and violence founded that domination which was the first distinguished by the name of a kingdom on the face of the earth.

34 Strong's Numbers and Concordance: OT:1368 gibbowr (ghib-bore'); or (shortened) gibbor (ghib-bore'); intensive from the same as OT:1397; powerful; by implication, warrior, tyrant:
KJV - champion, chief, excel, giant, man, mighty (man, one), strong (man), valiant man.

35 See Ralph Woodrow's excellent and concise book Babylon Mystery Religion: Ancient and Modern (Riverside, CA: Ralph Woodrow Evangelistic Assoc., 1981).

36 The Tower of Babel: From Albert Barnes, Barnes' Notes on the Old and New Testaments; In PC Study Bible: Advanced Reference Library (Seattle, WA: Biblesoft, 2002). Gen. 11:1–9, Verse 4

The purpose of their hearts is now more fully expressed.

"Let us build us a city, and a tower whose top may be in the skies." A city is a fortified enclosure or keep for defense against the violence of the brute creation. A tower whose top may be in the skies for escape from the possibility of a periodical deluge. This is the language of pride in man, who wishes to know nothing above himself, and to rise beyond the reach of an overruling Providence. "And let us make us a name." A name indicates distinction and preeminence. To make us a name, then, is not so much the cry of the multitude as of the few, with Nimrod at their head, who alone could expect what is not common, but distinctive. It is here artfully inserted, however, in the popular exclamation, as the people are prone to imagine the glory even of the despot to be reflected on themselves. This gives the character of a lurking desire for empire and self-aggrandizement to the design of the leaders—a new form of the same selfish spirit which animated the antediluvian men of name (Gen. 6:4). But despotism for the few or the one implies slavery and all its unnumbered ills for the many. "Lest we be scattered abroad upon the face of the whole land." The varied instincts of their common nature here speak forth. The social bond, the tie of kinsmanship, the wish for personal safety, the desire to be independent, perhaps even of God, the thirst for absolute power, all plead for union; but it is union for selfish ends.

37 When man does not embrace the truth, he is given over to demonic delusions like Nimrod and those who followed him:

"The coming of the lawless one is according to the working of Satan, with all power, signs, and lying wonders, and with all unrighteous deception among those who perish, because they did not receive the love of the truth, that they might be saved. And for this reason God will send them strong delusion that they should believe the lie that they all may be condemned who did not believe the truth but had pleasure in unrighteousness." 2 Thess. 2:9–12

38 From The Online Bible Thayer's Greek Lexicon and Brown-

Driver-Briggs Hebrew Lexicon. Copyright © 1993, by Woodside Bible Fellowship, Ontario, Canada. Licensed from the Institute for Creation Research.

> Ur means "flame," and is a city in southern Babylonia, a city of the Chaldeans; the center of moon worship; the home of Abraham's father, Terah, and the departure point for Abraham's migration to Mesopotamia and Canaan.

UR (from Nelson's Illustrated Bible Dictionary, Copyright © 1986, Thomas Nelson Publishers):

> Abraham's native city in southern Mesopotamia; an important metropolis of the ancient world situated on the Euphrates River. Strategically situated about halfway between the head of the Persian Gulf and Baghdad, in present-day Iraq, Ur was the capital of Sumer for two centuries until the Elamites captured the city. The city came to be known as "Ur of the Chaldees" after the Chaldeans entered southern Babylonia after 1000 BC.

> Abraham lived in the city of Ur (Gen. 11:28, 31) at the height of its splendor. The city was a prosperous center of religion and industry. Thousands of recovered clay documents attest to thriving business activity. Excavations of the royal cemetery, from about 2900 to 2500 B.C., have revealed a surprisingly advanced culture, particularly in the arts and crafts. Uncovered were beautiful jewelry and art treasures, including headwear, personal jewelry, and exquisite china and crystal.

> The Babylonians worshiped many gods, but the moon god Sin was supreme. Accordingly, the city of Ur was a kind of theocracy centered in the moon deity.

39 From Fausset's Bible Dictionary, Electronic Database Copyright (c)1998, 2003 by Biblesoft).
HEBREW; HEBREWS:

Shem is called "the father of all the children of Eber," as
Ham is called "father of Canaan." The Hebrews and
Canaanites were often brought, into contact, and exhibited
the respective characteristics of the Shemites and the
Hamites. The term "Hebrews" thus is derived from Eber
(Gen 10:21, compare Num. 24:24). The Septuagint
translated "passer from beyond" (peratees), taking the
name from `eeber "beyond." Abram in Palestine was to
the inhabitants the stranger from beyond the river (Gen.
14:13). In entering Palestine he spoke Chaldee or Syriac
(Gen. 31:47). In Canaan he and his descendants acquired
Hebrew from the Hamitic Canaanites, who in their turn had
acquired it from an earlier Semitic race. The Moabite stone
shows that Moab spoke the same Hebrew tongue as Israel,
which their connection with Lot, Abraham's nephew, would
lead us to expect. In the patriarchs' wanderings they never
used interpreters until they went to Egypt.

In New Testament the contrast is between "Hebrews" and
those having foreign characteristics, as especially the Greek
or any Gentile language (Acts 6:1; Phil. 3:5 (see GREEK,
GRECIAN), 2 Cor. 11:22; Luke 23:38). The name Hebrews is
found in Genesis and Exodus more than in all the other
Books of the Bible, for it was the international name linking
Jacob's descendants with the nations; Israel is the name
that separates them from the nations. After the
constitution of Israel as a separate people (in Exodus)
Hebrews rarely occurs; in the national poetry and in the
prophets the name does not occur as a designation of the
elect people among themselves. If, as seems implied in
Gen. 10, Eber be a patronymic, his name must be prophetic
(as Peleg is) of the migrations of his descendants.

Jew: "At first one belonging to the kingdom of Judah, as
distinguished from northern Israel (2 Kings 16:6). After the
captivity, all members of the one new state were "Jews,"
i.e. in God's outward covenant, as contrasted with
"Greeks" or Gentiles (Rom. 1:16; 2:9, margin). "Hebrews"

on the other hand expressed their language and nationality, in contrast to "Hellenists," i.e. Greek speaking Jews. Again the term" Israelites" expresses the high theocratic privileges of descent from the patriarch who "as a prince had power with God" (2 Cor. 11:22; Rom. 9:4).

40 When God manifests Himself in the Old Testament, it is through His manifest self which is Jesus Christ; as is evident now that we have the fullness of the Bible. For more on this subject, see the excellent work "The Unseen Realm" by Michael S. Heiser.

41 God made a covenant with Abraham and his physical descendants (Gen. 12:1–5; 15:9–21; Acts 7:1–8).

One of the covenant promises was the gift of the land of Canaan to the people of Israel, and this promise was repeated to Isaac and Jacob (Gen. 28:13–17). This covenant will last forever (Deut. 7:9).

This covenant also applies to Abraham's spiritual children (Luke 1:68–79; Gal. 3:1–9, 29).

42 The prophet Ezekiel said that Jerusalem, representing the entire nation, is "in the center of the nations" (Ezek. 5:5, NIV) and that the nation of Israel dwelled at the "center of the earth" (Ezek. 38:12, AMP).

Commentary From Warren W. Wiersbe, The Bible Exposition Commentary: Old Testament (Colorado Springs, CO: Victor, 2003).

> The Hebrew word translated "center" also means "navel," suggesting that Israel was the "lifeline" between God and this world; for "salvation is of the Jews" (John 4:22). God chose the land of Israel to be the "stage" on which the great drama of redemption would be presented.

43 Some of the detestable practices of the nations of Egypt and the Canaanites are listed in Leviticus 18:1–30. From Merrill F. Unger, et. al., The New Unger's Bible Dictionary (Chicago, IL:

Moody Press, 1988):

> Canaan, religion. New vistas of knowledge of Canaanite cults and their degrading character and debilitating effect have been opened up by the discovery of the Ras Shamra religious epic literature from Ugarit in N. Syria. Thousands of clay tablets stored in what seems to be a library between two great Canaanite temples dating from c. fifteenth—fourteenth century BC give a full description of the Canaanite pantheon. Canaanite fertility cults are seen to be more base than elsewhere in the ancient world. The virile monotheistic faith of the Hebrews was continually in peril of contamination from the lewd nature worship with immoral gods, prostitute goddesses, serpents, cultic doves, and bulls. El, the head of the pantheon, was the hero of sordid escapades and crimes. He was a bloody tyrant who dethroned his father, murdered his favorite son and decapitated his daughter. Despite these enormities, El was styled "father of years" (abu shanima), "the father of man" (abu adami, "father bull"), (i.e., the progenitor of the gods.) Baal, the widely revered Canaanite deity, was the son of El and dominated the Canaanite pantheon. He was the god of thunder, whose voice reverberated through the heavens in the storm. He is pictured on a Ras Shamra stela brandishing a mace in his right hand and holding in his left hand a stylized thunderbolt. The three goddesses were Anath, Astarte, and Ashera, who were all three patronesses of sex and war. All were sacred courtesans. Other Canaanite deities were Mot (death); Reshep, the god of pestilence; Shulman, the god of health; and Koshar, the god of arts and crafts. These Canaanite cults were utterly immoral, decadent, and corrupt, dangerously contaminating and thoroughly justifying the divine command to destroy their devotees (Deut. 20:17).

44 The population of the Israelites at the Exodus: From Merrill F. Unger, et. al., The New Unger's Bible Dictionary (Chicago, IL: Moody Press, 1988):

"According to the Law of Moses (Exod. 30:12–14) every male Israelite of twenty years old and upward was enrolled in the army and was to pay half a shekel as atonement money. The following instances of a census being taken are given in the OT: (1) Under the express direction of God (Exod. 38:26), in the third or fourth month after the Exodus during the encampment at Sinai, chiefly for the purpose of raising money for the Tabernacle. The numbers then taken amounted to 603,550 men."

45 Date according to James Ussher's The Annals of the World: May 5, 1491 BC.

46 Some Jewish teachers believe the first animal sacrifice made by God was a lamb. Jesus the Lamb: John 1:29; John 1:36; 1 Peter 1:19; Rev. 5:6; Acts 5:30–31.

47 From A.R. Fausset, Fausset's Bible Dictionary; In PC Study Bible: Advanced Reference Library (Seattle, WA: Biblesoft, 2002):

SHECHINAH; SHEKINAH Not found in the Bible, but in the targums. From shakan, "to dwell," from whence comes mishkan, "the tabernacle." God's visible manifestation in a cloudy pillar and fire; the glorious light, enveloped in a cloud and thence bursting forth at times (Exod. 16:7–10), especially over the mercy-seat or capporeth. (See CLOUD, PILLAR OF, and Exod. 13:21–22; 14:19–20). Its absence from Zerubbabel's temple is one of the five particulars reckoned by the Jews as wanting in the second temple. In the targums, Shekinah is used as a periphrasis for God whenever He is said to "dwell" in Zion, between the cherubims, etc., to avoid the semblance of materialism. They anticipated the Shekinah's return under Messiah; Hag. 1:8 they paraphrase, "I will cause My Shekinah to dwell in it in glory"; Zech. 2:10, "I will cause My Shekinah to dwell in the midst of thee," etc. The continued presence of the Shekinah down to Nebuchadnezzar's destruction of the temple seems implied in Josh. 3; 4; 6; Ps. 68:1; compare

Num. 10:35; Ps. 132:8; 80:1; 99:1, 7; Lev. 16:2.

In the New Testament we find, corresponding to the Shekinah, "the glory of the Lord"; Luke 2:9; compare Deut. 33:2; Acts 7:2, 53, 55; Heb. 2:2; 9:5; Rom. 9:4, "the glory"; John 1:14, "the Word tabernacled (eskeenosen) among us, and we beheld His glory"; 2 Cor. 4:6; 12:9, "that the power of Christ may tabernacle (episkeenosee) upon me"; Rev. 21:3. His coming again with clouds and fire is the antitype of this Shekinah (Matt. 26:64; Luke 21:27; Acts 1:9, 11; 2 Thess. 1:7–8; Rev. 1:7). Angels or cherubim generally accompany the Shekinah (Rev. 4:7–8; Ps. 68:17; Zech. 14:5). Genesis 3:24 is the earliest notice of the Shekinah as a sword-like flame between the cherubim, being the "Presence of Jehovah" from which Cain went out, and before which Adam and succeeding patriarchs worshipped.

48 Read the author's first book, Epic Earth, for a full discussion on earth as a classroom for men and angels.

49 God chose Israel and her land:

When the Most High divided their inheritance to the nations, when He separated the sons of Adam, He set the boundaries of the peoples according to the number of the children of Israel. 9 For the LORD's portion is His people; Jacob is the place of His inheritance.—Deut. 32:8-9: 8 NKJV

50 (Exod. 12:40) God lives among Israel in the tabernacle tent until Solomon's temple is built: 2 Sam. 7:5–7

In Ezekiel, God speaks of an earthly throne in the future temple in Jerusalem: Ezek. 43:6–7

51 Hebrew 9 talks of the tabernacle and its furnishings that were a type and shadow of Jesus Christ.

52 As a prophetic parallel, Jerusalem is the center from which all nations orbit.

53 God is faithful to Israel forever: see Gen. 13:15; Jer. 31; Mic. 4; Mic. 7:18-20.

54 Moses delivers his final address to Israel and gives them

the choice of blessings and curses. See Deut. Chapters 28-30.

God promises to restore Israel to her land and gather her from the nations where she was scattered: Duet. 30:1-6.

55 Jesus is often called the son and root of David. In addition, all the learned men and the people knew that Messiah would come from the line of David: Scriptures that speak to this truth: Matt. 22:41-44; Matt. 1-20-21; Matt. 12:23; Matt. 21:9; Luke 2:4; Luke 2:11; Rev. 5:5; Rev. 22:16.

56 Joshua chapters 15 and 18 both describe the borders and towns given to the Tribe of Judah when they entered the Promised Land.

57 Hebrews 8 speaks of the priests of ancient Israel:

"[But these offer] service [merely] as a pattern and as a foreshadowing of [what has its true existence and reality in] the heavenly sanctuary. For when Moses was about to erect the tabernacle, he was warned by God, saying, See to it that you make it all [exactly] according to the copy (the model) which was shown to you on the mountain." [Exod. 25:40.]—Heb. 8:5, AMP

58 The typology of the earthly Temple shows us that God cannot be approached by the sinful for God is a consuming fire.

59 God does not always strive with man: Gen. 6:3

From Barnes' Notes, Electronic Database Copyright © 1997, 2003 by Biblesoft, Inc. All rights reserved). Gen. 6:1-8 Verse 3:

. . . From this passage we learn that the Lord by his Spirit strives with man up to a certain point. . . . He sends his Spirit to irradiate the darkened mind, . . . to bring back the heart, the confidence, the affection to God. He effects the blessed result of repentance toward God in some, who are thus proved to be born of God. . . . He will not strive perpetually. There is a certain point beyond which he will not go, . . . First, he will not touch the free agency of his rational creatures. . . Secondly, after giving ample warning, instruction, and invitation, he will, as a just judgment on the unbelieving and the impenitent, withdraw his Spirit and let them alone.

60 Jesus who is the Creator is also the Lamb slain before Creation (Rev. 13:8b). Therefore, He saw our sin before we were created and dealt with it. Jesus personally engages in the wrath of God and pours it on the unrepentant. This was done pre-Creation; it also appears on the pages of time when evil is rebuked and judged:

> "Now out of His mouth goes a sharp sword, that with it He should strike the nations. And He Himself will rule them with a rod of iron. He Himself treads the winepress of the fierceness and wrath of Almighty God. And He has on His robe and on His thigh a name written: KING OF KINGS AND LORD OF LORDS."—Rev. 19:15–16 (also Rev. 6:16)

61 Satan is the ruler of this Gentile Age:

> "For we do not wrestle against flesh and blood, but against principalities, against powers, against the rulers of the darkness of this age, against spiritual hosts of wickedness in the heavenly places."—Eph. 6:12

> "Again, the devil took Him up on an exceedingly high mountain, and showed Him all the kingdoms of the world and their glory. And he said to Him, 'All these things I will give You if You will fall down and worship me.' Then Jesus said to him, 'Away with you, Satan! For it is written, "You shall worship the LORD your God, and Him only you shall serve."' Then the devil left Him, and behold, angels came and ministered to Him."—Matt. 4:8–11

62 Jesus goes forth victorious after the tribulation of the last days when all the enemies of the cross are neutralized: Rev 19:11.

From Adam Clarke's Commentary, Electronic Database. Copyright © 1996, 2003 by Biblesoft, Inc. All rights reserved:

[A white horse] This is an exhibition of the triumph of Christ after the destruction of his enemies. The white horse is the emblem of this, and FAITHFUL and TRUE are characters of Christ. See Rev 3:14.

63 Assyria is an ancient land where Nimrod built cities. In history, the Babylonians and Assyrians are sometimes mingled together and sometimes separate. Today the area of Assyria corresponds to Iraq, parts of Syria, and possibly Turkey.

64 Man is appointed once to die (Heb. 9:27; Job 30:23). Elijah is removed in a chariot of fire (2 Kings 2:11). Enoch is removed without first dying (Gen. 5:24; Heb. 11:5).

65 Nazarite vow—Albert Barnes, Barnes' Notes on the Old and New Testaments, Grand Rapids, MI, 1949:

The Nazarite vow was usually taken for a season, but with a few individuals it was a lifetime commitment. The vow taker did not drink fermented products or cut his hair—the symbol of strength—among other things (Luke 1:13–17).

66 The genealogy of Jesus Christ in Matthew 1 shows the lineage of Joseph; Luke 3 shows the lineage of Mary. Both descended from the tribe of Judah and King David. Also, Jesus was born in Bethlehem, the legal home of the tribe of Judah, because Joseph and Mary had travelled there to register at the census as foretold by by Micah the prophet 700 years earlier (Micah 5:2).

67   Pulpit   Commentary   copied   on   8-12-19: https://biblehub.com/commentaries/matthew/17-11.htm

Matthew 17:11: . . . Christ is here alluding to his own second coming, which shall be preceded by the appearance of Elijah in person. This seems to be the plain meaning of the prophecy in Malachi, and of Christ's announcement, and is confirmed by St. John's statement concerning the two witnesses (Revelation 11:3, 6). . . .Of course, John in a partial degree reproduced the character and acts of Elijah, directing the people to the eternal principles of justice and righteousness, to a reformation of religion and morals; but he could not be said to have reconstituted, re-established all things . . .in what degree Elijah, again appearing and living on earth, will effect this great achievement, we know not. We can only fall back on the ancient prophecy, which affirms that "he shall turn the heart of the fathers to [or, 'with'] the children, and the heart of the children to [or, 'and'] their fathers" (Malachi 4:6), and expect that in some way, known unto God, he shall convert one and all, young and old, unto the Lord; or unite the Jews who are the fathers in the faith to Christians who are their children, and thus embrace Jew and Gentile in one fold under one Shepherd.

68 Isaiah's and Jesus's name:

From A.R. Fausset, Fausset's Bible Dictionary; In PC Study Bible: Advanced Reference Library, Seattle, WA: Biblesoft, 2002:

> In Isaiah, the Messiah appears as Prophet (Isa. 42:4), as Priest (Isa. 53), and as King (Isa. 49:7; 52:15). His sufferings are the appointed path to His glory (Isa. 53:11–12). The Messianic hopes in Isaiah are so vivid that Jerome (Ad Paulinum) calls his book not a prophecy but the "Gospel"; "he is not so much a prophet as an evangelist."

69 (2) Life of Jeremiah: Accessed and copied 5-3-19 from the following website link: https://www.internationalstandardbible.com/J/jeremiah-(2).html

> "Jeremiah was called by the Lord to the office of a prophet while still a youth (Jer. 1:6) about 20 years of age, in the 13th year of King Josiah (Jer. 1:2; 25:3)."

70 The prophet Habakkuk is believed to have prophesied just prior to and perhaps after Babylonian captivity. Obadiah prophesied after the destruction of Jerusalem and foretold God's judgment upon Edom for her treatment of Israel.

71 "Babylon is fallen" was spoken by Isaiah the prophet

around 722 BC.

The wrath of God that is poured on Babylon is depicted as "the cup of the wine of the fierceness of His wrath" in Rev. 16:19.

72 Ezekiel goes into captivity:

> "Nebuchadnezzar took captive to Babylon King Jehoiachin; his mother, his wives, his officials, and the chief and mighty men of the land [the prophet Ezekiel included] he took from Jerusalem to Babylon into exile."—2 Kings 24:15, AMP

73 From Barnes' Notes, Electronic Database Copyright © 1997, 2003 by Biblesoft, Inc. All rights reserved. Ezek. 1:1:

> "God strengtheneth" or "hardeneth," was the son of Buzi, a priest probably of the family of Zadok. He was one of those who went into exile with Jehoiachin 2 Kings 24:14, and would seem to have belonged to the higher class, a supposition agreeing with the consideration accorded to him by his fellow exiles (Ezek. 8:1, etc.). The chief scene of his ministry was Tel-Abib in northern Mesopotamia, on the river Chebar, along the banks of which were the settlements of the exiles. He was probably born in or near Jerusalem, where he must certainly have lived many years before he was carried into exile. The date of his entering upon the prophetic office is given in Ezek. 1:1; and if, as is not unlikely, he entered upon this office at the legal age of 30, he must have been about 14 years of age when Josiah died. In this case, he could not have exercised the priestly functions at Jerusalem. However, since his father was a priest Ezek. 1:3, no doubt he was brought up in the courts of the temple, and so became familiar with its services and arrangements.

74 From Barnes' Notes, Electronic Database Copyright © 1997, 2003 by Biblesoft, Inc. All rights reserved. Ezek. 9:4:

[A mark] literally, "Tau," the name of the last letter of the Hebrew alphabet. The old form of the letter was that of a cross. The Jews have interpreted this sign variously, some considering that "Tau," being the last of the Hebrew letters, and so closing the alphabet, denoted completeness, and thus the mark indicated the completeness of the sorrow for sin in those upon whom it was placed. Others again observed that "Tau" was the first letter of Torah ("the Law") and that the foreheads were marked as of men obedient to the Law. Christians, noting the resemblance of this letter in its most ancient form to a cross, have seen herein a reference to the cross with which Christians were signed. The custom for pagan gods and their votaries to bear certain marks furnishes instances, in which God was pleased to employ symbolism, generally in use, to express higher and more divine truth. The sign of the cross in baptism is an outward sign of the designation of God's elect, who at the last day shall be exempted from the destruction of the ungodly (Matt 24:22,31).

75 For more on this topic see authors book "Epic Woman."

76 God uses the "east" to refer to the way to heaven (Ezek. 11:23; Matt. 2:2; 24:27; Acts 1:9–12); the Mount of Olives is on the east side of Jerusalem (Rev. 7:2–10). Scripture often refers to a heavenly portal "east" of Jerusalem. In his vision, Ezekiel watched as God and His entourage prepared to ascend into heaven from the Mount of Olives on the east side of Jerusalem. At the birth of Jesus Christ, the three wise men reported seeing a star in the east that led them to His location. And, when Jesus returned to heaven after His resurrection, He departed from the same spot as God in Ezekiel's vision.

77 God pulls out a remnant before the destruction of Jerusalem:

"Thus says the LORD, the God of Israel: 'Like these good figs, so will I acknowledge those who are carried away

307

captive from Judah, whom I have sent out of this place for their own good, into the land of the Chaldeans. 6 For I will set My eyes on them for good, and I will bring them back to this land; I will build them and not pull them down, and I will plant them and not pluck them up. 7 Then I will give them a heart to know Me, that I am the LORD; and they shall be My people, and I will be their God, for they shall return to Me with their whole heart.—Jer. 24:5-7 NKJV

78 Jeremiah 30:7–11 speaks of the day when God delivers Israel and punishes her enemies. He also tells her that she does not go unpunished herself for all she has done.

79 Gog and Magog: From A. T. Robertson, Word Pictures of the New Testament, In PC Study Bible: Advanced Reference Library, Seattle, WA: Biblesoft, 2002.

"In the rabbinical writings Gog and Magog appear as the enemies of the Messiah. Some early Christian writers thought of the Goths and Huns, but Augustine refuses to narrow the imagery and sees only the final protest of the world against Christianity."

80 In Ezek. 27:12 and Isa. 23:1, Tarshish and Tyre are linked together in Bible prophecy as trafficking merchants.

81 See the Books of Ezra and Nehemiah for the history of the Jews as they returned to Jerusalem after their Babylonian captivity and built a new temple on the ruins of Solomon's temple.

82 The Jews were expecting a strong warrior king like David who would restore their power in the earth: Acts 1:6; Isa. 9:6-7; Jer. 23:5-6; Ezek. 37:24; Dan. 7:27; Mic. 5:2; Zech. 9:9.

83 After Josiah died, the people appointed his son Jehoahaz as king. This lasted three months before Pharaoh Necho appointed his older brother Jehoiakim in his place. Jehoiakim reigned four years and then Babylon conquered Egypt and Jerusalem and allowed him to stay for three more years.

Eventually he was killed while fighting against Babylon and was replaced by Jeconiah who was quickly replaced by Zedekiah—the last Judean king.

84 Daniel's age at captivity: Prof. Stuart on Daniel, p. 373. From Barnes' Notes, Electronic Database Copyright © 1997, 2003 by Biblesoft, Inc. All rights reserved.

> Dan. 1:4: His age at that time [captivity] it is impossible to determine with accuracy, but it is not; improbable that it was somewhere about twelve or fifteen years. In Dan 1:4, he and his three friends are called "children" (yᵉlaadiym). "This word properly denotes the period from the age of childhood up to manhood, and might be translated boys, lads, or youth."

85 Imperial Rome describes the period of the Roman Empire from 27 B.C. to A.D. 476. At its height in A.D. 117, Rome controlled the land from Western Europe to the Middle East. See https://www.nationalgeographic.org/encyclopedia/imperial-rome/

86 The number ten: From Jamieson, Fausset, and Brown Commentary, Electronic Database. Copyright © 1997, 2003 by Biblesoft, Inc. All rights reserved.

> Rev. 2:10: Ten is the number of the world-powers hostile to the Church: cf. the beast's ten horns, Rev. 13:1

87 In John's vision in Revelation, the saints that come out of the Great Tribulation are in heaven wearing white robes (Rev. 7:9-17). Then in Revelation 19, the saints are in the throne room rejoicing over the fall of Babylon.

88 Son of Perdition: See John 17:12 Jesus speaking of Judas Iscariot. See also: 2 Thess. 2:3, speaking of Antichrist.

The word used for perdition from Strong's Numbers and Concordance: NT:684 apoleia (ap-o'-li-a); from a presumed derivative of NT:622; ruin or loss (physical, spiritual or eternal): KJV - damnable (-nation), destruction, die, perdition, perish, pernicious ways, waste.

Of note, the name Apollyon is used for Satan in Rev. 9:11 and is a derivative word.

Matt 11:19, from Barnes' Notes:

"Thus Judas is called a son of perdition because he had the character of a destroyer. He was a traitor and a murderer."

89 Throughout ancient history, Susa had been constantly inhabited, suffering fire and destruction many times only to be rebuilt. At the time of this vision, Susa was already in the hands of Cyrus the Great, also called Cyrus the king of the Medes and Cyrus the Persian. Historians believe Cyrus may have built a royal residence in Susa. Some eleven or twelve years after the death of Cyrus the Great, his second cousin Darius the Great took over the empire and built an elaborate palace in Susa which was well-known in ancient times. Today we have ample artifacts from his palace.

For history on Cyrus the Great and Darius the Great and Susa, see Keil and Delitzsch's commentary.

90 An excellent history of the House of Seleucid that includes the history of Antiochus Epiphanies can be found in the book called The House of Seleucus, written by Edwyn Robert Bevan and published in 1902. This important work has exhaustive footnotes and an appendix, and the research that went into the history is exemplary. To read and download this work: http://archive.org/stream/houseseleucus00bevagoog#page/n10/mode/2up.

91 Ussher paragraph 2376

92 An excellent history of the people, places, and events during Antiochus's life can be found in Bevan's The House of Seleucus. He draws from various ancient historians and

resources to give an all-encompassing and objective history and uses firsthand accounts when possible. During the reign of Antiochus Epiphanies, Cleopatra II was ruler with her husbands and brothers; the reign fluctuated several times because of power struggles and also the influence and dictates of Antiochus.

93 The office of high priest was first conferred on Aaron (Exod. 28). At first hereditary, it descended to the oldest son (Num. 3:10).

94 Antioch was an ancient Greek city on the eastern side of the Orontes River. Its ruins lie near the modern city of Antakya, Turkey.

95 The massacre of young and old and a total of 80,000 were lost to the army of Antiochus (2 Macc. 5:11–14). Also see www.jewishencyclopeida.com and the Books of the Maccabees for the full story on Antiochus Epiphanes and his ruthless destruction of Jerusalem and the true worshippers of God.

96 The Books of the Maccabees 1 and 2 give historical context for the times of Antiochus Epiphanies who is mentioned by name.

97 2,300 mornings and evenings: the number may be interpreted as symbolic (Dan. 8:13–14). If we reduce 2,300, we have six years, three or four months, and some days. This tells us that the oppression of God's people by the little horn was to last just short of seven years. In Scripture, the times of God's visitations, trials, and judgments are often measured by the number seven; see Dan. 4:13; 7:25.

- Seven years' famine came upon the land as a punishment for King David's sin of numbering the people (2 Sam. 24:13).
- During Elisha's time, Israel was visited with seven years' famine (2 Kings 8:1), etc.

98 Ussher paragraphs: 3419-3420.

99 Daniel references and quotes from The Law of Moses and

the Book of Jeremiah (Dan. 9:2, 13).

Jeremiah sends a message to the captives in Babylon that Daniel most likely read: see Jer. 29.

100 Lucifer is addressed in Isa. 14:12. He is a fallen angel and therefore not holy.

101 In the Bible, only Michael is called an archangel. In the Book of Daniel, Gabriel is referred to as "the man Gabriel," while in the Gospel of Luke, Gabriel is referred to as "an angel of the Lord" (Luke 1:11).

F. Godet, D. D.; from The Biblical Illustrator Copyright © 2002, 2003 Ages Software, Inc. and Biblesoft, Inc.:

"I am Gabriel." Names of angels

The part of Gabriel is positive; that of Michael is negative. Michael is, as his name indicates, the destroyer of every one who dares to equal, i.e., to oppose God. Such is his mission in Daniel, where he contends against the powers hostile to Israel; such also is it in Jude and in the Apocalypse, where he fights, as the champion of God, against Satan, the author of idolatry. Gabriel builds up; Michael overthrows. The former is the forerunner of Jehovah the Saviour; the latter, of Jehovah the Judge.

102 Of special note is the layered and thunderous voice of Jesus Christ. He is the Son of Man and His followers are members of His body. I believe His voice includes our voice. After all, we are His ambassadors in the earth and we have been commanded to "speak as speaking the very oracles of God" (1 Peter 4:11). The fact that Jesus includes our voices in His identity, underscores the love and honor that He has given us.

103 In the New Testament, after Jesus Christ was resurrected, the apostle John had his Revelation that corresponds closely to the Book of Daniel. John knew Jesus as an earthly man, but in this vision, He is glorious.

And in the midst of the seven candlesticks one like unto the

Son of man, clothed with a garment down to the foot, and girt about the paps with a golden girdle. His head and his hairs were white like wool, as white as snow; and his eyes were as a flame of fire; and his feet like unto fine brass, as if they burned in a furnace; and his voice as the sound of many waters. And he had in his right hand seven stars: and out of his mouth went a sharp two edged sword: and his countenance was as the sun shineth in his strength. And when I saw him, I fell at his feet as dead. And he laid his right hand upon me, saying unto me, Fear not; I am the first and the last: I am he that liveth, and was dead; and, behold, I am alive for evermore, Amen; and have the keys of hell and of death.—Rev. 1:13–18, KJV

Keil and Delitzsch Commentary on the Old Testament:

This heavenly form has thus, it is true, the shining white talar common to the angel, Ezek 9:9, but all the other features, as here described-the shining of his body, the brightness of his countenance, his eyes like a lamp of fire, arms and feet like glistering brass, the sound of his speaking-all these point to the revelation of the yᵊhaaowh kᵃbowd, the glorious appearance of the Lord, Ezek 1, and teach us that the 'iysh seen by Daniel was no common angel-prince, but a manifestation of Jehovah, i.e., the Logos. This is placed beyond a doubt by a comparison with Rev 1:13-15, where the form of the Son of man whom John saw walking in the midst of the seven golden candlesticks is described like the glorious appearance seen by Ezekiel and Daniel.

104 In this book, I use demons as a generic term for the entirety of the fallen angels, and creatures, and their ilk. They are the spiritual horde of those in treason who will be thrown into the lake of fire in the very end.

105 Jude 9: Michael is called an archangel. Michael as the Archangel over Israel: see Dan. 10:13, 21; 21:1; and Rev. 12:7.

106 Keil and Delitzsch Commentary on the Old Testament;

from Dan 11:28-32:

> "Ships coming from Cyprus are ships which come from the west, from the islands and coasts of the Mediterranean. In 1 Macc. 1:1 and 8:5 kitiym is interpreted of Macedonia, according to which Bertholdt and Dereser think of the Macedonian fleet with which the Roman embassy sailed to Alexandria. This much is historically verified, that the Roman embassy, led by Popillius, appeared with a fleet in Alexandria, and imperiously commanded Antiochus to desist from his undertaking against Egypt and to return to his own land (Liv. xlv. 10-12)."

107 According to early Church Fathers, many Christians took the words of Jesus seriously and fled Jerusalem before it was invaded by Titus and thus their lives were spared. See Matt. 24:15–22; Mark 13:14–20; Luke 21:20–24; Eusebius, Church History 3, 5, 3; Epiphanius, Panarion 29,7,7-8; Epiphanius, Panarion 30, 2, 7; Epiphanius, On Weights and Measures 15.

108 Dan. 11:29–32 speaks of Antiochus and the ships of Rome. Dan. 11:33–35 speaks of persecution. Dan. 11:36–39 is a character sketch of the king who persecutes Israel and it is so broad that it could be applied to Antiochus Epiphanes, or a modern king who starts the future Middle-Eastern war, or the Antichrist. In Dan. 11:40, a modern king invades the Middle East and Israel.

For a discussion on the identity of the northern king and Antichrist, see the commentary on Dan. 11:40–43. From Carl Friedrich Keil and Franz Delitzsch, Commentary on the Old Testament (Peabody, MA: Hendrickson, 1996).

109 Paul the apostle calls the days after the resurrection of Jesus "the last days" (Heb.1:2).

For a discussion on the time of the end specifically referenced in this vision and other parts of Daniel, see the commentary on Dan. 8:17. From Robert Jamieson, A.R. Fausset, and David Brown, A Commentary, Critical and Explanatory, on the Old and New Testaments (Seattle, WA: Biblesoft, 2003).

110 DAY OF THE LORD: From International Standard Bible Encyclopaedia, Electronic Database Copyright © 1996, 2003 by Biblesoft, Inc. All rights reserved.

> Day of the Lord: (yom Yahweh; he hemera tou Kuriou): The idea is a common Old Testament one. It denotes the consummation of the kingdom of God and the absolute cessation of all attacks upon it (Isa. 2:12; 13:6,9; 34:8; Ezek. 13:5; 30:3; Joel 1:15; 2:11; Amos 5:18; Zeph. 1:14; Zech. 14:1) It is a "day of visitation" (Isa. 10:3), a day "of the wrath of Yahweh" (Ezek. 7:19), a "great day of Yahweh" (Zeph. 1:14) . . .

> . . . In the New Testament it is eminently the day of Christ, the day of His coming in the glory of His father . . .John 5:27: "And he gave him authority to execute judgment, because he is a son of man" (compare Matt. 24:27, 30; Luke 12:8) . . . "day of wrath" (Rom. 2:5-6), a "great day" (Rev. 6:17; Jude 6), a "day of God" (2 Peter 3:12), a "day of judgment" (Matt. 10:15; 2 Peter 3:7; Rom. 2:16). Sometimes it is called "that day" (Matt. 7:22; 1 Thess. 5:4; 2 Tim. 4:8) . . .

111 The Sudanese are called by their ancient name, the Nubians, in this scripture.

112 Edom, Moab, and Ammon: From Carl Friedrich Keil and Franz Delitzsch, Commentary on the Old Testament Peabody, MA: Hendrickson, 1996

> Daniel 11:40–43; Edom, Moab, and Ammon, related with Israel by descent, are the old hereditary and chief enemies of this people, who have become by name representatives of all the hereditary and chief enemies of the people of God.).

Also, Syria, Moab, and Ammon helped Nebuchadnezzar of Babylon raid and subdue Israel: 2 Kings 24:1-4.

From Keil and Delitzsch Commentary on the Old Testament: Ps. 137:7-9:

> "The second part of the Psalm supplicates vengeance upon Edom and Babylon. We see from Obadiah's prophecy, which is taken up again by Jeremiah, how shamefully the Edomites, that brother-people related by descent to Israel and yet pre-eminently hostile to it, behaved in connection with the destruction of Jerusalem by the Chaldaeans as their malignant, rapacious, and inhuman helpers."

113 John the Beloved is told to seal up the words of the seven thunders, indicating that message was not ready for release—see Rev. 10:4.

114 The place where this king is killed: Barnes' Notes, Notes on the Old Testament, Job, Psalms, Isaiah, Daniel, by ALBERT BARNES, (Albert Barnes, 1798-1870):

> Dan 11:45 "So far as the phrase used here - "between the seas" - is concerned, there can be no difficulty. It might be applied to any place lying between two sheets of water, as the country between the Dead Sea and the Mediterranean, or the Dead Sea, and Persian Gulf; or the Caspian and Euxine Seas; or the Caspian Sea and the Persian Gulf, for there is nothing in the language to determine the exact locality."

115 Satan is called the great dragon who rules over the Roman / Babylonian beast of the book of Revelation (Rev. 13:1-11; Rev. 20:2).

116 The holy angels are given charge over the fiery cleanup. They are the ones who have been given charge over humanity during this age and our lives have had a major impact on their quality of life (Ps. 91:11; Heb. 1:14; Gen 28:12; John 1:51; Ps. 34:7). Also see authors book Epic Earth.

Made in the USA
Columbia, SC
19 July 2020